W9-AAE-549

Partnering for the Environment

Partnering for the Environment

*Multistakeholder Collaboration
in a Changing World*

ERIC C. PONCELET

ROWMAN & LITTLEFIELD PUBLISHERS, INC.
Lanham • Boulder • New York • Toronto • Oxford

ROWMAN & LITTLEFIELD PUBLISHERS, INC.

Published in the United States of America
by Rowman & Littlefield Publishers, Inc.
A wholly owned subsidiary of The Rowman & Littlefield Publishing Group, Inc.
4501 Forbes Boulevard, Suite 200, Lanham, MD 20706
www.rowmanlittlefield.com

P.O. Box 317, Oxford OX2 9RU, UK

Copyright © 2004 by Rowman & Littlefield Publishers, Inc.

All rights reserved. No part of this publication may be reproduced, stored in a retrieval
system, or transmitted in any form or by any means, electronic, mechanical,
photocopying, recording, or otherwise, without the prior permission of the publisher.

British Library Cataloguing in Publication Information Available

Library of Congress Cataloging-in-Publication Data

Poncelet, Eric C.
Partnering for the environment : multistakeholder collaboration in a changing world /
  Eric C. Poncelet.
    p. cm.
  Includes bibliographical references and index.
  ISBN 0-7425-0158-2 (cloth : alk. paper)
  ISBN 0-7425-0159-0 (paper : alk. paper)
  1. Environmental management. 2. Interprofessional relations. 3. Environmental
management—Planning. 4. Environmental management—Social aspects. I. Title.

GE300.P66   2004
363.7'05—dc22

                                                                              2003019861
Printed in the United States of America

♾™ The paper used in this publication meets the minimum requirements of American
National Standard for Information Sciences—Permanence of Paper for Printed Library
Materials, ANSI/NISO Z39.48-1992.

For Susie, Kira, and Maya

Contents

Figures

Tables

Abbreviations

CIMNR   Collaboration for the Improved Management of Natural Resources
EU   European Union
EUPEC   European Union Partnership for Environmental Cooperation
GBP   Gascoigne Biodiversity Project
NGO   nongovernmental organization
PCSD   President's Council on Sustainable Development
TRC   Toupin River Contract

Preface

My path to the study of multistakeholder environmental partnerships has been circuitous. It has included significant forays into the not always strongly aligned fields of power systems engineering and cultural anthropology. As a mechanical engineer designing wastewater treatment systems for the electric utility industry in the 1980s, I came to the realization that many of the biggest hurdles to resolving society's continuing environmental problems lie not in the technological or financial realms but in the domains of human communication and cooperation. This recognition was stimulated by observations from my engineering work that the diverse actors in society who play roles in either causing or remedying current forms of environmental degradation often have substantially different perceptions of and approaches to these issues. I also came to believe that the ultimate success of environmental problem-solving efforts depends largely on the capacity to improve the coordination and integration of these disparate perspectives and approaches.

Over time, I became more and more interested in these meaning-oriented— or what I later came to view as *cultural*—components of environmental action. This led me to pursue a doctoral program in anthropology in the 1990s. I began my studies in anthropology by exploring the varied ways by which humans interact with the natural environment in different cultures throughout the world. Later, I commenced a multiyear research project examining the impact that culturally based meanings and practices have on collaborative action in the environmental domain. This book constitutes a culmination of this research.

Since completing this research, I have begun a career as a professional mediator designing, coordinating, and facilitating multistakeholder collaborative environmental problem-solving processes in the United States. The research and analysis described in these pages has heavily influenced my approach to this work. It has also provided a foundation of knowledge, insight, and experience upon which I continually draw to help inform my efforts to bring these processes to successful resolution.

One of my main objectives in writing this book—and, indeed, in researching multistakeholder environmental partnerships in the first place—has been to present this topic in a fresh way. In particular, I have attempted to introduce an anthropological orientation to the public policy, planning, management, dispute resolution, and negotiation-based perspectives that have dominated past study of this subject. I believe that anthropology has much to offer in this regard. As intimated above, anthropology emphasizes the cultural dimensions of human activity. It views the world as imbued with meaning and approaches the people who inhabit it as both the creators and interpreters of this meaning. Anthropology also relies heavily on ethnographic methods. Many important insights can be gained by spending large amounts of time observing and participating in actual collaborative processes and getting to know personally the people who compose them. These are insights that might be missed if one were to rely solely on surveys and after-the-fact interviews. Finally, anthropology places a premium on conducting research cross-culturally. This enables researchers to approach their subjects of interest from a position of relative *strangeness*. I tried to cultivate this feeling of strangeness by selecting a specific topic—in this case, multistakeholder environmental partnerships—about which I knew relatively little and by commencing the research outside of my home country of the United States. My hope was to be able to view these partnerships from the standpoint of a novice so that my analysis of them would be less clouded by the assumptions and expectations that "experts" inevitably take with them into their research. It is my sincere hope that the people who read this book will also approach its ideas and arguments from a similar "beginner's mind" perspective.

Nonetheless, certain challenges reside in any analysis aimed at exploring people's underlying perspectives and belief systems. In particular, it is inherently difficult to portray how individuals perceive and think about things. To overcome this, I have tried to use people's own words whenever possible so that the reader, too, can evaluate the meanings intended behind the words. Using direct quotations is, alas, not always feasible or even appropriate, as people do not always speak clearly and concisely. In these instances, I have striven to paraphrase the ideas expressed as faithfully as possible.

In producing this exposition on multistakeholder partnerships, I make no pretenses of being a perfectly neutral observer of environmental action. I hold certain views and bear specific convictions that led me to select this topic of study in the first place and to pursue the line of inquiry that I did. I believe, for instance, that significant human-induced natural resource exploitation and pollution problems exist and that if these are not addressed in a serious, integrated, and timely fashion, they will severely undermine the health and well-being of humans as well as other life forms on this planet. I believe that these problems arise in large part from the continued prevalence of unsustainable systems of production and consumption in today's societies. In my view, the responsibility for addressing these issues falls on the shoulders of many. I believe that both industry and individual citizens must conduct themselves in a manner that better attends not only to their private needs but also to the needs of their greater communities. I also believe that government has an important role to play in helping to regulate appropriately the environmental burdens placed upon society. Finally, I believe in the importance of cooperative action among these diverse social actors. This does not mean that I consider collaborative, consensus-based strategies of problem solving to be inherently superior to all other modes, such as those of authoritarian rule or divisive activism. It just means that I believe that multistakeholder collaborative processes may well play a critical role in ensuring the long-term resolution of the complex array of environmental problems facing humanity in the twenty-first century.

Given my background and interests in both the study and practice of environmental collaboration, I have attempted to write this book to be of value for both students and practitioners of multistakeholder collaboration. For academic scholars, I present an important and, I believe, underused theoretical perspective for thinking about these processes, an alternative methodological approach for researching them, and concrete data revealing how specific case-study partnerships actually work in practice. For decision makers and leaders responsible for initiating multistakeholder partnerships, I present an analysis of some of the advantages and disadvantages of these processes that will assist them in deciding when a collaborative approach is most appropriate. For partnership coordinators and facilitators responsible for producing successful partnership outcomes, I examine some of the challenges facing collaboration-based initiatives and present useful suggestions for how to surmount these. For stakeholders from government, business, or the environmental community who might be considering participating in a multistakeholder partnership, I provide an analysis of some of the risks and benefits that such collaboratives pose for interests from these three sectors. Finally, for stakeholders of all kinds currently participating in these types of partnerships, I present an examination of the relationship between sociohistoric forces and partnership practices that might help these individuals become more aware of the functioning of their own initiatives.

With the advantages of trying to reach so many diverse readers, however, come certain hazards. In attempting to provide meaningful information to all of these potential audiences, I risk failing to address each of their most pressing interests in adequate detail. Similarly, in trying to speak to each potential reader's particular concerns, I risk presenting information of less significance or import to others. I have nevertheless gone ahead with this multiaudience strategy in the hopes that readers will take the opportunity to learn and benefit from each other's points of view.

The following chapters present an account that derives from my experience conducting ethnographic research with four multistakeholder environmental partnerships in Europe and the United States. I learned a tremendous amount from the scores of individuals who welcomed me into their projects and, in some cases, their personal lives as they strove to partner for the environment. It is my sincerest hope that this learning will inspire other readers as well.

Acknowledgments

The word in language is half someone else's.

—Mikhail M. Bakhtin

This book, like all writing, has been a collective effort. It is the product of an intensely interesting research project, numerous authors, scholars, and practitioners who influenced my own thinking, and dozens of dedicated colleagues and friends who graciously considered and shared their views on my own ideas and writings. I would like to single out those individuals and organizations that have been the most influential and who deserve so much of the credit.

The research was performed under the auspices of dissertation fellowships from the Belgian American Educational Foundation and the University of North Carolina Graduate School. It was also supported by a Grant-in-Aid of Research from Sigma Xi, The Scientific Research Society. I am beholden to all three organizations for their generous financial assistance.

Special thanks go to those who provided thoughtful and insightful feedback on the many iterations of the manuscript. Included are Willett Kempton, Don Nonini, Bruce Winterhalder, Francois Nielsen, John Wise, Ed Stafford, Cathy Hartman, Fran Lynn, and Pete Andrews. I am especially grateful to several others, including Carole Crumley for her confidence in championing the project from the beginning, Dorothy Holland for her steady inspiration and guidance on theoretical matters, Juliana Birkhoff for her particularly thorough review of the manuscript, and Scott McCreary both for his astute comments and for his mentorship and camaraderie during my transition to the world of environmental collaboration practitioners.

There are also many friends and family I would like to recognize. I want to acknowledge Robin Dalsheimer for her generous assistance with the cover design. To all of my friends and especially my siblings who gently (and not so gently) kept prodding me to keep plugging away on the manuscript, I say: thanks for the undying encouragement. To my parents, Noelle and Claude Poncelet, you have influenced this book in ways that I am sure I still do not fully appreciate. Mom, thanks for sharing your experience on the awesome task that is writing a book. And Dad, the only thing more valuable than your feedback on the manuscript has been your enduring faith in the value of what I was trying to accomplish. To my daughters, Kira and Maya, I want you to know that all of the weekends and evenings when I was less than available because I was working on "the book" have resulted in something of which I am very proud and that I hope will bring insight and understanding into your own lives. And to Susie, my wife, I feel the deepest gratitude. I could never have brought this endeavor to fruition without your dedicated and multifaceted support.

Finally, I want to express my great indebtedness to all of the partnership coordinators and members who participated in and contributed to the study. You welcomed me into your collaboratives and took the time to share important parts of yourselves. This book is as much yours as it is mine. May it contribute to the better world that you are all so honorably seeking.

Introduction

It is better to work *with* than *against* one another. This is the logic driving increasing levels of collaboration among diverse interests in the environmental realm.[1] This book takes as its topic a particular form of environmental collaboration—*multistakeholder environmental partnerships*. Broadly defined, multistakeholder environmental partnerships are voluntary attempts among representatives of the government, business, and nongovernmental organization (NGO) sectors[2] to address, in a proactive and cooperative fashion, environmental issues of mutual concern. These partnerships are consensus based and characterized by common goals. Stakeholders from any sector can initiate them. And they can be used for implementing as well as producing collaborative decisions.

Goals

This book has two main goals. The first is to improve current understandings of how multistakeholder environmental partnerships work, especially at the level of social interaction. To pursue this goal, I adopt a distinct analytical approach to this topic. Although most studies tend to focus primarily on the organizational and personal *interests* at stake in multiparty efforts to address environmental problems,[3] my analytical perspective concentrates more on what cultural anthropologists would describe as the realm of *meaning*.[4] From this point of view, participants enter environmental partnerships not only with disparate interests in mind but with varying socially, culturally, and historically based perspectives, conceptualizations, expectations, and values as well. These *sociohistoric*[5] differences, as I call them, cause people to derive meaning from, and attribute meaning to, particular ideas, situations, and actors in the environmental partnership setting in potentially distinct ways. They also affect *practice*—i.e., what people actually do in particular settings.[6] This book advances the proposition that sociohistoric factors constitute *a*, and at times *the*, key determinant of individual behavior in partnerships.

To explore the relationship between sociohistoric factors and behavior or practice in collaborative environmental problem-solving settings, I draw on ethnographic research conducted with four multistakeholder environmental partnerships in Europe and the United States. I focus my attention on the following issues:

- how participants interpret the various elements involved in multistakeholder environmental collaboration (e.g., the issues at stake, each other, each other's actions);
- how these interpretations are expressed and drawn upon in the process of social interaction;
- the power dynamics associated with competing interpretive frameworks;
- the degree to which new meanings are constructed;
- how these interpretations change over time; and
- how these changing interpretations, in turn, alter the people who possess them.

The book's second goal derives from the first and is to explore the implications that the findings generated by my particular analytical perspective present for multistakeholder environmental partnerships as decision-making tools. My aspiration here is to clarify the advantages and disadvantages associated with multistakeholder partnership approaches to environmental problem solving, the effect that partnerships have on past conflict in the environmental arena, and the significance that partnerships have for the different sectors engaging in them.

As indicated by these goals, my focus in this book is primarily on the practices adopted in the partnership setting and the sociohistoric factors that inform them. Unlike more conventional case-study analyses of multistakeholder collaboration, I devote less attention to the contextual specificities of the case-study partnerships themselves. I limit this detail both for reasons of protecting the confidentiality of the participants and their organizations and because this information contributes less significantly to my main arguments.

Outline

In Chapter 1, I situate my particular analytical approach to multistakeholder environmental partnerships relative to other studies and then describe in greater detail the research project on which the book is based. This includes a review of my methodology as well as a more in-depth description of the theoretical orientation guiding my analysis.

Chapter 2 sets the context for the rise of multistakeholder collaboration in the environmental arenas of Europe and North America by describing the forms of environmental conflict to which the modern environmental movement and the development of environmental policy owe their historical origins. I then explore other factors that have contributed to the creation of societal conditions conducive to collaborative approaches.

Chapter 3 describes the four case studies on which this inquiry into the practice and implications of multistakeholder environmental partnerships is based. I include information on the historical origins, objectives, structure and composition, and typical operations of the case studies.

Chapters 4 through 6 form the core of my analysis of multistakeholder environmental partnerships. In these chapters, I present the major findings of the research. Chapters 4 and 5 demonstrate the effects that sociohistoric forces can have on behavior in these interactive settings. Chapter 4 focuses in particular on the common practice of conflict[7] and addresses specific instances of disagreement and dispute among the participating actors. I draw primarily from two specific case-study examples of conflict to demonstrate the partiality of interest-based explanations and to show how sociohistoric-based explanations help provide a more complete account of why conflicts happen and how they play out. I describe these examples of conflict in terms of competition among alternative meaning systems, where different actors promote different ways of knowing, speaking, and acting with regard to the environment and environmental problem solving.

Chapter 5 investigates the even more prominent practice of conflict management.[8] It explores various modes of conflict management, drawing on examples from all four case-study partnerships for illustration. To explain this practice, I again direct attention toward key sociohistoric factors at play. I focus in particular on the roles played by (1) the existence of a commonly held cultural model for how partnerships are supposed to work, and (2) the existence of a particular discourse—that of *ecological modernization*—that was generally accorded more credence and legitimacy than any other in the partnerships studied.

Chapter 6 addresses the formative quality of environmental partnerships, exploring them as sites of personal transformation. The chapter examines structural as well as sociohistoric factors that encourage partnership participants to change. It also describes in significant detail three major ways by which these transformations take place, including the processes of social learning, cultural production, and identity change. Here, I present evidence demonstrating how multistakeholder environmental partnerships have the effect of inducing altered perceptions of self and other, changed understandings of and approaches to the environment, and reformulated social relations.

I leave critical analysis of the implications that follow from this study and its findings to the final chapter. Chapter 7 reviews the research's contributions to the study of multistakeholder collaboration and considers at greater length some of the implications for environmental decision making more broadly. In particular, I examine the benefits and detriments of multistakeholder partnerships as an environmental problem-solving tool, the extent to which these partnerships represent a possible reconfiguration of the long-term struggles that have characterized past action in the environmental arena, and the significance that these partnerships have for the various stakeholders participating in these initiatives. Finally, this chapter reflects on the appropriate role for multistakeholder environmental partnerships in society and offers suggestions regarding how they might be more effectively used and managed in today's changing world.

Notes

1. This logic is driving increasing levels of collaboration among diverse interests in other policy realms—such as education, public health, and urban renewal—as well.

2. I recognize that in singling out the business, government, and environmental NGO sectors as I do, I risk presenting them as monolithic structures—a construct that is obviously false, as each of these sectors is characterized by diverse, incongruous, and evolving organizations. Nevertheless, I do allude to each sector as a whole for the sake of discussion and therefore ask the reader to keep the hazards of this practice in mind.

3. Ross (1993a), Schwarz and Thompson (1990), Winslade and Monk (2000).

4. This predominant focus on meaning and the influence that meaning has in guiding human behavior is common to anthropological studies in general (e.g., Geertz 1973, Peacock 1986) and to the anthropological study of human-environment relations in particular (e.g., Crumley 2001, Milton 1993). It is also common to studies that concentrate on the social construction of reality (Berger and Luckmann 1967) and the environment in particular (Hajer 1995, Röling 1994, Simmons 1993, Hannigan 1995, and Röling and Wagemakers 1998). See Winslade and Monk (2000) and Shailor (1994) for examples of how this is being applied to the study of cooperation and conflict.

5. I describe the concept of "sociohistoric" differences in greater detail in chapter 1.

6. Holland et al. (1998). See also Roy (1994) and Ross (1993a).

7. I define "conflict" broadly here as a state of disharmony between incompatible or antithetical persons, ideas, or interests.

8. I define "conflict management" as a series of actions and reactions between disputants and other parties intended to control levels of disagreement or antagonism (Ross 1993b, 80). The goal of conflict management is to improve a problematic situation, although conflict management may or may not involve actual resolution of a conflict or a dispute (Daniels and Walker 2001, 35; Ross 1993b, 80).

Chapter 1

Multistakeholder Environmental Partnerships

Multistakeholder environmental partnerships come in many forms and refer to themselves via many different names. Some of these initiatives use the actual word partnership, while others employ the terms "collaborative," "dialogue," "alliance," "group," "forum," or "stakeholder process." Regardless of the title, multistakeholder environmental partnerships are part of a general trend toward increasing cooperation and collective action in the environmental arena that has varyingly been called "collaboration,"[1] "public participation,"[2] "participatory governance,"[3] "consensus building,"[4] and "cooperative management."[5] In this book, I use the term "collaboration" to refer to this broader movement.

Multistakeholder environmental partnerships share many of the fundamental features of collaboration.[6] They are founded upon constructive, noncompulsory cooperation among actors representing a wide variety of societal interests. They are unbounded politically and can occur at the local, regional, national, or international levels. They are problem oriented and function with the goal of producing and/or implementing mutually beneficial environmental management decisions. The problems that they face are of common concern and typically difficult to resolve alone. Multistakeholder environmental partnerships operate via direct, face-to-face interaction and pursue the ideal of consensus formation. This means that they encourage participants to develop shared understandings of the problems at issue and to come to agreement on proposed solutions. Some partnerships make use of third-party facilitation, although this is not a requirement.

Further clarity of the meaning of "multistakeholder environmental partnerships" comes by examining the phrase's constituent parts. The notion of "stake-

1

holder"[7] denotes that the participants in these initiatives are individuals or organizations that benefit from, are adversely affected by, or in some other way are able to affect particular environmental issues of concern.[8] The term "multistakeholder" indicates that these processes go beyond intrasectorial or bilateral type initiatives to involve representatives, at a minimum, from the government, business, and NGO sectors.[9] In this book, I treat the business sector as consisting of enterprises, both large and small. I consider the government sector to include public officials from legislative and regulatory bodies at the local, regional, national, and international levels. I regard the NGO sector as subsuming a wide variety of societal interests represented by formal not-for-profit organizations, informal community-based groups, and individual citizens. In multistakeholder environmental partnerships, each of these sectors is assumed to bring significant and necessary perspectives, experience, and knowledge for addressing the problems at issue.

The word "partnership" signifies that these initiatives are predicated upon different interests coming together in a proactive manner to pool resources and work cooperatively in pursuit of commonly agreed upon goals.[10] In partnerships, as opposed to consultation-based processes, decision making and implementation are jointly undertaken, power is shared, and participants take collective responsibility for results. Partnerships also demand a high degree of commitment, participation, trust, and respect among the partners.[11]

Finally, the term "environmental" defines the boundaries for the topical focus of these partnerships. "Environmental" is interpreted broadly here to include a wide range of environmental protection issues, ranging from pollution control to nature conservation, and from land use management to environmental justice.[12] A summary of the key attributes distinguishing multistakeholder environmental partnerships is listed in table 1.1.

Multistakeholder environmental partnerships, as defined above, constitute but one form of collaborative decision making currently being found in the envi-

Table 1.1. Key Attributes of Multistakeholder Environmental Partnerships

- Function to produce and/or implement environmental management decisions.
- Multisectorial: involving minimally the government, business, and NGO sectors.
- Organized around environmental problems of common concern.
- Decision-making power and responsibility are shared.
- Can be initiated by participants from any sector.
- Proactive rather than reactive in orientation.
- Voluntary/noncompulsory.
- Participants are defined as being affected by or capable of affecting the environmental matters of concern.
- Face-to-face interaction.
- Operate via consensus formation.
- Require the development of trust, respect, and shared understanding among participants.

ronmental policy arena. Others include environmental mediation and dispute resolution processes;[13] voluntary environmental agreements and covenants;[14] green alliances;[15] public-private partnerships;[16] community-based collaboratives;[17] citizen advisory committees;[18] community advisory panels;[19] policy dialogues;[20] regulatory negotiations;[21] collaborative natural resource management and conservation;[22] and collaborative or participatory planning more generally.[23]

Multistakeholder partnerships share many of the collaborative qualities of these other forms of environmental cooperation, but they also deviate from them in significant ways. They differ from environmental dispute resolution and mediation efforts, for instance, in that, unlike these latter processes, partnerships do not necessarily arise out of or in response to specific, preexisting conflicts. Instead, they are more commonly directed toward proactively improving environmental management and policy decisions in situations where shared environmental concerns and goals prevail.

Multistakeholder environmental partnerships also diverge from some of these other cooperative processes in that they are less restricted in the range or types of stakeholders that they typically involve. Traditionally, voluntary environmental agreements or covenants have been limited to representatives of the regulating and regulated communities,[24] green alliances have been confined to bilateral negotiations between individual corporations and environmental NGOs,[25] and public-private partnerships have been restricted to collaborations between either government and business or government and NGOs.[26] Multistakeholder partnerships, by definition, involve actors from all three of these major sectors. In addition, unlike community-based collaboratives,[27] multistakeholder environmental partnerships are not required to be organized around local stakeholders.

Multistakeholder environmental partnerships differ from most citizen advisory committees, community advisory panels, and policy dialogues in that partnerships serve more than a simple advisory function. Whereas decision-making authority in these other processes ultimately falls to the respective governmental or corporate representatives convening them, environmental partnerships operate as actual decision-making bodies that may also be responsible for implementing these same decisions.

Finally, multistakeholder environmental partnerships depart from regulatory negotiations, collaborative management, and participatory planning processes in that the decision to create a partnership does not reside with one sector only. While these other fora are commonly initiated by government, partnerships may be launched by any of the three sectors.

A Better Approach to Environmental Management?

Much has been written on the benefits and drawbacks of collaborative processes such as multistakeholder environmental partnerships. Proponents have touted them for a variety of reasons.[28] Some advocates laud them for producing solutions to environmental problems that are more fair, well informed, and likely to be implemented and sustained and that are generally more acceptable to and beneficial for all parties concerned. Others extol them for being well suited to the uncertainty and complexity that characterize contemporary environmental problems. Still others claim that they result in better communication; better understandings of the issues, interests, and other stakeholders involved; stronger relationships; and deeper levels of trust and commitment that will enhance the capacity of parties to deal with problems in the future.

Such claims are supported by evidence that shows these cooperative efforts produce economic benefits, positive environmental results, and favorable experiences for the people and organizations involved.[29] Certain of these advocates also argue that these new forms of environmental governance are critical to achieving the goal of sustainable development.[30]

Critics have countered such claims, however, on a variety of fronts. Some charge, for instance, that collaborative processes are not always more effective in terms of time, cost, or ease of implementation; that they often suffer from being exclusive, especially of non-local stakeholders; and that some interests tend to benefit more than others.[31] Others maintain that the potential for co-optation of these forms of environmental governance makes them easy targets for powerful special interests seeking to control the regulatory process and legitimate prevailing patterns of power.[32] Finally, still others warn of potential erosion of the accountability of elected and administrative officials and the threat that collaborative processes place on preexisting regulatory or public participation processes.[33]

Although this debate over the value of multistakeholder, collaborative approaches to addressing the complex array of environmental problems facing humankind in the twenty-first century is by no means resolved, it does point toward the need for better understanding of these processes. This book seeks to make a contribution in this direction. But collaborative processes such as multistakeholder environmental partnerships merit our attention for another reason as well. They are unique as policy instruments in that they do more than simply produce solutions to environmental problems. They also assemble particular interests from society's diverse sectors, often for the first time, and frame these encounters in a manner that diverges from the antagonistic formulations of the past. In this way, these partnerships present possibilities for new forms of environmental action. This book also explores what these possibilities may be.[34]

An Alternative Look at Environmental Collaboration

Given the significant attention that has already been directed toward the topic of multistakeholder environmental collaboration, readers will want to know how this book is different and what added value it brings to practitioners and scholars in this domain. This book departs from past analyses of this topic in two primary ways. As mentioned in the introduction, the first concerns its concentration on the sociohistoric factors affecting multistakeholder processes. The second comes with the analytical attention that I place on the *process*, rather than the origins or outcomes, of environmental collaboration. In focusing on process, however, my goal is not to delineate particular stages by which partnerships typically proceed.[35] Rather, I am concerned with the actual interaction that takes place when people of different backgrounds, personal experiences, and worldviews attempt to work together.

To better understand my approach to environmental collaboration, it is helpful to relate it to what might be considered as the mainstream analytical approach to the topic. Two main, though related, features characterize this prevailing approach. The first is a primary concern with stakeholder *interests*—that is, the preferences, desires, or concerns with which individual stakeholders enter a collaborative proceeding—and the manners by which these interests are pursued in these settings.[36] The mainstream approach either explicitly states or implicitly assumes competition among interests—whether political or economic in origin—to be the most important features driving these processes.

This predominant focus on interests is evident, for instance, in the literature on interest-based negotiation. Fisher, Ury, and Patton's classic book, *Getting to Yes*,[37] provides a nice example, as the authors in this text make the now well-known claim that achieving successful negotiations is predicated upon participants being able to focus on people's "interests" (their underlying needs and concerns) rather than their "positions" (their stated demands).[38] This concentration on interests is further illustrated by rational choice-based or microeconomic-oriented analyses of collaboration.[39] These analyses portray individual agents as rational, strategic maximizers of desires, preferences, or goals. Finally, this interest-based approach is also apparent in the many case-study analyses that presume interests to be the key drivers of environmental conflicts and disagreements.[40] These analyses focus on the struggle among competing stakeholders, be they farmers who fear restrictions on the use of pesticides, environmentalists who fear threats to biodiversity, or governmental agencies that fear losing regulatory control over industrial polluters. In fact, the ubiquity of the term "stakeholder" as a reference to participants in collaborative processes is itself an indication of the prominence of the interest-based perspective. After all, what is a stakeholder if not someone who has an interest in the issues of concern?

The second main feature characterizing the mainstream approach to environmental collaboration is an overarching concern with the *instrumentality* of such processes. By this I mean that these analyses tend to direct a great amount of attention toward the relationships between the *means* and *ends* of multistakeholder collaboration.[41] Emphasis is placed on the outcomes of these processes, and analytic priority is given to determining why particular projects succeeded or failed as they did. This focus on instrumentality is evident in the "how to" orientation of so many of these analyses and in their preeminent goal of making multistakeholder collaborative efforts more effective.[42]

Although interest-based approaches help make sense of multistakeholder cooperation, one of my main arguments is that these explanations are only partial.[43] An important limitation of this approach is that a prevailing focus on interests causes one to lose sight of some of the other significant factors also influencing collaborative action.[44] Often overlooked are the different habitual ways of thinking about, talking about, and acting with regard to the environment and environmental issues that individual participants also bring with them to these collaborative processes.[45] More and more texts are now pointing to the importance of these *sociohistoric* factors, as I am referring to them here.[46] For some of these scholars, sociohistoric factors are primarily significant in their capacity to influence people's interests. [47] This book, on the other hand, views sociohistoric factors as also directly affecting the actual process of social interaction in the collaborative process. [48]

A second limitation of the mainstream approach concerns the questions that it tends to ask. The instrumentalist orientation leads these types of analyses to concentrate on why partnerships are initiated in the first place or why they are successful or not in achieving their stated goals.[49] My focus is directed instead toward the *practice* of multistakeholder environmental collaboration—i.e., how partnerships play out as a social process. I am primarily interested in how people behave in these settings, in what they say, and in the meanings behind their words and actions. This book focuses on three practices in particular: how people engage in conflict, how they act to manage conflict, and how they change over the course of their collaborative experiences.

This principal focus on practice does not mean, however, that I am not concerned with how these partnerships turn out. Indeed, drawing links between actual practice and the products of collaboration remains one of my main goals. The difference between my approach and the prevailing model is that my analysis starts by focusing on practice and then moves toward partnership outcomes rather than the other way around.

Finally, while this book focuses on sociohistoric factors and their effects on partnership practices, my intention is not to build a prescriptive or predictive model. I am not interested, for instance, in developing a framework that ascribes particular sociohistoric characteristics to specific stakeholders. As I discuss in the following section, such a static, coherent portrayal of sociohistoric traits neglects the fact that people's ways of knowing and acting in the world differ in different contexts. Rather, my objective is to raise people's awareness of the importance of these sociohistoric factors by showing how patterns exist and how these affect partnership actions and outcomes. Nor is it my aim to categorize existing or former environmental partnerships in terms of particular sociohistoric features or predominant processes. Instead, I draw upon new research with previously unstudied partnerships to help illustrate how multistakeholder environmental partnerships can and indeed do work in practice.

Project Design

The arguments presented in this exposition draw upon firsthand research of four multistakeholder environmental partnerships in the middle and late 1990s. These include an EU-level initiative aimed at promoting sustainable development in Europe, a regional-level initiative focused on watershed protection in Belgium, a local-level initiative directed toward preserving biodiversity within a particular area of Belgium, and a national-level initiative fixed on improving natural resource management practices in the United States. The first three were studied over a one-year period in 1994-1995, while the fourth was researched over a two-year interval in 1997-1999.

My primary method for studying the case-study partnerships was ethnographic[50]—a method that emphasizes the systematic description of social and cultural processes based on direct observation and participation.[51] My focus, again, was not on the formation or completion phases of the partnerships but on the "operation"[52] or "execution"[53] stages in which participants were actually involved in collective problem solving.[54]

My research strategy was to start by focusing on what I call the *practice* of environmental partnerships—i.e., on what people were actually saying and doing when interacting in the collaborative process. To study this, I observed all collective partnership activities that took place during the research period. This meant attending formal meetings as well as participating in more informal activities such as communal meals, media events, and group recreational activities. My approach was to concentrate on the practice of environmental partnerships for at least six months before turning my attention toward the sociohistoric forces at play.[55] These I researched by conducting semistructured interviews with a cross section of partnership participants and collecting textual materials produced by both the participating organizations and the partnerships themselves.[56] This approach allowed me to relate people's sociohistorically based understandings to their behaviors in practice. It also helped me to distinguish between what people actually did in the partnership setting and what they said about it in the very different context of the personal interview.

My reasons for selecting the four case studies mentioned earlier are closely tied to the objectives of this book. As my primary goal was not to analyze the successes or failures of particular environmental partnerships but to highlight some of the links between sociohistoric forces and practices in the multistakeholder collaborative setting, I was not restricted to studying one particular partnership or another. There were two principal benefits to be gained, however, by examining more than just one case. First, studying a small number of diverse partnerships provides for a greater breadth of data on the sociohistoric factors influencing the practice of partnerships. Second, a focus on multiple case studies permits me to speak about the possible existence of particular trends that span multistakeholder partnerships in general. To ensure a diversity of case studies, I chose partnerships operating at different political levels, focusing on different environmental issues, and located in more than one country.[57] My decision to limit the study to four partnerships was a direct consequence of the time and cost constraints facing the research.

Despite my adoption of such a "collective case study" approach,[58] this investigation of multistakeholder partnerships was never meant to be comprehensive or fully representative of the great variety of multistakeholder partnerships currently in existence. Nor was this inquiry intended to be rigorously comparative. Instead, my intent was to use the individual cases in a "heuristic" fashion so that the data uncovered might stimulate new and improved understandings of these types of collaborative processes.[59]

Theoretical Approach

My approach to the study of multistakeholder collaboration is responding to the partiality of what might be summarized as the *instrumental rationality* perspective dominating many of the studies coming out of the disciplines of environmental policy, planning, management, dispute resolution, and negotiation.[60] This perspective treats actors as rational maximizers of preexisting preferences or goals and portrays decision-making outcomes as the result of strategic bargaining efforts among these self-interested actors. The presumption is that if one wants to make sense of multistakeholder collaboration efforts, one should just pay attention to how people are negotiating their interests.

Although this predominant perspective has made many valuable contributions to the study of multistakeholder collaboration, it also has its critics. Some object to the tendency of instrumental rationality to abstract behavior from its contextual settings and reduce it to the mechanistic actions of assumedly autonomous, utility-maximizing individuals.[61] What gets ignored here is the cultural embeddedness of social, economic, and political life.[62] In response, many analysts have emphasized the cognitive and interpretive dimensions of environmental conflict and cooperation by calling into attention the diverse values, attitudes, ethics, worldviews, and belief systems that inform people's understandings of and approaches to environmental issues. Exemplifying this analytical orientation are studies demonstrating the multiple interpretations that exist for such important concepts as "nature,"[63] "pollution,"[64] "climate change,"[65] and "environmentalism."[66]

As with the instrumental rationality perspective, however, these more culture-based approaches also suffer certain shortcomings. One major deficiency is that they, too, tend to be abstracted and decontextualized. These types of analyses commonly highlight particular cultural traits, such as people's varying interpretations of specific environmental concerns, but they do so without linking these interpretations to the situations in which they apply and, in particular, to the specific practices associated with them. This is important because the fact that people hold certain beliefs or ascribe to certain meaning systems does not mean that they will necessarily *act* on or consistently with them. A second related weakness of these culture-based approaches is that they often tend to treat cultural attributes and people's use of them as stable and consistent over time. Lost in the presentation is attention to the way in which people adopt cultural traits, change them, and in turn become shaped by them.

An Alternative Approach

Like the culture-based perspective, my analytical orientation approaches multistakeholder collaboration as a process in which interpretations and the meanings attached to them matter. My focus is on the sociohistoric factors at play. These sociohistoric factors refer to the disparate conceptualizations that individual actors have of the environmental problems at issue, each other, each other's organizations, and themselves; the divergent ways by which these actors habitually talk about these problems; and the distinctive types of actions they conventionally take to address them. These understandings, discourses, and behaviors are historically derived, having been developed in past personal experience and institutional activity with regard to environmental issues and struggles. This institutional activity includes one's formal education, professional training, organizational background, common interest-group affiliation, and past experiences with collaborative processes.[67] It should be noted that I prefer the term "sociohistoric" over other related analytical constructs based on the word "culture"—such as "political culture"[68] or "psychocultural"[69]—due to the tendency described earlier for cultural features to be viewed in a decontextualized and ahistorical manner.

Where I depart from past culture-based approaches is in my attempt to ground my analysis of sociohistoric differences in the context of actual partnership *practices*—i.e., in the context of what participants actually say and do in these collaborative settings.[70] Following the writings of Pierre Bourdieu,[71] I define practice more abstractly as the product of the dialectical interaction between the sociohistorically informed dispositions of actors and the social and material constraints that confront them (see figure 1.1). A practice-based approach thus acknowledges that people will adopt different ways of thinking, talking, or acting or will occupy different subjective positions in different social contexts. Stakeholders participating in collaborative settings, for example, can be expected to react differently from how they would in an adversarial setting or when alone.

Figure 1.1 Definition of Practice

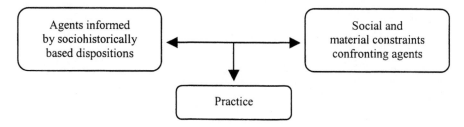

In this book, I focus my attention on two key factors constraining the actions of sociohistorically informed actors in multistakeholder environmental partnerships. The first concerns the asymmetrical and continuously evolving power relations that exist among different actors in the environmental arena.[72] Power relations are important because they affect how individuals will behave vis-à-vis one another in the collaborative setting. Power relations are structured according to the *capital*—both economic and symbolic—maintained by the actors involved.[73] Economic capital refers to the material resources accessible by any one individual. Symbolic capital, on the other hand, is expressed by the relative authority, prestige, credibility, and respect that a stakeholder is able to command from others. This symbolic capital, and the degree to which it is attained, is influenced by a variety of factors.[74] It is affected by the particular constituencies that a stakeholder represents, the stakeholder's credibility with the public and ability to mobilize public opinion, and the degree of democracy and transparency within his or her organization. It is influenced by a stakeholder's relationships with other actors in the environmental arena, such as with influential political decision makers or with the other participants in a particular collaborative process. It is also shaped by a stakeholder's perceived levels of skill, expertise, and knowledge—with regard to both environmental issues and other stakeholders in the environmental arena. Finally, symbolic capital can arise from a stakeholder's history and track record of environmental action, the stakeholder's ability to affect future environmental conditions, and his or her own personal integrity.

The second important structural constraint under consideration concerns the multiple, competing *discourses* that also define the possibilities for action in the environmental domain.[75] Discourses, here, are defined as particular collections of ideas, beliefs, categorizations, and reasoning through which meaning is given to social and physical realities.[76] The status of any particular discourse depends on two things: the power and authority of the actors who use it, and the degree to which the discourse is itself "privileged"—i.e., "deemed more appropriate or efficacious than others" in a given social setting.[77] In processes of social interaction, competing discourses often become organized into dominance hierarchies that, via the forces of selection, exclusion, and domination, influence what can and cannot be said in any particular situation.[78]

The result of sociohistorically informed stakeholders interacting in the context of these structural constraints is the practices that make up the multistakeholder collaborative process. In its most elemental form, the primary practice under examination in this book is that of interpersonal communication.[79] Multistakeholder environmental partnerships represent situations in which participants endeavor to recognize and incorporate each other's sociohistorically based interpretations.[80] From this essential practice emerge other related ones, such as developing shared understandings, exploring ideas, identifying key issues and obstacles, and producing decisions.

Both sociohistoric factors and structural constraints influence the communicative action residing at the core of multistakeholder collaboration. This influence, however, is not unidirectional. In the interactive practice of communication, participants have the capacity to reformulate sociohistoric factors and structural constraints in return.[81] Through the processes of dialogue and debate, participants may modify their understandings of the problems at issue, the ways that they express themselves with regard to these issues, and the actions that they choose to take in response. Similarly, these interactions may produce alterations both in the credibility and authority attained by different actors in the environmental domain and in the legitimacy and status accorded to the various competing environmental discourses. My theoretical orientation to the study of multistakeholder partnerships thus portrays such collaborations not as mechanistic bargaining efforts among participants holding timeless and consistent values, beliefs, and worldviews but as dynamic and emergent processes in which people, their ideas, and their actions can and do change.[82]

I conceptualize such changes as occurring at two basic levels: at the interpersonal level, and at the intrapersonal level. Interpersonal-level transformations involve changes to a person's understandings of and relations to things beyond him- or herself. Intrapersonal-level transformations, conversely, involve changes to a person's own self-conceptualizations.

At the interpersonal level, these transformations occur in two primary ways. First, they are induced by the process of *social learning*.[83] In multistakeholder collaborative processes, participants, over the course of talking, debating, and otherwise interacting with others, are exposed to new ideas, views, and practices brought by these other actors. In some cases, this causes these participants to alter their own thinking and behavior. Some of this learning is "single-loop learning," where, via error detection and correction, participants use new information gained to modify their approaches toward achieving set objectives.[84] Other aspects of this learning fall into the category of "double-loop learning."[85] Here, learning involves critical self-reflection and the transformation of one's underlying values or assumptions. This may induce participants in multistakeholder partnerships to change their basic arguments about the issues at stake as well as their relationships to and understandings of each other.

The second way by which personal transformation takes place at the interpersonal level is through the process of cultural production[86] and, in particular, through the generation of new *cultural forms*. These cultural forms consist of the new meaning systems, practices, and group processes that are often generated when people characterized by different sociohistoric features interact.[87] The point here is that participants do more than learn from their interactions with others in multistakeholder collaborative processes. They also actively participate in creating new ways of knowing, acting, and being together.

Deriving from these first two sources of change, but this time taking place at the intrapersonal level, is a third way that personal transformations occur in partnership settings. This involves participating actors forming new or altered identities. This notion of identity, however, goes beyond the in-group versus out-group notions of identity often emphasized in the literature on group processes,[88] as individuals do more than simply adopt a group's collective identity vis-à-vis other groups. Partnership participants must also be conceived of as dynamically "authoring" or (re-)creating themselves anew on a continual basis.[89] To express themselves and communicate among themselves in interactive settings such as multistakeholder environmental collaborations, participants must constantly choose from among the words, ideas, and behaviors that they each use for giving meaning to and acting in the world.[90] Social learning and cultural production are key processes by which this takes place. Social identities are also attached to particular words, ideas, and behaviors. Consequently, when actors selectively, although not necessarily consciously, adopt certain ways of knowing, acting, and talking, this may lead them to develop altered perceptions of themselves.[91]

Although personal transformation is an integral part of collaborative processes, significant alteration of a person's subjective understandings is by no means guaranteed or inevitable. Certain participants will undoubtedly be transformed more than others in these processes, and some will hardly shift at all. Nevertheless, such changes are possible, and I argue in this book that environmental partnerships are conducive to them.

Summary

Given this protracted description of the particular analytical lens through which I approach the study of multistakeholder environmental partnerships, a more concise review is in order. I see the diverse actors participating in multistakeholder collaborative processes as drawing upon sociohistorically based understandings in their efforts to address particular problems. Participants express these understandings via diverse, differentially privileged, and potentially conflicting meaning systems, discourses, and practices, and these actors may do so differently depending on the contextual constraints in effect. In the partnership process, participants engage in social interaction, dialogue, and debate. This creates the possibility for social learning as well as the production of new or altered meanings, discourses, and practices. Participants selectively, although not necessarily consciously, use this cultural information to creatively explore and understand different subjective positions or identities, thus creating the possibility for the transformation of both the sociohistoric factors and the structural constraints that influenced participant behavior in the first place. This entire iterative process constitutes what I call *the practice of multistakeholder collaboration*.

Notes

1. Daniels and Walker (2001), Gray (1989), Wondolleck and Yaffee (2000).

2. Coenen et al. (1998), Smith et al. (1997), Van den Hove (2000).

3. O'Connor and Van den Hove (2001).

4. Susskind et al. (1999), Susskind and Cruikshank (1987), Pellow (1996).

5. De Jongh and Captain (1999), Glasbergen (1998c).

6. For more on the description of environmental collaboration, see Daniels and Walker (2001), Gray (1989), Lober (1997), Selin and Chavez (1995), Snow (2001), Winer and Ray (1994), and Wondolleck and Yaffee (2000).

7. I use the word "stakeholder" with some caution here. This is due to the non-neutral origins of this term. In particular, it comes out of the business community, which has been redefining the consuming public, and citizens more generally, as stakeholders in corporate affairs. This reconceptualization demonstrates a particular worldview regarding economic relations that is not universally shared by actors outside of business (see Karliner 1997).

8. Gray (1989), Ozawa (1993).

9. Long and Arnold (1995).

10. Hartman et al. (1999), Long and Arnold (1995), U.S. Department of Labor (1998).

11. This understanding of partnership departs from more traditional and limited views of the term, such as Winer and Ray's (1994, 23) definition of partnership as "an association of two or more who contribute money or property to carry on a joint business and who share profits or losses."

12. Long and Arnold (1995).

13. Blackburn and Bruce (1995), Crowfoot and Wondolleck (1990a), Dukes (2001), Susskind and Cruikshank (1987), Weidner (1995).

14. Biekart (1998), Glasbergen (1998b), Liefferink and Mol (1998).

15. Hartman and Stafford (1997), Hartman et al. (1999), Livesey (1999), Lober (1997), Stafford and Hartman (1996).

16. Endicott (1993), Hawkins and Benedict (1990).

17. Conley (2001), Moote et al. (2000).

18. Lynn and Busenberg (1995).

19. Lynn et al. (2000), Milliman and Feyerherm (1999).

20. Bingham (1986), Dukes (1996).

21. Ryan (1995), Weber (1998).

22. Brick et al. (2001), Borrini-Feyerabend (1999), Pinkerton (1989).

23. Carr et al. (1998), Forester (1999), Healey (1997), Kearns and West (1996), Selin and Chavez (1995).

24. Biekart (1998), Glasbergen (1998b).

25. Stafford and Hartman (1996).

26. Endicott (1993), Hawkins and Benedict (1990).

27. Moote et al. (2000).

28. See, for example, Daniels and Walker (2001), Glasbergen (1998a), Gray (1989), Long and Arnold (1995), O'Connor and Van den Hove (2001), O'Leary (1995), Stern and Hicks (2000), Van den Hove (2000), and Wondolleck and Yaffee (2000).

29. Cardskadden and Lober (1998), Crowfoot and Wondolleck (1990b), Curtis (1998), Long and Arnold (1995), Van den Hove (2000).

30. Achterberg (1996), Baker et al. (1997), O'Connor and Van den Hove (2001), Young (1997).

31. Bingham (1986), Dukes (2001), McCloskey (1996), O'Leary (1995), Stafford et

al. (2000).

32. Amy (1987, 1990), Blowers (1998), Mazza (1997), O'Leary (1995).

33. Driessen (1998), Dukes (2001), O'Leary (1995).

34. This book is responding to various calls for increased investigation of multistakeholder collaboration. In the domains of environmental policy, planning, and management, Amy (1987), Dukes (2001), Lober (1997), Long and Arnold (1995), and Röling (1994), among others, have called for greater critical examination of multistakeholder collaborative processes in general and how they actually work in particular. In anthropology, Bennett (1990) and Brosius (1999a, 1999b) have solicited increased study of the institutions that are increasingly mediating human relations with the environment.

35. See Long and Arnold (1995) for such an approach to environmental partnerships. See also Brown et al. (1995) and Gulliver (1979) for a similar approach to conflict resolution.

36. Ross (1993a), Schwarz and Thompson (1990), Winslade and Monk (2000).

37. Fisher, Ury, and Patton (1991).

38. For other examples of this interest-based approach to negotiation, see Susskind et al. (2000), Ury et al. (1988), U.S. Department of Labor (1998).

39. For example, see Axelrod (1984), Bolton and Chatterjee (1996), Ellickson (1991), Maida (1995), Ostrom (1990).

40. For example, see Bacow and Wheeler (1984), Brick et al. (2001), Brown et al. (1995), Crowfoot and Wondolleck (1990b), Glasbergen (1995b), Gould et al. (1996), Long and Arnold (1995), Sloep and Blowers (1996).

41. This argument is also made by Gulliver (1979), Healey (1997), O'Leary (1995), Shailor 1994, and Woodhill and Röling (1998).

42. For examples of this "how to" approach, see Bingham (1986), Blackburn and Bruce (1995), Cardskadden and Lober (1998), Curtis (1998), Daniels and Walker (2001), de Bruijn and Tukker (2002), Dukes et al. (2000), Glasbergen (1995b, 1998c), Gray (1989), Littlejohn and Dominici (2001), Lober (1997), Long and Arnold (1995), Lynn et al. (2000), McNeely (1995), Selin and Chavez (1995), Stern and Hicks (2000), Stolton and Dudley (1999), Susskind et al. (2000), Ury et al. (1988), U.S. Department of Labor (1998), Venter and Breen (1998), Winer and Ray (1994), Wondolleck and Yaffee (2000), Yosie and Herbst (1998).

43. See also Ross (1993a), Roy (1994), and Winslade and Monk (2000) on this point.

44. See Ross (1993a) for a more in-depth discussion of these limitations.

45. Ross (1993a), Schwarz and Thompson (1990), Wildavsky (1987), Winslade and Monk (2000).

46. See, for example, Blackstock (2001), Chia et al. (2001), Daniels and Walker (2001), Dukes et al. (2000), Gulliver (1979), Kressel and Pruitt (1989), Littlejohn and Domenici (2001), Pearce and Cronen (1980), Ross (1993a, 1993b), Roy (1994), Schwarz and Thompson (1990), Shailor (1994), Wildavsky (1987), Winslade and Monk (2000).

47. Many of these analyses limit their attention here to stakeholder "values" (see, for example, Stern and Hicks 2000).

48. Ross (1993a) argues that the entire social sciences have tended to ignore the effect of sociohistoric factors on social action.

49. Gulliver (1979).

50. Ethnographic research is characterized by the following features: "a strong emphasis on exploring the nature of particular social phenomena, rather than setting out to

test hypotheses about them; a tendency to work primarily with 'unstructured' data, that is, data that have not been coded at the point of data collection in terms of a closed set of analytic categories; investigation of a small number of cases, perhaps just one case, in detail; [and] analysis of data that involves explicit interpretations of the meanings and functions of human actions, the product of which mainly takes the form of verbal descriptions and explanations, with quantification and statistical analysis playing a subordinate role at most" (Atkinson and Hammersley 1994, 248).

51. Atkinson and Hammersley (1994), Baba (1988), Denzin (1989).

52. Arrow et al. (2000).

53. Long and Arnold (1995).

54. There has not been a great deal of ethnographic research directed specifically toward multistakeholder environmental collaboration per se. There has been, however, a significant amount of ethnographic research directed more generally toward conflict (e.g., Brosius 1999b, Gulliver 1979, Roy 1994).

55. This six-month time frame was strategically chosen as the minimum amount of time that I thought was needed for partnership participants to become familiar and comfortable with my research project and me. The trust that was engendered played a critical role in encouraging frank and open discussion in the interviews themselves.

56. Supplementary methodological information is listed in appendix A. This includes information on the selection criteria for the partnerships, the types of data collected, and the design of the interviews.

57. I elected to confine the study to partnerships occurring in the industrialized West for reasons of personal interest and because this is a part of the world in which many such initiatives are currently taking place. Of course, numerous examples of environmental collaboration within the developing world also exist, especially in the area of nature conservation (see Gamman 1994, McNeely 1995, and Stolton and Dudley 1999).

58. Stake (1994, 237).

59. George (1979, 51).

60. Healey (1997), Shailor (1994), Schwarz and Thompson (1990), Weale (1992), and Woodhill and Röling (1998) make a similar argument regarding how instrumental rationality has become the dominant paradigm of these disciplines.

61. Abelson (1996), Green and Shapiro (1994), Healey (1997), Schwarz and Thompson (1990), Taylor (1996), Tversky (1996).

62. Ross (1993a), Schwarz and Thompson (1990), Wildavsky (1987), Winslade and Monk (2000).

63. Schwarz and Thompson (1990).

64. Warren (1993).

65. Kempton (1991), Kempton and Craig (1993), Kempton et al. (1995).

66. Grove-White (1993), Silverstein (1993).

67. Holland et al. (1998), Holland and Lave (2001), Piven and Cloward (1979).

68. Almond and Verba (1963).

69. Ross (1993a).

70. In the planning literature, practice-based approaches are being advocated by Forester (1993, 1999) and Innes (1995). In the communication and small group processes literature, they are being promoted by Frey (1994), Pearce (1989), and Pearce and Cronen (1980). In the literature on conflict and dispute resolution, they are being advanced by Cobb (1993) and Roy (1994).

71. Bourdieu (1977, 1990).

72. This notion of power draws from Bourdieu's (1983, 1985, see also Bourdieu and Wacquant 1992) notion of "field." From this analytical perspective, environmental stakeholders operate within an "environmental field" defined by the relationships that exist among them and structured according to the distribution of economic and symbolic capital maintained by them. Individuals are seen as continually, though not necessarily consciously, acting in consideration of preserving the value of their capital in this field. As such, they may also be seen as producing and reproducing both the field and its structure.

73. Bourdieu (1977, 1990).

74. See Daniels and Walker (2001), Fisher (1983), Folger et al. (1997), and Roy (1994) for more on the diverse factors that influence a stakeholder's authority and prestige in the collaborative process.

75. Much has been written about the role of competing discourses in the construction of environmental issues. See, for example, the work by Dryzek (1997), Hajer (1995), Litfin (1994), Peace (1993), Prato (1993), Swaffield (1998), Williams and Matheny (1995), and Winslade and Monk (2000).

76. Hajer (1995).

77. Wertsch (1991, 124).

78. Bakhtin (1981), Bourdieu (1982), Brosius (1999b), Foucault (1970), Weedon (1997).

79. This focus on communication as a product rather than simply as a medium is also being advocated in the literature on communication and small group decision making by Pearce and Cronen (1980), Poole and Hirokawa (1996), and Seibold et al. (1996).

80. My theoretical orientation parallels Habermas's (1984) theory of communicative action in both my attention to practices of interpersonal communication and in my focus on communicative rationalities and the pursuit of intersubjective understandings rather than instrumental rationalities and the pursuit of self-interest.

81. Giddens (1984), Holland et al. (1998), Holland and Lave (2001). In the literature on conflict and collaboration, the argument that culture-based factors affect dispute resolution just as the social interaction in these processes affects these culture-based factors in return is also being made by Chia et al. (2001), Dukes (1996), Dukes et al. (2000), Ross (1993a, 1993b), and Roy (1994).

82. See Dukes (1996), Dukes et al. (2000), Healey (1997), Forester (1999), and Winslade and Monk (2000) for similar portrayals of multistakeholder collaboration as an emergent process.

83. Daniels and Walker (2001), Forester (1996), Friedmann (1987), Glasbergen (1996a), Innes (1999), Maarleveld and Dangbégnon (1999), Woodhill and Röling (1998).

84. Argyris and Schön (1996).

85. Argyris and Schön (1996), Woodhill and Röling (1998).

86. This cultural production perspective, while drawing heavily on social constructionist roots, stems most directly from the domain of cultural studies. This perspective portrays the cultural information—i.e., the particular ways of knowing, talking, or acting—that individuals and groups draw upon in daily social interaction not as preexisting and stable but as undergoing active, collective, and continual formation, revision, and reproduction. This perspective situates cultural production in the context of dynamic and asymmetrical power relations, yet it also presents the process as engendering the alteration of these very same constraining structures (Holland and Lave 2001).

87. Although my discussion on cultural forms draws predominantly from the work of Johnson (1987) and Willis (1977, 1981), many other scholars have also written on the

production of new meanings and senses of self and community that occur in collaborative processes. See, for example, Bush and Folger (1994), Cobb (1993), Daniels and Walker (2001), Dukes (1996), Dukes et al. (2000), Littlejohn and Domenici (2001), and Ross (1993b).

88. Brewer and Gardner (1996), Hogg (1996).

89. Holland et al. (1998); see also Bruner (1990), Roy (1994), and Winslade and Monk (2000).

90. Bakhtin (1981), Holland and Lave (2001).

91. Holland et al. (1998).

Chapter 2

Conflict and Collaboration in the Environmental Arena

In February 1995, the British government approved a proposal by the U.K. division of Royal Dutch/Shell, a major oil company, for deep-sea disposal of the 16,000-ton, 463-foot Brent Spar oil storage and tanker-loading platform in the north Atlantic. The Brent Spar was one of over 400 North Sea oil platforms and the first to receive such a license. Less than three months later, fearing destruction of the surrounding marine ecosystem, activists from the environmental group Greenpeace began illegally occupying the oil rig as part of a high-profile media crusade and consumer boycott against Shell. At the height of the campaign, Shell filling stations in Germany were shot at and firebombed. Political leaders throughout Europe joined a large public outcry in declaring their opposition to the proposed sinking of the Brent Spar.

This high stakes environmental campaign cost Greenpeace over $2 million (U.S.), while the boycott threatened to cost Shell even more.[1] German sales of Shell products, for instance, declined by 30 percent in the month of June alone.[2] In the end, Shell elected to drop its plans for deep-sea dumping of the Brent Spar and began reconsidering on-land dismantlement, a move projected to increase disposal costs by as much as 40 percent.[3]

Greenpeace's campaign against Shell achieved international media attention. Some members of the press portrayed it as a great victory for Greenpeace and for environmental protection, in general, and as a humiliating defeat for both Shell and the British government, which had supported deep-sea disposal of oil platforms.[4] Other analysts criticized Greenpeace's use of science and decried the environmental group's pressure tactics as a threat to liberal democracy.[5] The petroleum industry, for its part, depicted the entire incident as a blow not only to the oil and gas business but also to the consuming public and saner environ-mental organizations elsewhere.[6] Whatever the interpretation, this event en-trenched the mistrust and contentiousness that was already pervasive among these environmental actors.

At the same time the Brent Spar episode was playing out in the North Sea, a very different mode of environmental action was under way in the Sierra Ne-vada Mountains of the United States. The setting was the town of Quincy, Cali-fornia, where animosity between the logging and environmental communities over timber harvesting in the surrounding forests had been growing for years. Relations had deteriorated to the point that fistfights, stone throwing, vandalism, and even the exchange of gunfire between the two sides were not uncommon. Against this backdrop, several members from the timber industry, local envi-ronmental groups, and local government began meeting regularly and voluntar-ily in the town library. They gathered to address some of the logging issues fac-ing the region in a cooperative rather than conflictual fashion. Calling themselves the Quincy Library Group, they adopted the goal of coproducing a tree harvesting and forest fire management plan that would protect both the re-gion's logging-based economy and its forests. In this way, they hoped to pre-serve the town's social fabric as well.[7]

Although the Quincy Library Group collaborative effort was noteworthy for the extreme enmity out of which it grew, it was by no means unique. Similar initiatives in which representatives from government, business, environmental groups, and other community organizations were gathering to cooperate rather than fight were gaining momentum in many other regions of Europe, North America, and the rest of the world. Many of these were local or regional initia-tives, like the Quincy Library Group, geared toward managing or preserving local resources. Others, however, were taking place at the highest policy levels. Among these were the European Commission's General Consultative Forum on the Environment[8] and the U.S. President's Council on Sustainable Development (PCSD).[9]

The simultaneous existence of both conflictive and cooperative styles of environmental action continues to be a distinctive feature marking the environ-mental policy arenas of Western industrialized nations at the turn of the twenty-first century. Why this dynamic persists and what it portends for the future of environmental problem solving are questions explored in this book.

Environmental Conflict

Although distinctive in its financial impact and media coverage, the Brent Spar episode typifies the type of environmental *dispute* that has become quite com-mon in the industrialized West. At the center of these disputes are particular actors who disagree over how to address particular environmental dilemmas.

Often underlying the disputes, however, are longer running, deep-rooted environmental *conflicts*.[10]

Broadly defined, environmental conflicts involve "some degree of incompatibility arising from issues relating to the environment."[11] They reflect persistent differences in the way that people value and use natural resources, in how environmental quality is assessed, and in what is at stake for people in environmental and natural resource management decisions.[12] Environmental conflicts also arise out of differing views as to the severity of environmental problems, the risks involved, and the types of changes needed to resolve these problems.[13]

In the industrialized West, the environmental problems currently giving rise to these conflicts are quite varied and include air and water pollution, waste production (toxic and otherwise), agrochemical use, urban sprawl, and natural resource depletion. Although complex, these problems are by no means new. For Europe and North America, they hark back to the industrial revolution and the development of resource-intensive modes of industrial and agricultural production. These problems are also the legacy of an extended period of economic growth and mass consumerism that has marked Western society since World War II.

A final key characteristic of environmental conflicts is their longevity. Unlike most of the particular disputes that arise from them, environmental conflicts tend to be *enduring*.[14] This is evident in the confrontational and antagonistic dynamic that has long marked relations among the business, government, and NGO sectors—a dynamic that owes its source to deep-rooted differences in the sectors' respective approaches to the use and care of the natural environment.

Contributing Factors

Four key sources of tension contribute to the enduring quality of environmental conflict that are of particular relevance to this book.[15] The first source concerns a belief commonly found in the business, government, and environmental NGO sectors that holds that an inexorable opposition exists between *economic* and *environmental* interests.[16] This belief is demonstrated by the pervasiveness of such aphorisms as "jobs versus trees" or "short-term profit versus long-term gain." The dual presumptions underlying this belief are (1) that continued economic growth is destined to result in environmental degradation, and (2) that excessive environmental regulation or forced inaccessibility to the resource base will inevitably lead to lessened availability of goods and services, increased inflation, and unemployment. Both of these presumptions were evident in the Brent Spar case. Greenpeace and its supporters believed that continued oil development in the North Sea would pose a great threat to the region's ecosystems. For their part, Shell and other representatives of the oil industry assumed that environmentally sensitive disposal of oil rigs would impair their ability to be profitable.

A second important source of tension underlying the enduring quality of environmental conflicts is tied to fundamental philosophical disagreements that people have over what constitutes the rightful relationship between humans and nature. Some people value the intrinsic worth of nature, holding that humans are no more important or entitled than any other life form. This position has its roots in the ecocentric ideals of many indigenous cultures. Other people, however, see nature anthropocentrically as subservient to and existing for the instrumental use of humans.[17] This view, at least in the West, draws its inspiration from two different sources. The first is the Judeo-Christian doctrine granting humans dominion over the earth.[18] The second concerns philosophical ideas stemming from the Enlightenment,[19] which view control over nature—and over other humans, for that matter—to be a necessary condition of human self-realization and progress.[20] In the Brent Spar case, the "intrinsic worth of nature" view was held by those members of Greenpeace and it supporters who felt that Shell had no right to place other life forms at risk. The "instrumental use" position was embodied in Shell's approach to natural resources, in which the oil company saw itself as entitled to extract, appropriate, dispose of, and otherwise manage petroleum purely for the benefit of people.

A third major source contributing to continuing environmental struggles emerges from diverging views over the suitability of *capitalism*, and especially a capitalist system founded upon the profit motive and free market ideals, as the predominant guiding force for society. A long-standing conflict persists between two general positions. On one side are proponents of capitalist structures, who claim or at least assume that the competitive market is the most effective system around which to organize society and manage the environment.[21] On the other side are opponents, who argue that an irreconcilable contradiction exists between the capitalist prime motive of unceasing economic growth and the earth's ultimately finite natural resources and limited capacity to absorb pollution.[22] In the Brent Spar affair, these two positions were represented by supporters of Shell's right to maximize economic efficiency in disposing of the Brent Spar platform, on one side, and by assailants of indeterminate dumping who argued that such actions constituted an irresponsible threat to the health of the planet, on the other.

The fourth and final underpinning of environmental conflict to be explored here involves a tension between human motivations guided purely by self-interest and those oriented toward ensuring the common good.[23] This opposition between private and common interests exists at two levels. First, it operates *between* people, as when individuals driven by private interest risk overexploiting scarce, commonly held natural resources.[24] Such would be the case if Shell derived its profits from dumping the Brent Spar at sea at the expense of future exploitation of the same marine ecosystem for the benefit of society at large. Second, this opposition exists *within* individual actors as well. Witnesses to the Greenpeace-Brent Spar conflict may have experienced tension between their preferences as *consumers* to continue using petroleum-based products for their own personal gain and their preferences as *citizens* to oppose actions that might lead to the destruction of common resources.[25]

Key Consequences: Social Movements and Public Policy

These tensions, and the enduring environmental conflicts that they support, have had important societal effects. One key outcome has been the rise of the modern environmental movement, which emerged in Western Europe and the United States in the 1960s. The modern environmental movement arose in response to issues of ecological instability and environmental degradation associated with the period of economic expansion and mass consumerism following the Second World War. The pivotal players in this movement were the great number of environmental groups, ranging from local-level citizen action committees to international-level nonprofit organizations, that sprang up to meet this challenge. Grounded in grass-roots and activist orientations, these groups used public awareness campaigns, popular protests, and legal actions to attack what they perceived as environmental excesses and injustices and governmental ineffectiveness.

Unlike the land and wildlife conservation movement that emerged at the turn of the twentieth century,[26] the modern environmental movement arose in conjunction with several other popular movements, including the peace, anti-nuclear, student, welfare rights, and feminist movements.[27] All of these so-called new social movements were reacting to various effects of the postwar boom. The movements were all characterized by a general mistrust of the marketplace, private investment, and the achievement ethic. They were also marked by "postmaterialist" values emphasizing personal and political freedom, participatory democracy, egalitarian redistribution, and the departure from traditional authoritarian structures. Finally, all of them drew upon grass-roots organizing and a strong activist orientation to promote new ideas in search of a more caring society.[28]

A second important consequence of enduring environmental conflicts has been the rise of environmental policy regimes. Starting in the 1960s and 1970s, policy makers in regions such as Western Europe and the United States began turning their attention to environmental concerns.[29] The result was the production of a broad array of landmark legislation banning or controlling the pollution of water, land, and air. Examples include the United States' Clean Air Act of 1970, Belgium's Toxic Waste Law of 1974, and the U.K.'s Control of Pollution Act in 1974.[30] Policy makers also established regulatory institutions to help implement and enforce these laws, such as the Environmental Protection Agency (1970) in the United States, the Environmental Ministerial Committee (1972) in Belgium, and the Council of Environmental Experts (1972) in West Germany.[31] These changes were part of a trend toward top-down, regulatory rule that would remain dominant within the environmental policy realm throughout the 1970s.[32]

One important ramification of this standardized, rule-based approach to environmental problem solving, however, was that it established a decision-making structure that encouraged antagonistic relations. It pitted an environmental community in favor of strict and enforceable regulations against a business community generally opposed to actions viewed as economically inefficient. Both of these communities, in turn, used lobbying and litigation to pressure governmental officials into satisfying their interests.

Such antagonistic relations continue to play out at every sociopolitical level where public policy decisions get made. At the international level, they are evident in politically volatile conflicts among countries over such issues as carbon dioxide emissions standards or acid rain restrictions. At more local levels, they are evident in recurring "NIMBY" (Not-in-My-Back-Yard) protests over the siting of industrial facilities and in pro-growth versus no/slow-growth disputes over land development. Since the 1960s, this context of hostility and opposition has been the setting for much of the activity in the environmental arena.

Contextualizing the Rise
of Multistakeholder Environmental Collaboration

Environmental Policy Reactions

The environmental laws and regulations of the 1960s and 1970s had, and continue to have, an enormous impact on environmental quality in the United States and Western Europe. The success of this so-called command-and-control approach, however, has not been without its consequences, as the entrenchment of environmental regulatory regimes has provoked a wide array of criticism.[33] One main complaint is that regulatory strategies are inherently inflexible and economically inefficient because they impose uniform reduction targets and technologies that ignore the actual pollution abatement situations facing individual firms.[34] Critics making this point have also argued that the prescriptive quality of these regulations stifles incentives to develop innovative pollution control methods or to reduce emissions beyond mandated levels.[35] A second main criticism is that regulatory-based approaches have reached the limits of their environmental effectiveness. Some analysts speak of this in terms of a diminishing rate of return, as most of the easy gains from regulations have been achieved.[36] Others point to the chronic problems of weak political commitment, deficient coordination among regulatory agencies, and poor records of implementation and enforcement.[37] A final main criticism is that direct regulatory approaches lack democratic legitimacy. Critics, here, point toward a general lack of transparency, poor accountability, and inadequate participation of actors from outside of government.[38]

Not willing to stop at criticism alone, many of these policy analysts have gone a step further and begun calling for new policy instruments that are more effective in addressing current environmental concerns. Some advocate greater adoption of market-based tools such as tax incentives and market trading of emissions permits.[39] Others promote the increased use of so-called voluntary instruments,[40] including eco-labeling,[41] third-party certification of environmental performance, as under the EU's Environmental Management and Auditing Scheme (EMAS) and ISO 14001 Environmental Management Systems Certification,[42] and voluntary or negotiated agreements between the regulating and regulated communities.[43] More broadly, still others are calling for the increased use of collaborative planning and management processes[44] and alternative dispute resolution methods to help make effective and long-lasting environmental decisions.[45]

As a result of these reactions, the environmental policy domains of the European Union and the United States have witnessed a shift since the late 1970s away from regulatory regimes focused solely on top-down control and toward more differentiated policy strategies also including substitute or parallel processes based upon stakeholder voluntary action, cooperation, and shared responsibility.[46] In the eyes of many, this shift also constitutes movement away from environmental decision-making processes based upon contestation and opposition and toward those more grounded in camaraderie, relationship building, social learning, and mutual gain.[47]

Supporting Societal-Level Trends

While these changes in the environmental domain have been significant, they have by no means been unique or isolated. They have also been affected by a number of important societal-level trends that have marked the industrialized West over the past several decades. This section highlights the influence of three of these in particular: the transformation of the predominant system of capitalism, the rise of the ideology of neoliberalism, and the proliferation of modern management techniques.

The Evolving Capitalist System

The first trend involves changes to the prevailing system of capitalism and, in particular, to relations among corporations, labor, and the state that have taken place over the last half-century.[48] In the domain of economic production, this transformation has entailed a shift from a system reliant upon standardized mass production and economies of scale to one valuing flexible, small batch production of variable product types, intensified technological and organizational innovation, entrepreneurship, and new market development.[49] Supply-driven, high inventory strategies and top-down decision-making methods have giving way to demand-driven, just-in-time "lean" production systems, a customer-oriented focus, and, most significantly for this discussion, more communicative and cooperative styles of management. In the 1990s, this shift toward cooperative management was evidenced by a substantial increase in the formation of strategic partnerships and alliances among firms that had existed only in competition beforehand.[50]

In the domain of labor, this evolution of the system of capitalism has involved a shift away from high degrees of job specialization and vertical labor organization toward an emphasis on the adaptability of skills, horizontal job movement, and retraining. Most significantly, the influence of trade unions in industrial relations and national policies has declined accordingly. This has opened the door for other special interest groups, such as those promoting environmental protection and nature conservation, to play a more significant role.[51]

Finally, in the domain of governance, this capitalist transformation has involved the decline of the Keynesian welfare state.[52] Governmental functions, particularly in the domain of social services, have been devolving to the business sector via privatization and to both the business and nonprofit sectors via cooperative arrangements.[53] This transformation is part of a relative shift in governance patterns away from "big government" and centralized rule and toward more localized decision making.

The Rise of Neoliberalism

A second major trend helping contextualize recent changes within the environmental policy domain, and one intricately related to the first, involves the ascendance of the ideology of neoliberalism. This ideology gained traction in the United States and the European Union with the rise to power of conservative political administrations in the late 1970s and early 1980s. It values the efficiency and freedom of the market, gives preference to economic competitiveness (e.g., over other social or environmental concerns), and favors the reorientation of state activities to satisfy the needs of the private sector.[54] Neoliberalism is evident in policies promoting the termination of trade barriers, such as the EU's single market and the North American Free Trade Agreement. It is also apparent in efforts made to relax or even do away with some of the regulations governing economic activity. This deregulatory pressure has been felt within all areas of public policy, including environmental policy. It is largely responsible for the recent promotion on both sides of the Atlantic of incentive-based, market-oriented policy tools and business "self-regulation."[55]

Under the ideology of neoliberalism, governments are being called upon to help structure the marketplace so that private-sector activities may assist in the advancement of public policy objectives. Public authorities are being asked to "steer" rather than "row" and to serve as facilitators and brokers of economic and social activity rather than as commanders and controllers.[56]

Proliferation of Modern Management Techniques

A third societal-level trend that has influenced changes within the environmental policy arena and, in particular, that has helped bring about greater levels of cooperation among environmental stakeholders involves the proliferation in recent decades of modern management paradigms and their underlying ethic of *managerialism*. Managerialism refers to the problem-solving-oriented manner, guided by economic rationality and bureaucratic thinking, by which organizations approach environmental, economic, political, or social issues.[57] It involves objectifying elements of the world—be they capital flows, production processes, human behaviors, or natural resources—so as to be better able to *control* them. The ultimate goal is increased efficiency.

Although managerialist ideas are by no means new (the business sector has long applied management theory to economic production and labor issues, and governments in the West have a long history of applying management techniques to the natural resources domain itself[58]), what has changed over the past several decades is the degree to which corporate, governmental, and even NGO actions are being driven by such strategies.

Among corporations, we see this increasing dependency on managerialism in their growing adoption of total quality control and, more recently, environmental management practices.[59] We also see it in their growing efforts to strategically manage a broader range of stakeholders in the domains of governmental and community relations.[60]

Among policy makers and regulatory agencies, we see this increasing reliance on managerialism in their promotion of ecosystem management strategies[61] and in their more recent efforts to manage the public via expanded citizen participation procedures.[62] Both business and government are more frequently approaching environmental conflict as something to be managed rather than resisted.[63]

Finally, among environmental NGOs, we see elements of managerialism arising in their continuing efforts to control the actions of business and government. This is especially true for the larger environmental groups operating at the national and international levels. This ethic appears in their increasing reliance on scientific expertism as well as in their increased use of rational pollution and resource management tools such as cost-benefit analyses and environmental impact assessments in their policy debates.[64]

The Net Effect

The net effect of these societal-level trends has been an overall shift in the expectations of how societies should be governed. Whereas Western governments in the past were expected to function primarily as regulators and authoritarian rulers, citizens and businesses alike are now increasingly calling upon them to play the roles of enablers and collaborative managers in a world where power is more shared.

Evolving Environmental Relations

These broad historical trends, and the recent transformations within the environmental policy sphere that they inform, form the distinctive backdrop against which today's environmental actions are being considered and undertaken. This has led to significant changes *within* the environmental NGO, business, and governmental sectors. It has also led to the development of new relations *among* these sectors.

Intrasectoral Transformations

In the environmental domain, the political and litigation successes of environmental groups in the 1960s and 1970s helped establish these groups as potent voices in the public policy arena.[65] This was especially true for the larger, better-funded organizations that managed to acquire a lobbying foothold in the centers of political power. Their influence has continued in the decades that followed, bolstered in particular by increased access to the policy production process. More and more environmental organizations are having the opportunity to affect policy decisions via representation on a wide variety of advisory councils, consultative commissions, and other participatory structures.[66]

The very success of environmental groups, however, has led to diversification within the environmental movement. This was due in large part to some of the economic and social effects brought about by the very environmental regulations promoted by these groups. These regulations had a direct and, at times, negative impact on the livelihoods of farmers, miners, ranchers, and loggers who depend on natural resource exploitation. The regulations also impinged on the interests of other social groups, such as property owners and outdoor recreation enthusiasts such as hunters, fishermen, and off-road vehicle users. Many of these diverse actors believed that they had been hurt rather than helped by the flood of new environmental regulations. Some came to resent the environmental movement for ignoring their needs. Others began to preach alternative environmentalist beliefs that advocated not nature preservation but the wise and efficient use of resources, and that recommended not constraining the free market but using it for pollution prevention and natural resource management purposes.[67] This alternate view, often referred to as "free market environmentalism"[68] or "market-based environmentalism,"[69] now constitutes a new strand of environmentalism that has come to challenge the authority of some of the more traditional NGOs within the environmental policy realm.

As smaller-scale economic interests were affected by the promulgation of environmental regulations, so too were those of larger firms. Although regulated industries had always been involved to some extent in the production of environmental policy, individual corporations and business federations began taking on markedly larger lobbying and agenda-setting roles in the 1980s.[70] These corporations and federations began shifting their approach away from the traditional method of simply resisting all new environmental legislation toward the alternative strategy of promoting legislation more acceptable to them.[71] To achieve this goal of a more tolerable regulatory climate, these firms began adopting more sophisticated methods, some of which were specifically aimed at the environmental movement. These methods included the dual-pronged tactic of launching their own environmental pressure groups while at the same time working to undermine the credibility and arguments of the more mainstream movement.[72]

All of these actions have helped to increase the influence of the business sector within the environmental policy arena. This influence was already substantial to begin with, given both the expertise that firms bring to the policy production process as the primary implementers of environmental regulations and the enormous edge in material resources that firms have to support their lobbying efforts.[73] The standing of the business sector has grown to the extent that some policy analysts now argue that corporations occupy a position of greater authority within the environmental policy arenas of the European Union and the United States than does the environmental community.[74] This is evidenced, they say, by the fact that EU and U.S. environmental policy and law since the late 1980s more fully reflect the priorities and positions of corporate Europe and corporate America than they do those of the environmental community.

This rise in the influence of the business sector, it should be noted, has not been restricted to the environmental domain. Some scholars have gone so far as to proclaim that corporations have replaced governments as the most dominant actors in society.[75] This is due, in large part, to the partial retreat that governments in the United States and the European Union have made from the broader regulatory arena. This retreat, in turn, has led to a bifurcation within many governmental agencies and even within individual officials themselves between an older, more top-down style of decision making and a newer, more participatory way of governing. To the traditional governmental role of "leader," agency officials are increasingly being called upon to add the more unfamiliar roles of "partner" and "stakeholder."[76] Both of these newer roles lack the authority of their antecedent.

Intersectorial Transformations

In addition to the changes that have been taking place within the governmental, environmental NGO, and business sectors, there has also been a shift in the relations *between* them. In particular, the sectors are becoming increasingly interdependent.[77] In today's global economy, for instance, governments are increasingly using subsidies and other measures to promote the competitive advantage of the very firms that they are supposed to regulate.[78] Similarly, many environmental NGOs are now frequently turning to the same corporations and governmental agencies that they campaign and litigate against for financial and technical assistance in their environmental protection endeavors.[79] Finally, as noted above, the business community is increasingly treating the governmental regulations and environmental groups that they have opposed in the past as opportunities for competitive advantage and new markets.[80]

The upshot is that it is no longer possible for players in one particular sector to take unilateral environmental action without thought or consideration to the other two. The capacity for representatives of any one of these sectors to veto the actions of the others has risen accordingly. The result has been the generation of a state of gridlock in which it is becoming increasingly difficult for anyone to design, enact, revise, or implement environmental policy decisions.[81]

The Collaborative Solution

Frustration with this gridlock, however, has led representatives from all of these sectors to look for ways beyond this impasse. Many have called for cooperative efforts to replace the contentious approaches of the past. In the European Union, the European Commission espoused this position in 1993 with its request in the Fifth Environmental Action Programme for the development of new policy instruments involving all of the "economic and social partners" in a more "bottom-up" approach to environmental decision making.[82] More recently, in laying down the Sixth Community Environmental Action Programme, the European Parliament and Council of the European Union reiterated this message by calling for improved "collaboration and partnership" among public authorities, enterprises, consumer groups, and NGOs, with a view toward improving environmental performance in the economic sector.[83] In the United States, the President's Council on Sustainable Development (PCSD) endorsed this view in 1996 by calling for greater use of "collaborative decision-making processes" for managing the country's natural resources.[84] The PCSD has since repeated this promotion of increased multistakeholder collaboration, stating that "[t]houghtful dialogue among the representatives from traditionally adversarial stakeholder groups can help promote mutual understanding, allowing a better appreciation of each other's priorities and concerns, and building a foundation for collaborative problem solving."[85]

To be sure, relations among these three sectors are still marked by considerable tension. Governments, bound by a social contract to protect the welfare of their citizens, continue to regulate business activity. Environmental groups, as self-selected protectors of the natural environment, continue to pressure business and government to stop polluting. And corporations, as profit-seeking entities, persist in resisting actions by these other two sectors that may impede economic efficiency. Nevertheless, there appears to be a growing shared belief that collaborative action, and not conflict, among society's diverse interests may be the key to resolving many of today's complex environmental problems.[86]

Notes

1. Luyken (1995).
2. Singh (1995).
3. *Economist* (1996).
4. Abbott (1996), Clery (1996), Grove-White (1996), Paterson (1995).
5. Bennie (1998), Clery (1996), Culbertson (1995).
6. *Oil and Gas Journal* (1997).
7. See Kiester (1999), Marston (2001), and Mazza (1997) for more on the Quincy Library Group.

8. European Commission (1997). The General Consultative Forum on the Environment was succeeded in 1997 by the European Consultative Forum on the Environment and Sustainable Development (European Commission 2001a).

9. President's Council on Sustainable Development (1996, 1999).

10. I draw upon Daniels and Walker (2001, 40-41) to make this distinction between environmental disputes and conflicts.

11. Daniels and Walker (2001, 40).

12. Crowfoot and Wondolleck (1990c), Daniels and Walker (2001).

13. Crowfoot and Wondolleck (1990c).

14. Brown (1995), Crowfoot and Wondolleck (1990a), Daniels and Walker (2001), Schnaiberg and Gould (1994).

15. My discussion here is influenced by Holland and Lave's (2001) concept of "enduring struggle." My description of four key sources of tension, however, is not intended to be comprehensive. I have selected these four sources because they are most pertinent to the research conducted. Other important sources of tension also exist, such as interorganizational competition or competing conceptual modes of cause and effect.

16. Brown (1995), Maser et al. (1998).

17. For more on these two positions, see Callicott (1994), Norton (1992), and Rolston (1986).

18. White (1967).

19. For different accounts of the materialism of the Enlightenment, see Harvey (1996), Horkheimer and Adorno (1972), and Nonini (1985).

20. These Enlightenment beliefs later became embodied in the exploitation of natural and human resources that has marked the colonialist and later postcolonial imperialist enterprises.

21. For example, see Anderson (1997) and Anderson and Leal (1991).

22. For example, see Cahn (1995), J. O'Connor (1994), and Schnaiberg and Gould (1994).

23. See Dryzek (1995) and Brown (1995) for more on this point.

24. See Hardin's (1968) notion of the "tragedy of the commons" for more on this risk.

25. I draw on Sagoff (1988) to make this point.

26. See Costain and Lester (1995), Dalton (1993, 1994), and Dowie (1995) for the history of the environmental movement in Europe and the United States.

27. Buttel (1992), Freeman and Johnson (1999), Kriesi et al. (1995).

28. Kriesi et al. (1995).

29. During this period, the vast majority of European action took place at the nation-state level. European Community-level environmental policy was not initiated in an integrated fashion until 1973 with the institution of the First Environmental Action Programme (Vogel 1993).

30. Smet (1990), Weale (1992).

31. Gobin (1986), Weale (1992).

32. Andrews (1999), Hagland (1991), Switzer (1994), Weale (1992).

33. See Golub (1998) for a compelling summary of criticisms that have been forwarded against current environmental regulatory regimes.

34. Andrews (1998), Collier (1998a).

35. Glasbergen (1995a).

36. Dente (1995).

37. Andrews (1999), Collier (1998a), Eckersley (1995a), Krämer (1989), Vogel (1993), Weale (1992).

38. Baker (1996), Dryzek (1992, 1995), Fiorino (1996), Paehlke (1996).

39. Golub (1998), Moran (1995).

40. Paton (2000).

41. Eiderström (1998).

42. Benson (1996), Taschner (1998).

43. Biekart (1998), Glasbergen (1998c), Liefferink and Mol (1998), Ryan (1995), Weber (1998).

44. Gray (1989), Healey (1997), Selin and Chavez (1995), Wondolleck and Yaffee (2000).

45. Crowfoot and Wondolleck (1990a), Dukes (1996), Susskind and Cruikshank (1987), Susskind et al. (2000), Weidner (1995).

46. Andrews (1999), Collier (1998b), Eckersley (1995b).

47. Daniels and Walker (2001), Kearns and West (1996), Meadowcroft (1998), Susskind et al. (2000), Wondolleck and Yaffee (2000).

48. Buttel (1992), Ernste (1998), Harvey (1989); see also Amin (1994).

49. Buttel (1992), Ernste (1998), Harvey (1989).

50. Scheuing (1994), Urban and Vendemini (1992).

51. Buttel (1992).

52. Harvey (1989), Jessop (1994).

53. Gidron et al. (1992), Salamon (1995), Squires (1996).

54. Gill (1995), Group of Lisbon (1993), Jessop (1994).

55. Anderson (1997), Andrews (1998), Collier (1998b), Eckersley (1995b).

56. Osborne and Gaebler (1992); see also Grabosky (1995).

57. Brosius (1999a), Ehrenfeld (1997), Escobar (1995), Ernste (1998).

58. Andrews (1999).

59. Berry and Rondinelli (1998), Buchholz (1998), Feigenbaum (1988), Reinhart (2000), Rikhardsson and Welford (1997), Welford (1996).

60. Cardskadden and Lober (1998), Clutterbuck (1981), McIntosh et al. (1998), Post et al. (1999).

61. Gordon and Coppock (1997), Yaffee et al. (1996).

62. Curtis (1998), Nader (1995), Lynn and Busenberg (1995).

63. Brown et al. (1995), Glasbergen (1995b).

64. Dowie (1995), Escobar (1995), Gottlieb (1993).

65. Hagland (1991), Andrews (1999). Note that litigation, as a strategy, was pursued with greater frequency in the United States than it was in Europe.

66. Lynn and Busenberg (1995), Marks and McAdam (1996), Pollack (1997).

67. Rowell (1996). This new form of environmentalism is better institutionalized in the United States (e.g., in the form of the Wise Use Movement) than it is in Europe.

68. Anderson (1997).

69. Hartman and Stafford (1997).

70. Andrews (1999), Coen (1997), Cowles (1995).

71. Lodge (1989), Switzer (1994).

72. Butt Philip and Porter (1997), Dowie (1995), Rowell (1996).

73. In the European Union, industrial and commercial lobbying groups outnumber their environmentalist counterparts by a margin of twenty to one at the EU level (Butt Philip 1995).

74. Amy (1987), Andrews (1999), Butt Philip (1995), Butt Philip and Porter (1997), McCormick (2001), Switzer (1994).

75. Kulik (1999), McIntosh et al. (1998), Tichy et al. (1997).

76. Wondolleck and Ryan (1999).

77. Gray (1989) argues that increasing interdependence is itself a product of increasing levels of collaboration.

78. Cahn (1995), Schnaiberg and Gould (1994).

79. Endicott (1993), Goldsmith (1995), Lober (1997), Stafford and Hartman (1996).

80. Hartman and Stafford (1997), Welford and Gouldson (1993).

81. Long and Arnold (1995), Dukes (1996).

82. European Commission (1993, 43).

83. European Parliament/Council of the European Union (2002, 5-6).

84. President's Council on Sustainable Development (1996, 113).

85. President's Council on Sustainable Development (1999, 95).

86. Wondolleck and Yaffee (2000).

Chapter 3

Case-Study Environmental Partnerships

Collaborative environmental action among diverse societal interests can take a variety of forms. My focus is on one form in particular: multistakeholder environmental partnerships. Four case-study partnerships serve as the basis for this analysis. This chapter describes them in greater detail.

Throughout this book, I follow the ethnographic convention of using pseudonyms to refer to both the partnerships studied and the individuals and organizations that compose them. Protecting the identities of the partnership participants was an integral part of the research design. My access to each of the case studies was contingent on this promise of anonymity.

Two important benefits arise from this convention. First, gaining the trust of the people being studied is a critical element of ethnographic research.[1] Participants are more likely to express themselves freely and fully in meetings or in interviews if they believe no harm will come out of it. Second, this convention helps draw the reader's attention away from the features of the particular case studies and toward my primary focus—the processes by which partnerships operate. My overarching goal, again, is to improve understandings of how partnering for the environment works in practice. I am less concerned with analyzing or evaluating the performance of particular partnerships.

My descriptions of the case-study partnerships focus on four main areas: their goals, their historical backgrounds and reasons for being, their organizational structures and modes of operation, and their compositions. Summaries of the four case-study partnerships are presented in table 3.1.

Table 3.1. Summary Description of Case-Study Partnerships

	European Union Partnership for Environmental Co-operation (EUPEC)	Toupin River Contract (TRC)	Gascoigne Biodiversity Project (GBP)	Collaboration for the Improved Management of Natural Resources (CIMNR)
Area	European Union	Belgium (Walloon Region)	Belgium (Walloon Region)	United States
Time Frame	1994–present (Studied over a one-year period in 1994–1995)	1993–present (Studied over a one-year period in 1994–1995)	1994–present (Studied over a one-year period in 1994–1995)	1997–1999[1] (Studied over a two-year period in 1997–1999)
Key Participants	European-based multinational corporations and European and national-level environmental NGOs. Regional and sub-regional governmental federations also played important roles. Approximately fifty partners in total.	Local, regional, and national-level environmental NGOs and governmental representatives in the form of elected officials and agency personnel from the regional, provincial, and communal levels. Representatives from industrial and agricultural federations also played important roles. Approximately fifty partners in total.	Local government officials, NGOs focused on a wide variety of social, cultural heritage, and nature conservation issues, and school officials and teachers. Social services administrators, local farmers, beekeepers, hunters, and small business owners also played important roles. Approximately forty-five partners in total.	Resource-intensive and extraction-based industries, a range of international to state-level environmental advocacy groups for whom nature conservation was a major issue, and representatives of federal-level regulatory agencies and state-level environmental administrations. Approximately thirty-five partners in total.
Partnership Goals	To forward the practice of sustainable development in Europe by stimulating dialogue and cooperation among all sectors involved in or affected by the implementation of the European Commission's Fifth Environmental Action Programme. To serve as a model for future partnerships.	To develop and implement a plan protecting, restoring, and valorizing water resources associated with one of the region's main rivers. To integrate this plan with other provincial objectives in the domains of economic development, land-use planning, tourism, and cultural heritage.	To employ participatory processes for the purpose of preserving or improving the diversity of the local area's natural heritage while at the same time respecting and promoting the economic and social development of its inhabitants. To go beyond the isolated environmental actions of the past to address the biodiversity concerns of the commune as a whole.	To engage leaders from business, government, and the environmental NGO community in civil dialogue and the generation of innovative ideas for the purposes of informing and influencing policy making in both the public and private domains. To produce a report recommending new approaches to natural resource management that will better sustain natural systems, a healthy economy, and vital communities.

[1] An earlier phase of the CIMNR partnership ran from 1993 to 1996.

The European Union Partnership
for Environmental Cooperation (EUPEC)

The first case study was a European Union-level partnership headquartered in Brussels, Belgium. I call it the European Union Partnership for Environmental Cooperation (EUPEC). The EUPEC initiative's overarching goal was to forward the practice of sustainable development in Europe. It aimed to do so by raising the awareness of different stakeholders and by helping to catalyze progress toward the objectives and targets presented in the European Commission's Fifth Environmental Action Programme. The EUPEC initiative also hoped to serve as a model for similar partnership initiatives to be established at national, regional, and local levels. Finally, the partnership planned to use its multistakeholder collaborative forum to produce policy recommendations on a variety of sustainability-related issues in such domains as transport, agriculture, energy production, manufacturing, tourism, and environmental management.

Background

The EUPEC initiative grew out of two important trends converging in Europe in the early 1990s. The first was the rise of "sustainable development" as a focal issue in the EU policy arena.

The concept of sustainable development emerged onto the international policy stage in 1987 with the World Commission on Environment and Development's (WCED) publication of *Our Common Future*.[2] Unlike previous formulations of the term, the WCED's version integrated environmental concerns with the economic and social imperatives of development strategies.[3]

This idea of an integrated environmental approach began to take hold in Europe around the same time. In 1986, the European Union passed the Single European Act requiring the incorporation of environmental considerations into all other policy sectors. By 1993, sustainable development had itself become a key policy issue. It was the centerpiece of the EU's Fifth Environmental Action Programme, entitled *Toward Sustainability: A European Community programme of policy and action in relation to the environment and sustainable development*. In the context of global economic pressures, the policy of sustainable development was important to the European Union because it provided a way of reconciling the EU's historical commitment to economic growth with its rising concerns over environmental protection.[4]

The second major trend concerned the state of multistakeholder collaboration in the European environmental arena. In the late 1980s, environmental partnerships were still relatively scarce in Europe. This changed dramatically in the early 1990s, due in large part to the momentum generated by the 1992 United Nations Conference on Environment and Development. Not only did the "Earth Summit" call for accelerating sustainable development throughout the world, but it also advocated bottom-up cooperation among societal sectors as a key means for achieving this.[5] Although the period leading to and immediately following the Earth Summit saw the formation of many new collaborative environmental ventures in Europe, most of these involving the business sector remained either solely comprised of industrial corporations or limited to alliances between business and government.[6] Interaction between environmental NGOs and these other two major sectors remained for the most part relegated to the largely adversarial activities of lobbying, participation in advisory councils, litigation, and protest actions.

In 1993, in an attempt to address this dearth of collaboration between the European environmental and business communities, an environmental NGO initiated a series of roundtable discussions. These roundtables had the effect of bringing together two charismatic leaders from the European environmental domain: the executive officer of an influential European environmental group and a high-ranking executive from a prominent multinational corporation. In the face of weak economic growth and increasing global competition, these two individuals decided to launch a European-level, multistakeholder initiative aimed at fostering economic recovery based on what they called "green economics and green industries." They assembled a steering committee of prominent representatives from public authorities, trade unions, research institutes, and environmental consultancies as well as from business corporations and environmental NGOs to help officially launch the EUPEC initiative a year later.

The EUPEC initiative thus did not arise in response to a specific environmental crisis or event, as has been the case for many other multistakeholder collaborations. Nor did it spring from long-standing disputes over the disproportionate effects of pollution on certain populations or the unequal use and allocation of natural resources. Rather, certain key actors in the environmental realm simply came to the realization that there was much to be gained and little lost from increased intersectorial communication and cooperation. Taking a cue from the EU's Fifth Environmental Action Programme, these actors adopted the broader objective of sustainable development as their primary focus.

Structure and Operation

From the beginning, the EUPEC's initiators were concerned about the possibility that the partnership could be co-opted by special interests. The initiators consequently attempted to design the collaborative so as to ensure representativeness and balance among the varied sectors.

Structurally, the initiators organized the partnership into a general assembly and an executive committee (refer to figure 3.1 for a diagram of the EUPEC organizational structure). The general assembly included all of the partnership's official members. It was designed to contain roughly equal numbers of partners from four main sectors. These included the NGO, business, and governmental

Figure 3.1. EUPEC Organizational Structure

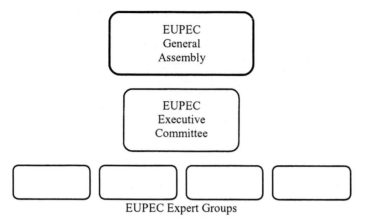

EUPEC Expert Groups

sectors as well as a fourth professional sector composed of representatives from trade unions, consumer organizations, think tanks, academia, and environmental consultancies. The general assembly convened once a year to decide on program and budgetary issues and to elect the members of the executive committee. Decisions required a majority of votes from each of these four sectors.

The executive committee consisted of twelve members recruited equally from the four sectors. The committee was led by a group of elected officers, also divided evenly among the different sectors, and met every three months or so. Decisions were made by majority voting, although at least one vote was required from representatives of each of the four sectors for a measure to pass. The main responsibility of the executive committee was to coordinate and run the partnership.

During my yearlong research with the EUPEC initiative in 1994-1995, the partnership was primarily involved in the process of institution building. Most of the executive committee meetings in the first part of the year were directed toward structuring the partnership, building membership, and developing a plan outlining the work to be covered in the future. As part of its membership-building responsibilities, the executive committee organized and hosted several informational seminars and partnership workshops. These seminars and workshops assembled representatives from the four sectors for the purposes of sharing experiences, increasing awareness of environmentally related issues, exposing these actors to each other's particular understandings of and approaches to these issues, and assisting them in identifying opportunities for initiating specific partnership activities together.

Starting in the second half of my research, the executive committee also undertook the task of creating expert work groups to address key environmental issues selected and approved by the general assembly. These expert groups comprised interested EUPEC members as well as technical specialists brought in from the outside. During this period, the EUPEC initiative created four expert groups. They were focused on tourism, leisure, nature protection, and agri-tourism; agriculture, food, retail, and solid waste issues; private and public transport, communication, and urban issues; and sustainability management and auditing instruments. These expert groups were to meet over a series of months or years and draw upon the multistakeholder collaborative process to produce innovative policy recommendations.

Procedurally, the EUPEC initiative operated largely without the assistance of third-party neutrals. The partnership's elected officials ran the general assembly and executive committee meetings, while the expert group meetings were facilitated informally by designated group members. Only in the large workshops were professional facilitators brought in to support the collaborative process.

Funding for the EUPEC initiative during the research period came from several main sources. Approximately half came from the annual membership dues required of all EUPEC participants. These dues were organized on a sliding scale, with large corporations contributing the most and smaller NGOs the least.[7] The other half of the funding was supplied by grants from the European Commission and the environmental ministries of several EU member states. The operating budget for 1994 was approximately 220,000 Euros (about $260,000 U.S.), while that of 1995 was about 500,000 Euros (about $600,000 U.S.).[8] In 1995, the project coordinators registered the EUPEC initiative as a not-for-profit organization, a move intended to establish the autonomy of the partnership and to make it eligible for additional funding sources.[9]

Composition

Participation in the EUPEC initiative was theoretically open to any organization, but official membership required approval by the general assembly and the payment of annual dues. Prospective candidates were evaluated based on whether they were adequately supporting the sustainability objectives delineated by the European Commission's Fifth Environmental Action Programme. The purpose behind this was to discourage those organizations with poor environmental records and negligible histories of proactive efforts in the environmental domain from seeking membership in the partnership solely for the benefit of good publicity.

By late 1995, over fifty partners were formally affiliated with the EUPEC initiative. Given the partnership's history, it was not surprising that the most active participants came from the business and environmental NGO sectors. The business sector members comprised largely major multinational corporations, many of which represented pollution-intensive petroleum, chemicals, agro-chemicals, and energy industries. Also common were representatives from the consumer products and biomedical sectors.

Although not as large as its business counterpart, the environmental NGO sector was marked by the presence of several prestigious international- and national-level environmental organizations with long histories of engaging in environmental policy formation. Many of these were either large nature conservation organizations or federations of national-, regional-, and local-level environmental NGOs. Nearly all of them, given their willingness to work with the business and governmental sectors, could be labeled as mainstream or moderate. Several environmental groups from the more radical wing of the European environmental movement were invited to join the EUPEC initiative, but these groups, which historically had taken more adversarial and hard-line approaches toward environmental issues, elected not to participate.

Public authorities were the least well represented of the three main sectors. Their members came primarily from international-level environmental agencies or federations of cities or regional areas. There was little representation from regulatory agencies at the national or EU level. The European Commission, as a major funder of the partnership, followed the initiative closely but did not participate actively. The environmental ministries of various EU member states also followed the partnership, sending delegates to some of the EUPEC functions, but they did not participate actively either. The EUPEC coordinators had elected not to encourage the participation of EU member states. The coordinators were mindful of the political difficulties that might arise out of having some but not all of the EU member states represented.

Of the EUPEC initiative's major participants, the business sector appeared to wield the most influence in the partnership.[10] Its authority and power stemmed from several sources. First, there were more participants from business than from any other sector, and they tended to be among the most active in the executive committee and expert groups. Second, corporations benefited from their role as the primary implementers of sustainability-oriented change. Large-scale sustainability cannot occur without the involvement of business. Last, while by no means pollution free, most of the corporate participants had already adopted proactive approaches to environmental action. They had, for instance, instituted sophisticated environmental management systems, undertaken small-scale process-oriented changes to improve resource use efficiency, or begun convening their own stakeholder-based processes to better coordinate and communicate with local communities. They thus had reputations as being among the business leaders in the environmental field. Only a few of the corporate members had reputations of being laggards, but even these were credited for attempting to improve their environmental behaviors.

Although the NGO representatives brought with them long histories of lobbying governments and influencing public opinion, they generally lacked the financial resources, manpower, or expertise to track, let alone challenge, many of the changes being adopted by such business leaders. They also were limited in their abilities to effectuate many sustainability-oriented actions without partnering with the business sector. They did realize, however, that while the EUPEC initiative's focus was on promoting sustainable development within the

EU, exactly what this meant or entailed had yet to be clearly defined. These NGO participants were present because they wanted to make sure that their views on sustainable development would balance the ideas coming from business.

The governmental sector participants, lacking representation from key EU or national-level regulatory agencies, exerted the least influence of the three main sectors. They entered into the partnership largely to leverage their capacity for environmental action. They hoped to do so by building coalitions among diverse constituencies.

Demographically, EUPEC members came from all over the European Union. Most of them, however, represented organizations situated in the environmentally progressive EU member states of northern Europe. These participants shared certain other characteristics in common as well. A large majority of them were male. Nearly all were racially classifiable as white or Caucasian. Participants ranged in age from their thirties to their sixties, with most being in their forties and fifties. They also typically held middle to high-ranking managerial or administrative positions within their organizations. None of them came from organizations dedicated to representing socioeconomically disfranchised populations within Europe.

The Toupin River Contract (TRC)

The second case study involved a watershed partnership located in the Ixtoup Province (a pseudonym) in the Walloon Region of Belgium. The Walloon Region is the southernmost of three semiautonomous regions comprising the Belgian federal state.[11] The goal of this partnership was to develop and implement a plan to protect, restore, and valorize water resources associated with the province's major river, the Toupin River (a pseudonym), and its tributaries. The partnership hoped to integrate this plan with other economic development, land-use planning, tourism, and cultural heritage objectives. I refer to this initiative as the Toupin River Contract (TRC) partnership.

Background

The Toupin River is a small river that runs through much of the Ixtoup Province, which comprises over two dozen separate communes, or local governments.[12] The Ixtoup Province is characterized by a mix of agricultural and industrial activities. Over the past forty years, it has become increasingly urbanized due to its proximity to a nearby expanding metropolitan area. Property values in the Ixtoup Province are now among the highest in Belgium. Population has also been on the increase. In 1995, the province had over 300,000 inhabitants.

The TRC partnership did not arise in response to a specific problem facing the river so much as it did to the presence within the province of several active environmental organizations that wanted to do something on behalf of their local environment. This is not to say, however, that the Toupin River was pollution free. Indeed, the river suffered from decades of agricultural runoff (primarily pesticides and nitrates from fertilizers); industrial waste discharges from paper mills, tanneries, breweries, and gravel mines; and the release of untreated sewage. For many years, the predominant governmental response to the foul smells and unsightly views caused by this pollution was to cover large parts of the river over. Even in the mid-1990s, significant portions of the river in some towns remained covered to shield local inhabitants from the waters.

Starting in the 1970s, the European Union began enacting directives targeting wastewater discharges.[13] This brought about increased levels of wastewater treatment in the Toupin River basin, including treatment of sewage by local governments. As a result, the water quality in certain parts of the river improved significantly. During the 1980s and 1990s, the European Union also passed several additional directives regulating industrial and agricultural discharges.[14] Implementation of these directives had a further beneficial impact on the river. When the TRC partnership kicked off in 1993, the overall health of the river was generally viewed as fair, although certain portions still remained stressed.[15]

The existence within the province of a relatively large and active environmental NGO community reflected a growing environmental consciousness in the region. The primary cause of this shift was the influx over the past four decades of new residents from nearby cities drawn to the area for its greenery and rural character. These new inhabitants, or "neo-rurals" as they were often called, came from higher socioeconomic standings than many of the province's longtime citizens. They brought with them a different kind of environmental sensibility—one that placed greater emphasis on the aesthetics and intrinsic value of the natural environment than on its instrumental utility.

Communication among government, business, and these citizens was never robust. The province made efforts to remedy the situation by mandating public inquiries for major construction projects, but certain segments of the population remained dissatisfied with the current state of affairs. Citizens were becoming increasingly apathetic toward their elected officials and their administrations and increasingly distrustful of the region's major economic actors. By the late 1980s, these new inhabitants began forming local citizen action groups to resist large public works and economic development projects, leading to an overall heightening of tensions among the three sectors.

The TRC partnership grew out of this context in 1992, when a federation of environmental groups in Wallonia, in anticipation of the United Nations Conference on Environment and Development and at the urging of the Belgian government, asked some of its member organizations in the Ixtoup Province to initiate a grass-roots environmental project for the region. Under the coordination of a local land-use planning institute, approximately twenty-five NGOs came together to pursue the prospect of working collaboratively on a major environmental project or campaign. After considering other pertinent issues such as waste management and transportation, they settled on the problem of water pollution, largely because many of them lived or worked close to the region's major river.

Borrowing an idea that had received a lot of positive press in the Dordogne River basin in France a few years earlier, the group decided to create and enact a "river contract" for the Toupin River. A river contract is a publicly recognized though not legally binding series of propositions for environmental action that its participants cooperatively create and voluntarily agree to implement. River contracts operate in parallel to existing governmental regulations but do not preempt them. The Toupin River Contract was one of several river contracts being initiated in the Walloon Region. Geographically, the contract was defined by the boundaries of the Toupin River watershed and the borders of the Ixtoup Province. It affected over 200,000 inhabitants and nearly 700 square kilometers of land area.

While not directly involved in creating the Toupin River Contract partnership, the Walloon government encouraged the project's formation. The enactment and implementation of river contracts supported the Walloon Region's broader goal of better integrating water quality objectives with other policies governing the use and management of the region's waterways, such as flood control and habitat protection.[16] The Walloon government also hoped that the TRC partnership would serve as a standing collaborative that could be used to address other local environmental and land-use planning issues in the future.

Structure and Operation

The NGO initiators of the TRC partnership decided that they wanted to create an initiative involving as many interested parties as possible. They organized the partnership into a series of task-differentiated committees (see figure 3.2 for a diagram of the TRC partnership's organizational structure).

At the heart of the TRC organizational structure was a multisectorial, plenary-level body that I refer to as the river committee. Comprising forty-five or so participants selected to represent the province's diverse interests, this committee was responsible for instituting, managing, and signing off on the river contract.

The river committee received logistical support from three distinct sources. The first was an expert group that I call the technical committee. Numbering about twenty participants, it was composed largely of technicians and engineers from the governmental agencies responsible for managing and maintaining the province's rivers. The second, which I call the NGO committee, was a group designed to serve as a public forum. Totaling approximately thirty participants, it consisted primarily of members of local- and regional-level environmental groups, although it also included representatives from agricultural unions, fish-

Figure 3.2. TRC Organizational Structure

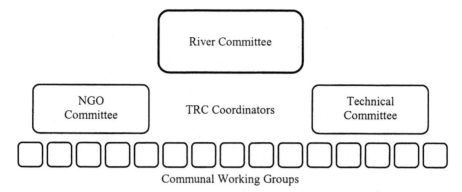

Communal Working Groups

ing associations, and social-sector NGOs. The third source of support for the river committee came from a series of communal-level working groups representing each of the participating communes. These working groups served several important functions: they permitted the participation of any interested individual or organization in the partnership, they provided direct access to the concerns and desires of local inhabitants, and they constituted a ready labor force to assist in the development and eventual implementation of the river contract itself.

Coordination of the partnership was assigned to the local land-use planning institute that had assisted in its formation. This institute also provided professional facilitation services for all of the partnership meetings.

Though not legally binding, river contracts have a basis in Belgian law in the form of a March 18, 1993, "Ministerial letter" issued by the Walloon Minister for the Environment, Natural Resources, and Agriculture. This document gives the terms and conditions for the establishment of river contracts in the Walloon Region and also lays out the specific procedures by which river contracts must be set up and operated. In line with these requirements, the first action undertaken by the TRC partnership was to assemble the various actors concerned with the river to produce an accord detailing the specific objectives, scope, methodology, budget, and plan of action for the proposed Toupin River Contract project. This accord was then circulated to the provincial and communal governments for signature.[17] In signing this agreement, the provincial and communal governments committed financial resources for three years beginning in 1993. The total budget for the project was approximately 13.5 million Belgian francs, or about $450,000 (U.S.).[18] The province assumed two-thirds of the cost, while the Walloon government covered one quarter. The remaining fraction was subdivided among the participating communes.

Once the accord initiating the partnership was signed by the communal, provincial, and regional authorities in late 1993, the project was required to proceed in three general phases. The first phase, the inventory phase, involved establishing a baseline environmental "state of affairs" for the Toupin River and its tributaries. The TRC partnership subdivided this inventory into four separate studies: a survey of surface water quality, a report of existing and potential flood zones, an account of particular pollution trouble spots along the river, and an evaluation of subsurface water quality. The next phase involved the development of a charter composed of a list of proposed environmental actions. These propositions were developed by the partnership coordinators based on input and feedback from all of the partnership's participants. The final phase involved the creation of a master plan detailing what environmental actions were going to be performed, by whom, by what date, and with what money. This multiyear implementation phase would require new financial support beyond the funds that had been committed by the regional, provincial, and communal levels of government for the first three-year period of the contract.

During my yearlong research with the TRC partnership, various work streams proceeded concurrently. Communal working groups and outside contractors were enlisted to conduct the survey work establishing baseline environmental conditions. At the same time, the technical committee and NGO committee began meeting every two months or so, providing logistical support to the survey efforts and developing the specific propositions that would become the basis for the charter. The river committee met twice a year to review, amend, and approve the charter's progress and to attend to administrative concerns. Throughout this work, the coordinators produced and disseminated publications informing the province's broader population of the project's goals and accomplishments.

The propositions composing the proposed charter fell into four different categories. The first set was geared toward better informing and involving the public regarding decisions affecting the river. Signatories would commit here, for instance, to notify and consult with the TRC partnership on future public works projects such as the construction of new water treatment plants or flood basins. The second set of propositions involved surface water quality improvements. Among these were projects that involved creating a permanent system for monitoring water quality throughout the river basin, restocking the river with appropriate species of fish, and establishing financial incentives to encourage best agricultural practices along the riverbeds. The third grouping of propositions was directed toward improving the management of the river basin, including better integration of flood control, pollution abatement, and ground water management practices. The final set of propositions was focused on the management of the province's natural heritage. Specific projects here included establishing new natural reserves in some of the region's wetland areas and creating a new team of voluntary "river-keepers" to help with the daily monitoring and upkeep of the river.

At a more procedural level, the project coordinators informed the participants that all of the meetings would proceed via the process of *concertation*. In their publications, they defined *concertation* as a mode of decision making that is consensus based and inclusive of a wide variety of interests and perspectives.

It involves not only compromise but also the possibility that views will change and that decisions will be made that bring satisfaction to all. Concertation seeks to avoid the rise of entrenched conflicts by requiring committed participation and dialogue on the part of the partners.

Composition

Participation in the TRC partnership was open to any individual or organization situated within the province. The coordinators tried to maximize the representativeness of the initiative by sending invitations to many of the area's diverse interest groups. The participants included representatives from all three major sectors. The major governmental participants included public officials from the regional, provincial, and communal levels. NGO participants came from communal citizen action groups as well as regional- and national-level conservation groups. Representing the business sector were delegates from agricultural alliances and industrial federations.

The most active and influential participants in the TRC partnership came from NGOs and government. They were also the most numerous. The business sector was represented by only a handful of participants. Most of these came from the agricultural sector, which was concerned that local farmers would be disproportionately blamed for the river's troubles. Representatives of industry participated only intermittently, claiming that they preferred to direct their collaborative efforts to the national and regional rather than subregional level.

The NGO participants—comprising largely environmental groups but also including social services organizations, fishermen's associations, and individual citizens—were the major drivers behind the project. They saw their primary role to be that of opening to the public the decision-making processes concerning the river. They donated significant amounts of time and labor to help conduct the studies establishing the state of the river. They participated actively in developing the propositions that formed the foundation of the charter. They typically served as leaders in the communal working groups. They also provided the pressure that brought the other major stakeholders, especially those from government, to the table and kept them involved. Although the NGO participants were generally lacking in financial resources, their power in the TRC negotiations came from their commitment to the process, their potential influence on public opinion, their scientific expertise on ecological matters, and their extensive knowledge of local environmental conditions.

The governmental representatives participating in the partnership were less proactive than their NGO counterparts but no less important. They were the primary managers of the region's waterways and had legal decision-making and implementation authority in this regard. They were also the primary funders of the project. Governmental enthusiasm for the partnership, however, was not uniform. Although higher-ranking officials in the Walloon and Ixtoup provincial governments generally expressed strong support for the partnership, many of the lower-level administrators and resource managers involved participated more reluctantly. They were also less than eager to subject their projects and decisions to greater public involvement and scrutiny.

The governmental authorities involved included a wide variety of public officials. The Walloon government sent functionaries to follow and provide logistical support for the partnership and also to serve as a link to the region's other ongoing river contracts. The Walloon government's authority derived from its role as the primary producer and enforcer of laws and regulations governing the region's waterways.

The provincial government, which owned the Toupin River and its major tributaries, sent several representatives, including elected officials responsible for water and environmental policy issues as well as employees from two resource management agencies. The first of these agencies, the Provincial Waterway Service, was responsible for supervising and maintaining the river system. This agency was the primary source of knowledge and expertise regarding the history and condition of the river. It dealt with flooding problems, repaired riverbed damage, and designed and constructed storm basins. The second agency, the Water Treatment Agency, was responsible for all sewage and wastewater treatment in the province. The Water Treatment Agency was a powerful player in the region. It had a lot of money, as its wastewater treatment work was fully subsidized by the Walloon government. Moreover, it was responsible for planning and managing all new economic development in the province.

The final group of governmental actors participating in the partnership came from the communes. The communes owned and were responsible for managing and maintaining the smaller tributaries flowing into the Toupin River. They were represented by elected environmental officials and local natural resource managers. Their influence in the partnership was hindered by a lack of both financial resources and manpower.

Demographically, the participants in the TRC project were overwhelmingly white and middle or upper-middle class. In both cases, this reflected the overall population of the province. Although the province was also home to lower-income groups, such as some small farmers and the inhabitants of several subsidized housing developments, these relatively disfranchised populations were not well represented in the partnership. The committees were predominantly male, although this was less the case for the NGO committee and the communal working groups than for the other committees. Participants varied in age from their twenties to their seventies, with most of the older people being retirees volunteering for environmental groups. These elderly NGO representatives tended to be among the most active participants in the partnership.

The Gascoigne Biodiversity Project (GBP)

The third case study consisted of a local initiative directed toward biodiversity conservation within a single commune, the commune of Gascoigne (a pseudonym), in the Walloon Region of Belgium. Referred to as the Gascoigne Biodiversity Project (GBP) partnership, its stated goal was to employ participatory processes to preserve or improve the diversity of the commune's natural heritage while at the same time respecting and promoting the economic and social development of its inhabitants. The project hoped to go beyond the isolated environmental actions of the past to address the biodiversity concerns of the commune as a whole.

Background

Gascoigne is a small commune measuring slightly over 3,100 hectares in size. Although its economy is largely agricultural, it has also experienced urbanization pressure over the past thirty years due to its proximity to several expanding metropolitan areas. In 1995, its population was slightly over six thousand, nearly double what it had been two decades earlier. This population contained an uneasy mix of longtime agriculturalists who had been growing beets and grains and raising pigs and chickens on family farms for generations and a relatively new group of inhabitants commonly referred to as neo-rurals. The neo-rurals included people who had relocated to the commune for its rural character and proximity to nature but who continued to commute to nearby cities for work.

A recent survey conducted by a research institute found the biological diversity within the commune to be relatively poor. Most of the biodiversity left was relegated to the riparian areas along the commune's two main rivers, some undeveloped prairies along one of these rivers, several small lakes, a few wetland areas, two forested zones around ten hectares in size, a number of other smaller forested sections, and many hedgerows. Among the flora in need of protection were numerous species of wildflowers, including heather, arnica, hollyhock, and orchids. Common fauna to be preserved included hedgehogs, a variety of shrews, bats, frogs, snakes, lizards, and butterflies, and over forty species of birds.[19]

The study attributed this paucity of biodiversity to two main causes. The first was the intensive agriculture taking place on the vast majority of the commune's surface area. Agriculture's threat to biodiversity had increased several decades earlier when the Belgian government began promoting a policy of farmland regrouping. This involved the removal of hedgerows and the transformation of a landscape characterized by numerous smaller plots into a new one featuring fewer, larger fields more conducive to industrial agriculture and monoculture. The second cause was burgeoning real estate development in the region. New housing development was threatening not only agricultural land but also some of the commune's forested, riparian, and wetland areas.

Although the diversity of biota in the commune of Gascoigne might have been hampered, this was not an issue that was galvanizing the area's six thousand inhabitants. In fact, the initial impetus for forming a partnership focused on biodiversity protection came not from within the commune but from outside. The catalyst was a prestigious philanthropic foundation in Belgium that in 1993 began offering a limited number of grants to qualified communes interested in conserving their biological diversity. These grants were part of the foundation's efforts, inspired by the 1992 United Nations Conference on Environment and Development, to promote sustainable development in Belgium. The grants required the development of a "biodiversity contract" by a multistakeholder partnership. A biodiversity contract, like the aforementioned river contracts, comprises a series of action items that the signatories collaboratively develop, agree upon, and commit to implement. Also like river contracts, it is intended to supplement but not preempt local policy and regulations.

Supporting this funding program, but not directly involved, was the Walloon government. Since the Earth Summit and the 1992 Convention on Biodiversity, the Walloon government had begun taking a more active role in encouraging biodiversity protection.[20] The government promoted the development of inventories of "zones of biological interest" and the issuance of local decrees to protect and manage these zones. It encouraged local governments to put into place "ecological networks" linking these zones. And it encouraged the formation of local-level partnerships to help produce "Communal Plans for Nature Development." The Walloon government hoped to use the biodiversity contract initiative as a pilot study to help inform these local nature conservation planning processes. Its hope was that these local partnerships would serve as standing collaborative bodies that could be used to address future environmental and land-use planning issues in the communes.

Also supporting this drive toward biodiversity protection were habitat protection directives coming from the European Union.[21] The European Union was also promoting a suite of agricultural best management practices in this regard.[22] These agro-environmental measures encouraged biodiversity-friendly agricultural practices such as delaying the harvesting of meadows, replanting and maintaining additional hedgerows, and decreasing livestock load.

When the philanthropic foundation announced its request for proposals, two separate individuals—the commune's elected official responsible for environmental affairs and a member of a social service and cultural affairs NGO—decided to respond independently. Upon discovering their mutual interest, they assembled a small steering committee of similarly interested individuals to submit a joint application. The steering committee included another representative from the social service sector as well as several members of local nature conservation groups.

Up until this point, environmental action within the commune had consisted largely of small-scale, independent projects. Most of these had been carried out by the communal government, but these tended to be reactive measures, such as clearing trash out of local streams. The GBP founders hoped through the grant to bring about environmental improvements on a larger scale and in a more integrated fashion. They also hoped to involve more of the commune's residents in doing so. Finally, they believed that establishing a formal biodiversity contract might encourage better land-use planning by the commune.

The fledgling GBP partnership was awarded funding at the beginning of 1994. It was one of only a half dozen or so communes in the Walloon Region to be so honored. The project initiators then immediately set about enlarging the partnership by sending invitations to every inhabitant in the commune.

Structure and Operation

The GBP partnership was guided by several requirements placed on it by the funding institution. It was obligated, for instance, to involve participants representing a broad range of the commune's diverse interests, including the communal government, and to operate by consensus. Once the partners were assembled, however, the partnership was free to organize itself as it wished. Here, the GBP partnership adopted the standard not-for-profit model of arranging itself into a general assembly and an executive bureau (refer to figure 3.3 for a diagram of the GBP organizational structure). The general assembly consisted of all of the partnership participants and was responsible for approving all work accomplished, ratifying funding decisions, and electing the executive bureau and its officers. The executive bureau was responsible for coordinating partnership activities. Participation in the executive bureau was open to all, and its meetings were chaired by the elected GBP president.

Figure 3.3. GBP Organizational Structure

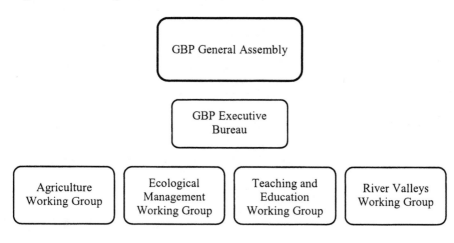

Once these preliminary structures were in place, the partnership polled its participants to uncover their principal interests and then used this information to establish four main working groups. These working groups were focused on the topics of ecological management, teaching and education, agriculture, and river valleys. It was their task to propose and eventually implement particular projects that forwarded the partnership's goals. Partners were free to participate in any or all of the working groups. Administration of these groups fell to particular executive bureau members who volunteered to lead them. The partnership did not make use of any external professional facilitation.

Once initiated, the GBP partnership devoted its first few general assembly meetings to introducing the project to interested participants and building membership. During these first meetings, participants were encouraged to describe at some length themselves, their organizations, and their interests in biodiversity conservation.

After this initial rush of introductory meetings, the general assembly began convening once or twice a year, the executive bureau around four times a year, and the working groups up to six times a year or as needed. Meetings were held in the town hall, local churches, and local schoolrooms as appropriate.

As part of the funding agreement, the GBP partnership was required to produce by the end of its first year a "biodiversity contract." This was to consist of a charter detailing all of the proposed projects, how they would be funded, and the people or organizations that would be responsible for their implementation. After the charter was signed by the general assembly at the end of 1994, the project then entered into an open-ended implementation phase. My research with the GBP partnership began just prior to the signing of the charter and covered much of the first year of the charter's implementation. Examples of projects initiated during this period included the commune's first annual "biodiversity day," an all-day fair designed to introduce the commune's general population to the concept of biodiversity; a project to clean up a local pond; a project to protect bats in local church belfries; a project designating certain roadsides as "late mowing" areas to allow for the blooming and propagation of local wildflowers; and a project encouraging the planting of new hedgerows by participating farmers.

The partnership's budget came largely from the grant of two million Belgian francs—or approximately $67,000 (U.S.)[23]—awarded by the supporting foundation. GBP participants also solicited additional funding throughout the project in the form of small, environmentally related grants from the Walloon government and the European Union. The communal government offered administrative support for the project and small budgetary allocations, and made efforts to combine GBP initiatives with its own environmental projects.

Composition

Participation in the GBP partnership was voluntary and open to all individuals and organizations located in the commune. Over forty individuals chose to take part in the project. These included communal government officials, regional resource managers, and members of a local land-use planning advisory committee; representatives from a relatively large and dynamic NGO community focused on a wide variety of social, cultural heritage, and nature conservation issues; social services advocates and administrators; school officials and teachers; local farmers, beekeepers, and hunters; small business owners; and other interested citizens.

The most active of these participants came from the governmental and NGO sectors. Of these partners, the most powerful was clearly the communal government. This was the institution responsible for managing important segments of the commune's natural environment, including all of the publicly owned lands and rivers. The communal government was also a primary source of resources—logistical, administrative, and otherwise—upon which the partnership depended heavily. The most important governmental representative was the elected official responsible for environmental affairs. This environmental deputy was one of the project's initiators. He was also the consensus choice to be the partnership's first president. Partway through the project, this individual was replaced by another official as a consequence of communal elections. The new environmental deputy, however, never showed the same interest in or commitment to the partnership. In fact, he saw the partnership as a potential threat to his authority. This had the effect of diminishing the influence of the communal government in the project.

Representatives from NGOs and the concerned public constituted a second influential group within the project. These participants were interested in maintaining a high quality of life in their commune. Their prestige and authority came from a variety of sources. As with the TRC partnership, the NGO participants were among the project's primary drivers. They made up a large fraction of the executive bureau and served as the leads for nearly all of the working groups. Along with the founding governmental official, they were the true motivators behind the project. These representatives were also very diverse. Some came from environmental protection or nature conservation groups, while others represented social services organizations. Still others represented the commune's schools. Finally, these NGO participants came from an active and relatively large NGO community within Gascoigne. Many of the commune's inhabitants were proud of this tradition, and this pride extended to the GBP partnership as well.

Another stakeholder group holding a position of relative importance, at least at the onset of the partnership, was the commune's agricultural community. These local farmers were considered to be critical partners, given their roles as managers of much of the commune's land. Their influence diminished over time, however, as many of them ceased to participate actively. The only other members of the business community who participated to any extent came from small businesses with direct links to biodiversity promotion. This included a restaurant serving native wildflowers and a nursery selling native plants to local gardeners.

Reflecting the demographics of the commune, the participants in the GBP partnership were almost exclusively white and ranged in socioeconomic standing from relatively poor farmers to wealthy suburbanites. Partners varied in age from their twenties to their sixties, and the overall composition, though still predominantly male, was relatively gender balanced. Some participants came from social service-based NGOs representing lower income populations living in the commune, but few of these inhabitants actually participated themselves.

The Collaboration for Improved Management of Natural Resources (CIMNR)

The final case study concerned a North American-based, national-level partnership directed toward improving natural resource management practices in the United States. Its intention was to engage leaders from business, government, and the environmental community in civil dialogue and the generation of innovative ideas to inform and influence policy making in both the public and private domains. Its specific objective was to produce a report recommending new approaches to natural resource management that would better sustain natural systems, a healthy economy, and local communities. I refer to this initiative as the Collaboration for Improved Management of Natural Resources (CIMNR) partnership.

Background

The natural resource management focus adopted by the CIMNR partnership actually constituted the second phase of the CIMNR initiative. The partnership was initiated in 1993 to explore alternatives to the conventional system for regulating industrial pollution in the United States. This first phase originated out of the growing concerns within the business sector that the existing system of environmental management in the United States was excessively expensive and inefficient. Convinced that an improved scheme could be developed only via open dialogue among a wide range of stakeholders, a small group of business executives took the initiative to assemble a small group of similarly concerned environmentalists and public officials. This steering committee then enlisted the support of a neutral coordinating body to help convene, coordinate, and facilitate a broader stakeholder process. Once more balanced representation was established, the enlarged partnership met regularly for three years, producing at the end a policy document recommending a series of innovative and more cost-effective approaches to pollution prevention.

The decision to initiate a second phase of the partnership grew out of unfinished business from the first phase. Phase one participants recognized that they had not adequately addressed the issue of natural resource management in their earlier deliberations. They acknowledged that despite decades of federal regulatory efforts—ranging from the National Environmental Policy Act, the Endangered Species Act, and the Clean Water Act to the Surface Mining Control and Reclamation Act, the Federal Land Policy and Management Act, and the Resource Conservation and Recovery Act—complex ecosystems were still being degraded. They also feared that threats to natural systems would continue to increase unless current patterns of economic development and human settlement were modified.

Approximately one-third of the phase one participants committed to continue their collaborative efforts and turn their focus toward natural resource management issues. They scheduled an additional two-year phase to run between 1997 and 1999. Like the first phase, the second phase aspired to look beyond more traditional regulatory means of natural resource protection. It aimed to focus particular attention on the wide variety of economic drivers—including tax policies, subsidies, private property interests, and public investment in infrastructure—serving to shape the demand for and use of natural resources. It hoped to explore a new suite of policy options—including full cost accounting, deed or title adjustment mechanisms for private landowners wishing to conserve, debt restructuring programs, property rights transfers, tax measures, and banking and trading approaches—that would encourage more sustainable natural resource management practices. It also aimed to draw attention to the wide variety of social and cultural factors driving individual behavior, including the value and ethical systems in operation, the impact of environmental education, and people's proclivities toward collaborative versus confrontational problem-solving approaches.

About two dozen new, interested participants from government, business, and the NGO community were invited to join the remaining phase one members. The focus remained on producing policy recommendations with regard to natural resource management that might have an impact in both the public and private sectors.

Structure and Operation

The CIMNR partnership was less formally organized than the other three case studies. Structurally, it consisted of a plenary group that would subdivide into temporary working groups as dictated by the group's general agreement on what needed to be done next to accomplish the partnership's overall goals. Foci for these various working groups covered a range of natural resource domains, including agriculture, development, extraction, land and water resources, and recreation. Participants commonly joined the working groups that interested them the most or for which they had the greatest expertise. Actors were not bound to any one group, however, and many transferred from one to another. The partnership convened every three months, and participants met for three days at a time. In between the quarterly meetings, participants continued to work remotely to advance particular tasks initiated.

The two most important and long-lasting working groups established during the second phase were the "prevention" and "mitigation" working groups (refer to figure 3.4 for a diagram of the CIMNR partnership's organizational structure). The prevention working group focused on ways of avoiding the adverse environmental and economic impact associated with development projects. The group explored ways of increasing environmental literacy, realigning economic drivers and price signals with environmental goals, increasing sustainable resource productivity, and enhancing community involvement. The mitigation working group focused alternatively on some of the problems facing current mitigation practices. This group examined the assumptions underlying current conventions for determining how much, where, when, and what kind of mitigation should take place and also explored new strategies for guiding future mitigation efforts. Both working groups independently discussed the need for a more stewardship-oriented ethic to guide individual and organizational environmental actions.

The organization responsible for coordinating the CIMNR partnership was an institute specializing in processes of multidisciplinary and multistakeholder dialogue and exchange. The key rule by which the institute ran the partnership meetings was a not-for-attribution edict requiring that each of the participants keep private the statements made by the other partners. The coordinating body described its roles to include facilitating the exchange of information, encouraging the discovery of others' values and interests, and building trust among the

Figure 3.4. CIMNR Organizational Structure

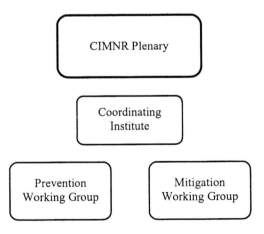

varied participants. This body also advocated that participants represent their own points of view rather than those of their organizations, arguing that only in this way could the partnership produce innovative and, indeed, improved environmental decisions and actions. To encourage these processes, the coordinators organized the three-day meetings to include a fair amount of leisure time so that participants would have opportunities to converse and relate in less formal settings. Professional facilitators were also used for all of the meetings.

Financial support for the first year of phase one of the CIMNR partnership was assumed by one of the original business participants. Afterward, the coordinating body took on the responsibility of raising funds to support the partnership. This funding came primarily from donations made by the major corporate participants and from grants solicited from several philanthropic foundations and the U.S. Environmental Protection Agency. The annual budget for the second phase of the partnership was approximately $300,000 (U.S.).

Composition

During the research period, the CIMNR partnership comprised thirty-five or so participants. Unlike the other case studies, participation in CIMNR was by invitation only. This responsibility was assumed by the project coordinators, who attempted to achieve a mix of participants that would maintain a balance among the interests at stake while at the same time satisfactorily representing pertinent areas of expertise and experience in the natural resources domain.

The CIMNR partnership had the best sectorial balance among the four case studies, both numerically and in terms of influence. Most of the participants from the business sector were environmental managers and executives from resource-intensive and extraction-based industries in such areas as energy production, mining, petroleum, forestry, ranching, and real estate development. Many of these actors came from large corporations whose business activities extended beyond U.S. borders, although several represented more local interests. Most of them had also invested significant amounts of money in environmental management activities.

The NGO sector participants came from a range of international- and state-level environmental advocacy organizations for which natural resource conservation was a focal issue. Some of these organizations, given their long histories of influencing environmental policy decisions and the significant technical and monetary resources at their disposal, were among the most powerful environmental NGOs in the United States. Others were small, issue-oriented or place-based associations.

Participants from the governmental sector included middle- and high-ranking representatives of federal regulatory agencies and state-level environmental administrations as well as federal legislative staff. Their voices carried a lot of weight in the partnership discussions due to their roles as regulators of both economic activity and environmental protection.

All of these participants shared the general view that the natural resource management strategies of the past were no longer sufficient to ensure robust ecosystems and economic prosperity. The business representatives were especially interested in exploring nonregulatory approaches to improved natural resource management. They hoped, following the successes of the partnership's first phase, to develop strategies that allowed enterprises more flexibility in protecting, mitigating the damage done to, and restoring critical water, land, and air resources. They also wanted to highlight the benefits associated with voluntary, stewardship-based practices.

The environmental organizations were a little more wary entering the partnership. They favored an approach directed toward preventing damage to natural resources rather than rectifying harm done. Many, though not all, assumed a rather defensive posture in the partnership meetings. Although interested in promoting a greater stewardship ethic within society, they did not believe that the nation's natural resource management problems would be resolved voluntarily, and they wanted to be sure that existing regulatory structures would be safeguarded. Nevertheless, few of the participating environmental organizations would have been considered to represent the "radical" or "extremist" wing of the environmental movement. Some of the individual participants did, at times, however, express ideas that went beyond mainstream environmentalism.

The governmental participants also resisted the idea of regulatory rollback. They were, at the same time, generally willing to explore alternative approaches to influencing the environmental performance of natural resource exploiters and users as long as these remained supplemental to a well-defined regulatory regime.

As with the other case studies, nearly all of the CIMNR participants were white and, with the exception of certain small NGOs, most represented organizations with substantial economic means. A vast majority of the participants were again male. Only one organization, a Native America defense group, represented socioeconomically disempowered populations in the United States. Approximately halfway through the first phase of the CIMNR partnership, the project coordinators made a concerted attempt to include members from the environmental justice community. They invited about a dozen such groups to participate, and most of these groups did send a representative to the next meeting. All but a couple of them, however, stopped participating shortly thereafter. The project coordinators expressed dismay at this result but did not attempt to invite some of these environmental justice representatives back for the second phase. The coordinators did not believe that these groups would be sufficiently interested by natural resource management issues.

A Basis for Analysis

Together, these four case studies constitute a small yet diverse sampling of the great variety of multistakeholder environmental partnerships in operation or taking form throughout Western Europe, North America, and beyond. Although these four partnerships are by no means representative of all of the multistakeholder environmental partnerships in existence, they do demonstrate the great breadth in problem focus, stakeholder characteristics, sociopolitical level, and geographic location currently displayed by these partnerships. Like all partnerships, they also constitute fertile sites for the study of the practice of multistakeholder collaboration.

Notes

1. Punch (1994).
2. World Commission on Environment and Development (1987).
3. Baker et al. (1997).
4. Baker et al. (1997).
5. Johnson (1993).
6. Refer to *The Green Keiretsu*, compiled by SustainAbility, Ltd., and the journal TOMORROW—Global Environmental Business (1994), for a compendium of international business alliances and networks for sustainable development.
7. Dues ranged from 10,000 Euros (approximately $12,000 U.S.) for large firms to 1,000 Euros (approximately $1,200 U.S.) or work in kind for NGOs.
8. This is based on an exchange rate of approximately one Euros per 1.2 U.S. dollars.
9. Starting in 1996, the EUPEC initiative began diminishing the percentage of funding that it was receiving from the European Commission and EU member states in an effort to establish greater independence from these governmental bodies. The financial difference was made up by increased membership.
10. My characterizations of the relative positions of power and influence of the different sectors within each of the case-study partnerships draw primarily from the comments of the partnership participants themselves and my own observations.
11. Belgium is subdivided into three semiautonomous political regions: Flanders to the north, Wallonia to the south, and Brussels in the center. These regions were created largely along ethnic (and especially linguistic) lines, with native Flemish speakers primarily inhabiting Flanders and native French speakers primarily inhabiting Wallonia. Brussels, which also serves as the nation's capital, is officially bilingual. With the exception of a few policy areas such as national defense that remain housed at the federal level, each of the three regions operates relatively autonomously.
12. The commune is the most local level of government in Belgium.
13. These directives included 75/440/CEE governing the quality required of surface water intended for the abstraction of drinking water, 76/446/EEC governing pollution by discharges of certain dangerous substances, 76/160/CEE governing the quality of bathing water (Press and Taylor 1990, Smith and Hunter 1992).

14. These directives included 82/176/CEE and 84/156/CEE governing mercury discharges, 83/513/CEE governing cadmium, 84/491/CEE and 86/280/CEE governing particular pesticides, 91/676/CEE governing nitrates, and 91/271/CEE governing urban wastewater treatment (Press and Taylor 1990, Smith and Hunter 1992).

15. This conclusion was supported by studies on the state of the river conducted by the TRC partnership itself.

16. See the Walloon Region's Environmental Plan for Sustainable Development (Ministre de l'Environnement, des Resources Naturelles, et de l'Agriculture 1995).

17. All but one of the communes situated within the river basin elected to sign the accord.

18. This is based on an exchange rate of thirty Belgian francs to one U.S. dollar.

19. The Walloon government published guidelines prohibiting the killing, damaging, or disturbing of most of the region's indigenous fauna and flora (Ministère de la Region Wallonne 1995).

20. See the Walloon Region's Environmental Plan for Sustainable Development (Ministre de l'Environnement, des Resources Naturelles, et de l'Agriculture 1995).

21. The most notable of these directives was 92/43/EEC governing the conservation of natural habitats and of wild fauna and flora.

22. See the Walloon Region's Environmental Plan for Sustainable Development (Ministre de l'Environnement, des Resources Naturelles, et de l'Agriculture 1995).

23. This is based on an exchange rate of approximately thirty Belgian francs to one U.S. dollar.

Chapter 4

Conflict in Environmental Partnerships

The scene was not unlike a shooting gallery. The shooters were leading NGO members from the Gascoigne Biodiversity Project (GBP) partnership. The target was the partnership's main representative from the Gascoigne communal government.

The setting was an executive bureau meeting taking place in the local town hall. The commune's new environmental deputy had arrived late, and this was not the first time that the commune's top official responsible for environmental affairs and the management of nonagricultural lands was tardy for a GBP meeting. The potshots were induced by the perception held by other executive bureau members that the communal government was insufficiently engaging in the partnership.

Prior to the environmental deputy's arrival, executive bureau members had been reviewing the status of several GBP projects, including new environmental education initiatives in the local schools, bat habitation in neighboring church belfries, and the cleanup of a nearby pond. In each of these cases, the participants reporting on these projects commented that they did not know where the commune stood on these issues. This led to a broader discussion in which participants complained about the environmental deputy's relative lack of engagement in the partnership to date. This concerned many of the executive bureau members, because they believed that the partnership would not succeed without the communal government's committed participation. They subsequently decided to schedule a presentation of the GBP partnership for the entire council of communal deputies.

Fifty minutes into the meeting, an executive bureau member was sent to remind the environmental deputy of the meeting. He finally joined the group ten minutes later, apologizing for his tardiness. For many executive bureau members, however, this was not enough. They thus began firing questions. One asked the environmental deputy if he had read the proposal sent to him on the topic of delayed roadside mowing intended to foster improved reproduction of wildflowers. The environmental deputy responded that he had not. Another executive bureau member asked the deputy to provide an update on communal government efforts to prepare an informational signpost for the local water treatment facility. Here, the environmental deputy pleaded ignorance. This led some executive bureau members to shake their heads while others rolled their eyes. When the environmental deputy then complained that a central person was needed to help coordinate all of these projects with the commune, the GBP president responded pointedly that the partnership was hoping that he, as the environmental deputy, would play this role. The environmental deputy seemed rather embarrassed by this remark and excused himself briefly to fetch some documents from his office.

Later in the meeting, after the topic returned to some of the partnership's educational initiatives, the environmental deputy took the offensive and described an education-based project that he had been working on for the past couple of months. The project was focused on raising student awareness of waste issues facing local schools. The deputy noted with pride his plans to present the project at an exposition in two months time. Rather than eliciting praise, however, this comment brought about a distraught look on the face of the executive bureau member in charge of the Teaching and Education Work Group. Stating that his work group had been discussing something similar to this, he asked the environmental deputy why he had not informed the partnership of his plans. Other participants joined the upwell of frustration and called for the commune to be more forthcoming in sharing information with the partnership. The environmental deputy became defensive again at this point and retorted that the communal government believed that it had to move quickly to get things done in a timely manner.

Finally, when the agenda shifted to a project involving the planting of indigenous wildflowers in a local cemetery, the environmental deputy admitted that he had not come prepared with the proper documents. He nevertheless went on to describe specific efforts that the communal government had taken independently of the GBP partnership. This led to more snickering and derisive whispers from other executive bureau participants, causing even greater discomfort for the now red-faced environmental deputy. When the meeting ended shortly thereafter, the environmental deputy quickly made his departure. After he had left, one executive bureau participant leaned over to another and stated quietly, "That's what is called revenge."

Making Sense of Conflict

This type of conflict, where diverse actors find themselves in antithetical or disharmonious positions, is fundamental to most multistakeholder activity. Analyzing it requires examining both its behavioral and perceptual components.[1] The behavioral component of conflict—or the *practice of conflict*, as I refer to it—involves how people actually *act* in conflictual situations. Observing such acts was a primary goal of my ethnographic research of multistakeholder partnerships. The perceptual component of conflict involves people's motivations for engaging in conflictual behavior. These motivations stem to some extent from perceived incompatibilities in interests, goals, or aspirations.[2] As I demonstrate in the following sections, they also derive from differences in the sociohistorically based frameworks by which participants approach issues, ideas, events, and each other.[3]

My analysis of conflict in multistakeholder environmental partnerships is a dispute-level analysis.[4] Rather than looking at societywide patterns, my focus is on a particular issue or event being contested, as was the case in the particular GPB partnership dispute just described. It is also at the dispute level that one can most clearly see how shared or divergent understandings and perceptions come to shape disputants' actions.[5]

Sociohistoric forces may help incite conflict in a variety of ways. One way is when participants' divergent or antithetical interpretations of issues, ideas, people, or events lead them to act in incompatible or oppositional ways.[6] Another way is for conflict to arise out of contestation over whose particular interpretations or preferred meanings, often expressed in the form of competing discourses, get to be dominant in any particular interaction.[7] This chapter looks at both of these.

In the sections that follow, I examine two examples of disputes involving stakeholders participating in environmental partnerships. In the first case, I return to the GBP partnership dispute over communal government commitment to the partnership. I show that interest-based explanations for the conflict, while important, are only partial, and I suggest that the dispute may be further explained by diverging sociohistorically based understandings that the contending parties had of the partnership itself. This is an interesting case because both sides of this conflict used the same language to describe the partnership. The problem was that this language held different meanings and elicited different types of actions from the participating actors.

In a second, more detailed case example, I explore a Toupin River Contract (TRC) partnership dispute centered on the issue of public participation in environmental decision-making processes. Again, I show the incompleteness of an interest-based approach and argue that the conflict also has its roots in participants' varying approaches to both environmental problem solving and multistakeholder participatory forms of decision making. This case illustrates in particular how conflict arises out of competition between alternative discourses.

Conflict over Stakeholder Commitment
in the Gascoigne Biodiversity Project

The dispute described at the opening of this chapter was not a one-time event. In fact, it recurred at various times throughout the stakeholder collaboration. The conflict out of which it grew has its roots in the partnership's early history. In the first months of the project, the GBP partnership was marked by a particularly close relationship between the commune's environmental deputy and the other leading participants in the initiative. A year into its existence, however, an event severely altered the partnership's course. This was the regularly scheduled communal elections that took place at the end of 1994. In these elections, the political party represented by the environmental deputy was ousted from power. This event was significant for several reasons. First, this official had been one of the project's initiators and greatest supporters. His role as the partnership's first elected president further guaranteed active participation on the part of the communal government. Second, this individual was an indisputable leader in the environmental arena. He was the first deputy official in the commune's history to add the environment to his list of public responsibilities, an act he initiated out of his own personal interest. Finally, and perhaps most important, his successor in the communal government was much less interested and experienced in environmental affairs.

This event led to a relative retreat by the communal government from the project. So while the partnership's executive bureau and four working groups continued to work toward implementing the specific projects laid out in the partnership's charter, the new environmental deputy, still the single most important player for many of these projects, no longer supported the process to the same degree. The deputy did attend some of the meetings, but these became marked by increasing levels of conflict between him and the rest of the partners. Tensions were especially high between the new environmental deputy and some of the NGO representatives who had helped initiate the partnership.

The new environmental deputy incited the anger of these other participants in a variety of ways. He consistently arrived late for meetings, he was unaware of many of his own responsibilities in the partnership, he was often negligent in responding to GBP activities demanding his attention, and as the commune's environmental deputy, he continued to initiate and carry out environmental actions parallel to those of the GBP partnership without informing the partners. Some of the partners responded to his lack of consideration by blatantly exposing his lack of preparation for the meetings. Others reacted to the deputy's own environmental projects not with acclaim, as the new deputy expected, but by admonishing him for failing to coordinate better with the partnership. These attacks, at times, visibly humiliated the new deputy in front of the other participants. The attacks led him to react angrily and defensively to the other participants' claims and had the effect of discouraging him from further involvement in the project. These attacks did not, however, cause him to withdraw completely from the stakeholder process. As a formal signatory to the actual biodiversity charter, the communal government had already committed its participation. In the end, the new environmental deputy opted for a strategy in which he followed the progress of the project, attended meetings periodically, and continued to provide some logistical support. He did not, however, take an active role leading the partnership.

Making Sense of the Conflict: An Interest-Based Approach

A common way of explaining conflictual behavior in cases such as these is to focus on the interests involved. To get at these interests, I asked participants on both sides of the dispute to discuss what they hoped to get from the GBP partnership. Interestingly, both sides described the partnership as having only advantages.

The members of the executive bureau challenging the environmental deputy to increase his involvement cited several environmental, economic, and social benefits brought by the partnership. First, and not surprisingly, they mentioned expected improvements in the areas of nature conservation and biodiversity enhancement. Second, they noted that the partnership placed at the disposal of the commune substantial resources for achieving these goals. Some of these resources were financial, including the initial foundation grant money received and the potential for future funding from both the Walloon regional government and the European Union made possible by the prestige of being one of only five communes in all of Wallonia to have a biodiversity contract. Other resources came in the form of free labor offered by both Walloon region governmental agencies and local environmental groups. One executive bureau member noted that the GBP partnership "brings together lots of motivated people whom we can count on to move things forward" (GBP.15.12).[8] Another NGO representative added that partnerships such as the GBP initiative enable small, volunteer-based organizations to work more effectively by "combining their forces" (GBP.9.5). Third, they remarked that, as a grass-roots initiative, the project offered residents of the commune an opportunity to grow as a community. One executive bureau member described the GBP partnership as a "door" through which newcomers to the commune can get to know their neighbors (GBP.15.20). Another representative described the partnership as helping normally solitary residents "come out of their shells" (GBP.9.6). Finally, they observed that the project brought with it other socioeconomic opportunities, such as the creation of new biodiversity-related jobs and the augmentation of tourism-based revenue.

When taken together with the vital role played by the environmental deputy in all of the commune's environmental affairs, these interests provide a compelling case for why these partners were willing to pressure the environmental deputy into playing a more active role in the project.

For his part, the environmental deputy also presented a series of reasons for why the GBP partnership was advantageous to him. First, he stated that, as a communal official, it was in his best interest "to participate in all projects that concern public life and its inhabitants" (GBP.16.10). He described himself as an "advocate" of the project and of "people organizing themselves and acting out their good will" (GBP.16.10). Second, he portrayed multistakeholder partnerships as having both financial and efficiency benefits. He noted:

> When we can work with other partners who have resources, we can avoid having to go through formal channels. We can accomplish things much faster. (GBP.16.8)

Finally, he noted that partnerships such as the GBP initiative allowed him to access the views and benefit from the experience of others. When asked to discuss some of the disadvantages of partnerships such as the GBP initiative, he responded only that these were minimal compared to the advantages.

As was the case for the executive bureau members, the environmental deputy presents compelling reasons for supporting the GBP partnership. This finding is problematic, however, for any interest-based explanation of this conflict. It raises the question: If the environmental deputy was so in favor of a partnership like the GBP, why did his participation remain so poor?[9]

Making Sense of the Conflict: A Sociohistoric Perspective

This apparent contradiction suggests that there are other factors underlying the recurring dispute. This section explores some of the sociohistoric influences at play. In particular, I forward the argument that the conflict also results from differences marking the two sides' respective conceptualizations of the partnership itself.

This argument stems from a critical finding regarding the different words that participants used to describe the GBP partnership. The research showed that both the new deputy official and his antagonists in the executive bureau employed the same term when talking about the project. They all described it as an "association"—that is, as an NGO. Where the two sides differed, however, was in the meaning that they attributed to "NGOs." The disputing parties diverged in their views on (1) the underlying interests of NGOs, and (2) the relationship between NGOs and the communal government. The findings are summarized in table 4.1.

Differing Perceptions of the Interests of the GBP Partnership

In his discussions of the GBP partnership and its participants, the new environmental deputy described NGOs, and environmental NGOs in particular, as special-interest groups. Although he characterized NGOs as comprising highly motivated, well-intentioned individuals, he also referred to their projects as "private initiatives" (GBP.16.2). He clearly distinguished these private initiatives from public projects being carried out by the communal government.

Table 4.1. Comparison of Sociohistoric Factors Influencing the GBP Conflict

Sociohistoric Factors	The Environmental Deputy	Other GBP Partnership Leaders (largely from the NGO sector)
1. Views on the underlying interests		
Of NGOs	• Special-interest groups. • Pursue private initiatives.	• Common-interest organizations. • Work for the general welfare. • Volunteer-based, altruistic.
Of the GBP Partnership	• Directed toward private initiatives. • Environmentally focused. • Return to environment of the past. • Against economic development. • Lack of respect for safety issues.	• Geared toward the public good. • More than just an environmental focus. Social and economic goals as well. • Intended to benefit future generations.
2. Views on communal governmental relations		
With NGOs	• NGOs do not have free rein. • Authority rests with elected officials. • Paternalistic relationship.	• Egalitarian ethos. • Relationships founded on participation and cooperation.
With the GBP Partnership	• Partnership is governed by rules. • Government makes final decisions. • Paternalistic relationship.	• Government is a partner like the others. • Environmental decision-making responsibility of commune is subsumed under the partnership.

The environmental deputy extended this perspective to his conceptualizations of the GBP partnership itself. In particular, he saw the partnership as being specifically focused on the environment to the exclusion of other important matters, namely, economic and safety issues. Along these lines, he commented:

> [The goal of the GBP partnership] is to help bring people back to a life that is less industrialized and more close to nature, to avoid all of the pollution caused by chemical fertilizers, and to just become more natural again. This needs to be done in different ways, such as by creating ponds to protect certain fish, preserving certain plants so they are not destroyed by industrial pollution and fertilizers, and restoring certain wildflowers that we were destroying via the elimination of hedgerows and the spraying of pesticides. But I must tell you that within the context of the [Biodiversity Project] . . . it is becoming more and more imperative that we respect [related] security measures as well. (GBP.16.10-11)

The deputy was bothered by the willingness of the other partnership members to protect the wildflowers that grew along the commune's roadsides regardless of the driving and pedestrian hazards that this presented.

For their part, the other GBP participants in the conflict, and especially those from the environmental community, tended to portray NGOs less as pressure groups pursuing special interests and more as common-interest organizations working for the betterment of the commune's general welfare. In their discussions, they described their own NGOs as volunteer based, future oriented, and global in perspective. They also depicted their own personal motivations for participating in NGOs as stemming not from the desire for self-advancement but from the enrichment that they experience by participating in civil society.

These participants spoke about the GBP partnership in the same way. With regard to the general interests of the partnership, participants made statements such as:

> The primary concern [of partnerships such as the GBP] is above all the public good. It is the interest of the people. It is the development of the commune, or it is maintaining our environment in a satisfactory state. So, there are no personal interests or personal stakes [in partnerships]. Everyone works in the service of the collective. (GBP.11.7)

Others made a point of depicting the partnership, like many of their NGOs, as being more than exclusively environmentally focused. One NGO member defined the GBP partnership's goal to be that of

> respecting the fauna and the flora of the commune without impeding the socio-economic development of the people who live there. (GBP.9.12)

Still others emphasized how, rather than being near-sighted and geared toward producing isolated effects, the GBP partnership was intended for the benefit of future generations. As one NGO representative put it, the goal of the partnership is to "assure sustainable development for the long term" (GBP.11.12).

Differing Views on the Relationship between the GBP Partnership and the Communal Government

The second major area of difference regarding the disputing parties' conceptualizations of NGOs, and hence the GBP partnership, concerns their views on the relations between government and NGOs. In the interview, the new environmental deputy clearly asserted that NGOs did not have free rein to do whatever they wanted in the commune. He declared, for instance, that these groups must remain in harmony with some of the commune's other interests, such as those of urban development. He also believed that ultimate authority must remain with the elected representatives of the communal government. Here, he remarked:

We don't all have the same power of decision. The commune is at a different level. We may or may not have the same ideas as others, but it must be known that the commune is there to make the final decisions. It is the commune who decides and is responsible for the general population. (GBP.16.14)

The deputy official portrayed his relationship with the GBP partnership in much the same way. He described the partnership's actions, as well as his support for them, as being governed by specific communal rules. Within these rules, he likened his role to that of a "catalyst" (GBP.16.2) in that he saw his main job to be that of encouraging the commune's citizens to exercise their goodwill. This role did not, however, include sharing power.

The other executive bureau participants, on the other hand, tended to conceptualize NGOs and the GBP partnership as rather egalitarian in orientation. They described both as being founded on processes of participation, cooperation, and consensus rather than the more hierarchical and unilateral modes portrayed by the new deputy official. One environmental NGO representative described the GBP partnership this way:

Equality of power exists [in the project]. Everyone has an equal right to speak, to give his or her opinions, to agree or not. In the Executive Bureau, we don't choose one voice over another. Everything is done with full consensus. We decide things together. . . . From the point of view of decisions, everyone is on equal standing. (GBP.19.13-14)

Within the partnership setting, these executive bureau members generally portrayed representatives from the communal government as "partners" like everyone else. These participants did not ignore or deny the governing role of the communal officials. They just saw it as subsumed within what they perceived to be the more comprehensive decision-making authority of the partnership itself.

Summary

Taken together, these sociohistoric factors help to clarify the conflict that arose between the GBP partnership's NGO leadership and the commune's new environmental deputy during his first year of participation. This perspective adds depth to an interest-based approach that, taken alone, appears contradictory. While an interest-base approach sheds light on why the various members of the executive bureau might have been willing to provoke the environmental deputy for the purpose of increasing his level of engagement, it is less successful in explaining why the deputy official nevertheless resisted committing to the partnership.

What a sociohistoric-based approach does in this case is present an alternative reason for the environmental deputy's recalcitrance. The previous analysis suggests that the deputy's interpretation of the partnership as a special-interest initiative benefiting mostly the NGOs involved led him to act in ways that would retain a certain distance and power asymmetry between the communal government and the partnership. He did not feel compelled to include the partnership in his decision-making processes because, as he understood it, the decisions were ultimately his to make anyway. He perceived the GBP partnership to be little more than a series of privately motivated projects. These projects merited encouragement, but not autonomy. They did not, in any event, require his ownership.

A sociohistoric approach also helps to explain further the hostile actions of the other executive bureau members involved in the conflict. For these participants, the partnership was not a private initiative but an altruistic endeavor dedicated to the long-term economic, social, and environmental benefit of the greater public. It was a powerful, consensus-based, problem-solving tool available to the commune that had the advantage of representing a broad range of interests and perspectives. For the communal official to refuse to share information or decision-making authority was extremely frustrating for these participants. This was clearly in violation of their view of the partnership as an egalitarian, participatory entity. They could not help but respond negatively to this untenable position.

Conflict over Public Participation in the Toupin River Contract

A second case example of conflict comes from the Toupin River Contract partnership. The disagreement here was over the appropriate role of the public in environmental decision making. At issue was the extent to which average citizens should have a say in the design, construction, and management of large public works and infrastructure projects. In the paragraphs that follow, I expand the discussion from the previous section to show how conflictual action in multistakeholder settings may be incited not just by different interpretations of particular issues, ideas, people, or events but also by tension among competing meaning systems.

As with the GBP case, the TRC conflict under examination encompassed two opposing camps. On one side were the most active environmental groups participating in the TRC partnership. They were in strongly in favor of increased citizen participation in environmental decision-making processes. These NGOs included long-established, national-level, nature conservation organizations characterized by their solid institutional ties to government and their reputations for credible scientific expertise in the area of ecology. They also included more recently formed citizen action groups notable for their activist orientations and knowledge of local conditions.

The opposing camp comprised those participants responsible for designing, building, and managing large public works and infrastructure projects in the Ixtoup Province. These participants generally opposed any increases in public participation. The two main actors here were the Provincial Waterway Service and the Water Treatment Agency.[10] The Waterway Service, a provincial governmental division responsible for the maintenance of the province's waterways and roads, was charged with providing flood control and water runoff measures for the area, which it did primarily through the construction of storm water basins. It also brought to the TRC partnership vast knowledge of the province's rivers. The Water Treatment Agency was a governmental institution responsible for treating sewage and other waste products entering the Ixtoup Province's rivers. This involved, among other things, constructing and managing wastewater treatment plants in the Toupin River valley. Both of these agencies were responsible for implementing existing regulations. The Provincial Waterway Service was also responsible for enforcing them. Neither of these agencies, however, had good reputations for involving the public in their work.

Conflict over public participation in the TRC partnership occurred most frequently and openly in the multisectorial river committee and technical committee meetings. Conflict was almost always initiated by environmental NGOs, who demanded two fundamental changes in the way environmentally related projects such as storm water basins, water treatment plants, and river maintenance were being conducted. First, they wanted environmental factors, such as habitat destruction and pollution in the form of noxious odors and loud noises, to be better taken into account in these projects and for this to be done earlier in the project design phase. Second, they wanted their groups to be better informed about and more involved in the actual decision-making processes for these projects. The Waterway Service and the Water Treatment Agency typically responded by resisting these demands, claiming sole authority in these areas and arguing that the existing consultation-based, public inquiry system precluded any need for further citizen involvement.

One particular dispute that arose out of this conflict occurred during a technical committee meeting organized to review a regulation governing non-navigable rivers in the province. The provincial government had approached the TRC coordinators and requested that the partnership provide feedback on proposed revisions to the regulation. The coordinators first submitted the proposed regulation to the NGO committee for comment. This committee, composed primarily of environmental group members, was designed to serve as a public forum for the partnership. After completing its comments, the NGO committee was asked to submit them for further review to the technical committee. The technical committee was composed largely of technicians and engineers from governmental agencies charged with managing the province's rivers. The technical committee also included several Waterway Service representatives who had helped write the regulation in the first place. Its responsibility was to provide technical advice to the partnership. Upon completion of its review, the technical committee was supposed to send back any final comments to the provincial government.

In the technical committee meeting, a lone environmental NGO representative presented a list of over forty comments to the technical committee members. The list covered a wide range of recommendations. Many of these were technical, warning of misguided and potentially damaging ecological practices present in the existing regulation. For instance, the Provincial Waterway Service's strategy for keeping the rivers flowing involved keeping the riverbeds clear of plant life such as tree roots, branches, and thickets. The NGO committee objected to this because plant life plays an important role in the auto-purification of the river. The NGO committee thus suggested new management practices for the Waterway Service, such as avoiding draining ponds during periods of high water. In its list of comments, the NGO committee also criticized the standard practices of information exchange and decision making provided by the regulation and advocated instead the increased use of consensus-based concertation processes. Under the existing regulation, the Waterway Service had the power to act unilaterally, with the consent of communal governments, to clear small rivers when the flow was being impeded. The NGO committee urged the Waterway Service to use collaborative procedures involving the public to make these decisions, just as the Waterway Service was required to do in the case of larger rivers.

The technical committee's reactions to the NGO committee comments were consistently negative. Ranking Waterway Service representatives appeared annoyed that they were being asked to consider these comments. Supported by the Water Treatment Agency representatives in attendance, they quickly countered most of the recommendations presented, thus forcing the NGO spokesperson to defend or explain the feedback in greater detail. They complained, for instance, that many of the NGO committee's comments unrealistically ignored the complex legalities of modifying a law. They expressed doubt that the members of the NGO committee had the expertise necessary to comment constructively on regulatory matters. They also discounted several of the NGO comments requesting changes in Waterway Service river management procedures because these suggestions failed to take into account the technical and logistical realities of Waterway Service work. Finally, they strongly resisted the NGO committee's recommendations for new environmental management and collaboration practices on the ground that this would result in a substantial increase in their workload.

In the face of the rejections and criticisms received, the NGO committee spokesperson struggled to maintain his composure during the meeting. The overwhelmingly negative response to the NGO committee comments forced the TRC coordinators, at times, to come to his assistance. Even this, however, did little to persuade the agency representatives to consider most of the recommendations in anything more than a cursory fashion. The meeting left several participants wondering if the entire idea of reviewing the regulation had been such a good idea.

Making Sense of the Conflict: An Interest-Based Approach

In this technical committee meeting, as well as in several other TRC partnership meetings, influential governmental agency officials from the Provincial Waterway Service and the Water Treatment Agency found themselves defending their historically held control over environmental decision-making processes against attempts by increasingly influential NGO members demanding more of a say in how environmentally related projects were to be done. The conflict boiled down to who gets to determine the environmental actions to be taken, and how these actions would be carried out.

In the meetings and the interviews, participants from the two opposing sides described some of the interests that were driving their positions. In the case of the governmental agency representatives, these interests centered on their desires to satisfy their organizational missions and to perform their jobs well. Provincial Waterway Service representatives described their overall mission to be that of supervising public works at the provincial and communal levels. This also included authoring and conducting projects where needed. Water Treatment Agency members described their primary mission to involve designing and operating water treatment plants in the province. For members from both of these agencies, fulfilling these missions meant having the freedom to do the best job possible. They did not want outside influences, especially from people perceived as having little or no experience or expertise in the environmental management domain, to impinge on the effectiveness of their work. Nor did they want to be forced to do what one Water Treatment Agency employee called "projects that are not the most appropriate" (TRC.27.12). These participants expressed the fear that citizens and citizen action groups might use the information shared by the agencies or their involvement in decision-making processes to force project goal revisions or design modifications that might, in turn, result in schedule delays, cost overruns, or even project closures. The concern was that this might lead to a subsequent loss of agency work responsibilities, funding, or contracts.

For their part, the environmental groups participating in the TRC described their primary interest to be that of protecting and preserving the natural environment and its diversity. The goal, as one environmental NGO representative put it, was to "have nature conservation adequately taken into account in [decision-making] areas where it has been largely ignored" (TRC.10.8). This was seen as necessitating greater public participation, especially on the part of the environmental community. Participating NGOs also expressed a clear interest in mounting successful environmental campaigns. Prompting the Water Treatment Agency to better integrate new water treatment facilities into their natural surroundings or forcing the Provincial Waterway Service to refrain from building a storm water basin that would unnecessarily destroy an existing wetland might lead to increases in membership and funding. As another local environmental group representative noted, the additional funding that this brings could help NGOs develop more privileged and less dependent relationships with local government.

As was the case in the GBP example, however, the interests held by these key stakeholder groups were not always consistent. Some of the agency representatives, for instance, also indicated their support for increased coordination with environmental groups. Several mentioned ecological learning and networking opportunities as important benefits that often arise from increased NGO participation. One Water Treatment Agency member added that better coordination would also "help others to see the beneficial results of Water Treatment Agency projects" (TRC.27.14). In addition to the public relations benefits, increased public awareness of agency actions projects might have the effect of decreasing the risk of future NGO protests.

Some of the environmental NGO members, likewise, cautioned against pushing for too much inclusion too fast. As one representative noted:

> My group can only go as far as we believe our members will allow. . . . At stake is our credibility with both our supporters and the communal government. And without credibility, we have nothing at all. (TRC.2.2)

These participants recognized that environmental NGOs have much to lose if the pressure that they place on the governmental agencies causes these agencies to be less rather than more accessible in the future.

Although this interest-based approach provides important reasons for why this conflict reoccurred as it did, it is not complete. In particular, it does not address contributing factors residing outside of the domain of interests that provide a deeper understanding for why environmental NGOs want to be more involved in environmental decision making, why NGOs favor broader public participation as a means of attaining this, why some agencies resist pressure to take environmental action, and why they disapprove of public participation and multistakeholder participatory processes more generally. Nor does it address why this conflict commonly played out as it did—i.e., with the NGOs repeatedly serving as the instigators. Reaching beyond an interest-based approach can also help explain why certain interests prevailed over others—for instance, why agency interests in resisting NGO participation outweighed corresponding interests in collaborating with NGOs, and why NGO pursuit of increased public participation outweighed the risks of doing so. In the remainder of this chapter, I again show that improved understanding of the conflict at issue comes from considering some of the sociohistoric differences at play. In particular, I demonstrate how clarity can be gained by viewing the conflict as the outcome of competition between alternative meaning systems or discourses.

Making Sense of the Conflict: A Sociohistoric Perspective

In the interviews conducted and meetings observed, representatives from both sides of the conflict revealed differences in their understandings of and approaches to the issues of environmental problem solving and multistakeholder collaboration. In this section, I focus on distinctions in four main areas. These relate to the questions: (1) Why does environmental action need to be taken? (2) What is the cause of current environmental problems? (3) How does environmental action proceed? and (4) What is the most appropriate form of environmental governance?

The alternative meaning systems examined in this section are also distinctive in that they hold together as more or less coherent discourses. The conflict that arises may thus also be viewed as resulting from competition over which side's discourse will be dominant. I will discuss how this depends on the specific contexts in which discourses interact.

Why Does Environmental Action Need to Be Taken?

The first area of difference concerns the conflicting parties' respective understandings of why there is a need for environmental protection and remediation in the first place. This distinction manifests itself in three ways: the first concerns the two parties' underlying motivations for addressing environmental issues, the second involves their differing interpretations of the state of the environment in the Toupin River valley, and the third relates to differences in their views on pollution. The results of this analysis are shown in table 4.2.

With regard to the first of these, the two parties' underlying motivations for addressing environmental concerns are distinguished by their respective views

Table 4.2. Alternative TRC Partnership Views on Why Environmental Action Needs to Be Taken

Sociohistoric Factors	Government Agencies	Environmental NGOs
Underlying motivation	• Anthropocentric orientation. • Environmental action for human benefit.	• Anthropocentric and biocentric orientation. • Benefits to both humans and nature.
Interpretation of the state of the environment	• Relativist view. • Conditions are fair but improving.	• Absolutist view. • Conditions are generally bad.
Views on pollution	• Realist standpoint. • Pollution as normal. • Goal is to control pollution.	• Both realist and idealist standpoints. • Pollution as both inevitable and an aberration. • Goal is a society without pollution. • Goal is a return to conditions of the past.

on the intended beneficiaries of such actions. The major difference is that the Waterway Service and Water Treatment Agency approached environmental action primarily from an anthropocentric orientation, while the NGOs did so from a biocentric viewpoint as well. An anthropocentric position views the natural environment as having value primarily in terms of its utility to humans, while a biocentric perspective sees nature as having its own intrinsic value.

Evidence for this is apparent from the contending participants' particular approaches to the Toupin River itself. When asked to describe what the river—or even water in general—meant to them, Waterway Service and Water Treatment Agency representatives commonly described it in terms of its service to or effect on local inhabitants. They discussed its utilitarian role and the pleasure it provides for people. When asked to comment on the benefits brought by the TRC partnership to the river and the environment more generally, a Water Treatment Agency representative responded:

> [The Toupin River] doesn't benefit; it is we who benefit. The environment doesn't derive pleasure from being better. (TRC.27.17)

Although members of environmental organizations frequently made similar types of anthropocentric comments, they also offered descriptions of the river that focused on its non- or extrahuman characteristics. They described it in terms of the fauna and flora that it supported and as part of a larger ecosystem. Along these lines, one environmental NGO participant described the river as the "blood of the territory" and as "giving life to the landscape" (TRC.21.9).

Further evidence for this distinction also comes from comparing the conflicting actors' organizational approaches to environmental action. Both the Water Treatment Agency and the Waterway Service acted on nature for the benefit of humans. The Water Treatment Agency built water treatment plants to purify water, while the Waterway Service managed the rivers to keep them flowing in an orderly fashion. The agency representatives described these actions as serving the local residents, not the river ecosystem itself. For their part, the environmental NGOs involved generally pursued organizational objectives that included but went beyond merely making nature more enjoyable for humans. Among the intended beneficiaries of their environmentalist actions, they listed "biodiversity," "the river," and "the North Sea."

The second difference distinguishing the contending views on why environmental action needs to occur emerges from contrasting interpretations of the state of the environment. The two camps diverged here in their impressions of the severity of water pollution in the Toupin River. The positions taken may be likened to the distinction between a glass half full and a glass half empty.

Representatives from the Water Treatment Agency and the Waterway Service took a relativist approach to the water quality of the Toupin River, commonly viewing it as fair but improving. They generally formed their opinions by comparing the river at present with its condition before sewage treatment began twenty years earlier. As one Waterway Service representative stated:

Since we've begun installing water treatment systems . . . the life of the river is becoming normal again. . . . This means that we've removed many of the harmful effects. Without these [burdens], the river is becoming natural again. (TRC.14.13)

These participants did not deny that some problems persisted, especially in places where sewage still entered the river untreated. They just tended to emphasize the gains achieved.

Most of the representatives from the environmental groups, on the other hand, tended to describe the river as being in a desperate state. They typically spoke about its condition in absolute terms, depicting it as "really bad," "totally polluted," "horrible," or "catastrophic." When asked why she was participating in the TRC partnership, a representative from a local-level environmental group answered:

Because we find the situation of the river to be deplorable, especially when compared to what the older people remember about the river. It's hard to believe. We take walks along the river and don't see any life at all. . . . We see the pollution. We smell the pollution. The reaction of the public authorities has been—and this was the case for [my commune, by the way]—to hide the river because it is so dirty. So they covered the river over . . . for a very long stretch. This was done about fifteen to twenty years ago. . . . The situation is such that we must do something. (TRC.2.7)

This crisis-oriented language was especially common in the NGO committee setting. It was not unusual for NGO members to complain about the degraded state of the river that they had witnessed while out walking or collecting data for the TRC survey. Moreover, comments made that contradicted this view were not afforded much credibility. This was clear in one particular NGO committee meeting when a member of a large nature conservation organization happily announced that results from a recent survey had shown good water quality in one of the Toupin River tributaries. This comment elicited doubts by a number of the other NGO representatives at the table, many of whom represented smaller, more activist-oriented environmental groups. These participants simply would not believe that the water quality in the Toupin watershed was anything but poor.

The third area of difference regarding why environmental action needs to occur derives from the second and concerns the two parties' respective outlooks toward pollution. Representatives from the Water Treatment Agency and Waterway Service generally expressed a worldview in which pollution, and environmental problems in general, were seen as normal. This self-described "realistic" viewpoint is evident in the comments of a Water Treatment Agency representative on the topic of wastewater treatment:[11]

When you talk about eliminating waste or purifying wastewater, this is not a mission that will end one day. Waste will always be produced. We have always

done so in history, though to a lesser degree than now. Hopefully, we will produce less in the future, though this remains to be seen. We will always need
some form of waste treatment. The methods may be different from those of today, but there will always be treatment. (TRC.17.14)

Many of the environmental NGO representatives made similar realism-based
statements in which they either acknowledged the existence of powerful economic or political constraints to improved environmental quality or accepted the
need for pollution minimization as well as prevention strategies. Nevertheless,
there were a number of environmental advocates who departed strongly from
this realist position. These participants treated pollution not as a norm but as an
aberration. This more self-acknowledged "idealistic" viewpoint on the place of
pollution in society is clear in the comments of a communal-level NGO representative on the TRC partnership:

> The goal [of the TRC partnership] is to have an unpolluted river—for the river
> and its banks to be in a more natural state and where the river is permitted to
> follow a path more natural, which would help to avoid flooding problems. . . .
> This would mean going a little bit backwards, but going backwards in this do-
> main is a sign of progress. . . . The ideal goal . . . would be to find fish as we
> did before 1900, with the birds and accompanying flora. (TRC.2.7)

For these participants, a society without pollution was the real objective.

What Is the Cause of Current Environmental Problems?

The second major area of sociohistoric difference marking the disputing
parties in the TRC conflict concerns their respective understandings of the
source of the environmental problems facing the Toupin River basin. In their
discussions on the topic, representatives from both the governmental agencies
and the environmental NGOs associated these problems with increasing popula-
tion-related growth issues and some of the "private" interests involved. They
diverged, however, in the aspects of growth that they chose to emphasize and in
how they defined the private interests at fault. In short, both sides implicated the
other as part of the problem while defining themselves as part of the solution.
The results of this analysis are shown in table 4.3.

The Water Treatment Agency and the Waterway Service placed most of the
blame for the environmental problems facing the Toupin River basin on the actual inhabitants of the province. In doing so, they shifted responsibility away
from the organizations involved in implementing residential development, including their own institutions, and toward the recipients of this development—
the residents themselves. In the eyes of these two agencies, members of local
environmental groups were just as guilty of environmental degradation as
everyone else because they too consumed resources and produced waste. This

Table 4.3. Alternative TRC Partnership Views on the Cause of Current Environmental Problems

Sociohistoric Factors	Government Agencies	Environmental NGOs
What is the root cause?	• Growth issues arising from rising population density.	• Growth issues arising from rising population density.
Who is primarily at fault?	• NGOs are part of the problem both for producing waste and opposing waste treatment efforts. • Governmental agencies are part of solution.	• Governmental agencies are part of the problem—for failing to enforce current regulations and designing ecologically insensitive public works projects. • NGOs are part of the solution.
What is the role of "private" interests?	• The private interests of local protest groups are being favored over the public interests of governmental agencies.	• The private interests of political and economic elites are being favored over the public interests of NGOs.

general belief was nicely illustrated by a Water Treatment Agency employee's comments criticizing the public for not recognizing the necessity of his agency's water treatment projects:

> I am relatively calm in nature, but also resolute. When [the Water Treatment Agency] comes to a place to build a water treatment plant, it is . . . because it is necessary to do so, because analyses . . . show that we must do something in that location. . . . Now, we are amenable to discuss with people whether to locate the plant in a specific place or a little further away or something like that, but if you tell me that we can't do the project, I'll respond to people by saying: "No . . . you need to stop polluting." (TRC.17.8)

These agencies saw themselves as playing a major role in the fight against pollution, as it was they who were treating the wastewater and dealing with storm water runoff problems produced by the increasing number of inhabitants in the area. They resented being blamed for negative environmental consequences arising out of their own water management efforts and considered the local environmental groups who were resisting these public works projects to be hypocrites.

For the environmental groups involved in the conflict, the source of the problems included not only irresponsible inhabitants but also a history of less than satisfactory efforts to resolve some of the problems associated with increasing population pressure. These NGOs blamed institutions such as the Water Treatment Agency and the Provincial Waterway Service for failing to implement and enforce existing laws and regulations. As one local NGO representative described it:

> We wouldn't need a river contract if only we applied existing laws and regulations. Because if we applied existing regulations of water preservation, there would be no pollution in our rivers. However, there are no controls. There are no sanctions. Everything goes. (TRC.13.8-9)

These NGOs also reproached the two agencies for creating new environmental problems in their efforts to resolve old ones. As examples, NGO representatives pointed toward the propensity of the Water Treatment Agency and the Waterway Service to propose building water treatment plants and storm water basins in ecologically sensitive areas. In protesting and resisting such projects, these NGOs saw themselves as protectors of the environment in the face of continuing governmental irresponsibility.

Another distinction between the two sides of the conflict concerns their views on the role of private interests. Although they made similar arguments that the environmental problems facing the river were due to prevailing tendencies to favor "private" interests at the expense of the "collective," the two sides differed with regard to how they defined these terms.

Employees of the Water Treatment Agency and the Waterway Service frequently expressed resentment regarding what they perceived as increasingly frequent citizen action group protests being directed toward their water treatment plants and storm water basins. They conceptualized this dynamic as a conflict between the good of the collective, represented by the public works projects, and the good of the few, represented by the individual objections to these projects. The governmental agency members did not consider these local protest groups to be representative of, let alone the voice of, the public. Instead, they saw these groups to be collections of self-interested individuals. A Water Treatment Agency representative voiced this opinion:

> Recently, we have had more and more opposition groups emerging under the cover of the "public interest." These are specific opposition groups concerned only with protecting private, particular interests. . . . Many NGOs are created and work for the purpose of having a majority intervene for the benefit of a minority. (TRC.27.13)

In the view of these governmental representatives, society as a whole benefits from sewage treatment and flood controls. If a small minority from within the collective suffers from such minor inconveniences as noise, foul odors, or visual displeasure, this should be treated as a small sacrifice that these few should willingly make for the benefit of the greater society.

For their part, the NGOs also saw the social collective as benefiting from a cleaner environment. They departed from the governmental agency view, however, in that they tended to portray themselves as part and parcel of the collective and even, at times, as direct representatives of the region's population. They supported this claim by pointing toward their volunteer status and by noting that, unlike the Water Treatment Agency and the Waterway Service, they did not have any professional interests in the issues at stake. The problem, as the NGOs saw it, was that private development interests were compromising a broader, collective desire for a better environment. NGO representatives described these private interests as constituted not by local citizens but by a politically and economically dominant minority whose environmentally related decisions were being made from a position of individual economic or political profitability rather than a concern for the common welfare.

This NGO conceptualization of private interests is, I argue, rooted in the organizational histories of many of these environmental groups. A large number of the NGOs participating in the TRC partnership actually started out as informal, local pressure groups that formed in response to specific instances of economic development in their communes. In the Ixtoup Province, this economic development often came in the form of sand mines, sugar refineries, or breweries. To the extent that these NGOs saw the Waterway Service and especially the Water Treatment Agency, given its institutional responsibility to promote economic development in the province, as associated with these types of private interests, these NGOs regarded them as detractors to, rather than facilitators of, a healthier environment. They therefore found them worthy of being opposed.

How Does Environmental Action Proceed?

A third major area of sociohistoric difference characterizing the disputing parties concerns their approaches to environmental problem solving. These differences took three forms. They pertained to (1) the contestants' varying conceptualizations of the environmental problem-solving process, (2) contrasts in their prioritizations of the factors involved in environmental problem solving, and (3) differences in their conventional strategies for problem solving. The results of this analysis are shown in table 4.4.

With regard to the first of these, there was a clear distinction between governmental agency and environmental NGO conceptualizations of the idealized process by which environmental problems typically get resolved. This distinction was most apparent between the Water Treatment Agency and the NGOs. In their descriptions of environmental problem solving, representatives from both sides revealed a shared model for how this process typically occurs. They each assumed a process with three steps. In the first step, there is the recognition of the existence of an environmentally related problem. In the second step, there ensues a political decision to do something about it. In the third step, there is the implementation of this decision. Where these two sides diverged was over the importance that they attributed to the different steps.

Informed by the protest experiences out of which many of these groups emerged, the environmental NGOs tended to value most the initial phase of problem awareness and definition. From their perspective, the process of environmental problem solving could be truncated to the following. An environ-

Table 4.4. Alternative TRC Partnership Views on How Environmental Action Proceeds

Sociohistoric Factors	Government Agencies	Environmental NGOs
Conceptualization of environmental problem-solving process	• Emphasis on latter phase of policy implementation and concretization. • Agencies as key environmental actor.	• Emphasis on initial phase of problem awareness and definition. • NGOs as key environmental actor.
Prioritization of environmental problem-solving variables	• Environment is one of many variables. • Environmental objectives seen as fixed and predetermined by existing standards. • Economic efficiency and political feasibility treated as most important variables.	• Environment is the most important variable. • Strive for continuous environmental improvement. • Less attention paid to economic or political constraints.
Environmental problem-solving strategies	• Reactive, curative. • Manage the river to maintain status quo.	• Proactive, preventive. • Manage the river to improve conditions and avoid future damage.

mental problem develops or exists. It eventually becomes the concern of affected citizens or members of the environmental community, who then set about informing the public and putting pressure on public authorities to do something about it. If the concerned citizens or environmental groups are persuasive or adamant enough, political action may be taken to address the situation.

The governmental agencies, on the other hand, tended to attach greatest importance to the later implementation phase. From the perspective of these actors, the standard environmental problem-solving process may be condensed in a different way. It focuses on the phases where policy makers respond to environmental concerns by producing environmental legislation and regulations and where key societal actors then implement these decisions. The representatives of the governmental agencies considered themselves to be among those actors who have the expertise and means to "concretize" and "operationalize" policy decisions.

Evidence for this particular sociohistoric distinction may be found in the many statements made by both NGO and agency participants describing themselves as the most important actors in the TRC partnership and, indeed, the environmental domain. The NGOs participating in the TRC commonly referred to themselves as the "motor" or "engine" of the project. For them, the keys to successfully cleaning up and protecting the river were increasing public awareness of environmental issues and convincing public authorities to actively address these matters. This perspective is apparent in the following comments made by a member of a communal-level environmental group:

> At a fundamental level . . . the environmental associations are the ones who push the communal authorities [to participate in the TRC project]. . . . We have to relaunch the project at every [communal working group] meeting. . . . And we have to do this from the background because the communal authorities want to take credit for anything that gets done rather than cede this to the NGOs. If we accept that whatever we do will be exploited by the communal authorities, things can still work. I think that the worst situation for NGOs participating in the [TRC partnership] would be if they refused to work just because the communes were refusing to participate. This would result in total blockage. We must accept to do the work, to motivate people to do the inventory fieldwork, even though this motivational work will be exploited by the commune. (TRC.9.13)

Representatives of the governmental agencies privileged their own role in the process of environmental action by frequently insisting that environmental problem resolution is most dependent on the realization of "concrete" actions, such as the actual treatment of sewage, the collection of solid wastes, or the building of storm water basins. They also extended this idea to the TRC project itself, as is evident in the comments of one Water Treatment Agency employee:

> [The success of the TRC project depends on] it becoming operationalized in a real way, so that the actors who participate can see the results of their actions and be encouraged and recompensed in this way . . . and so that their work means something. (TRC.27.17)

In short, both sides of the conflict believed that without them, little if anything would be accomplished on behalf of the environment.

The second main area of difference distinguishing agency and NGO approaches to environmental action involves their alternative prioritizations of the factors involved in environmental problem solving. These pertained to both their treatment of environmental factors and their large-scale approaches.

Historically, when the Water Treatment Agency built a sewage treatment facility or the Provincial Waterway Service constructed a storm water basin, their predominant preoccupation was not the overall health of the environment. As one Waterway Service representative explained:

> We do not have direct [environmental objectives]. . . . Our goal is not to improve the environment but above all to improve traffic. . . . With regard to waterways, our primary function is to guarantee the flow of rivers. But we have to take environmental components into account in our decisions. (TRC.4.2-3)

In effect, these actors dealt with the environment because they had to to accomplish their broader goals. They treated the environment largely as a design constraint, albeit an increasingly important one.

Complicating this was the fact that these agencies saw their environmental objectives not as arbitrarily defined but as largely predetermined and fixed in the form of governmental standards. As such, they generally cared less about their environmental accomplishments than they did their efficiency in carrying these out. This was plainly the case for the Water Treatment Agency, which clearly prioritized the time and cost effectiveness of its work over all other variables. As related by one Water Treatment Agency employee:

> [In the Water Treatment Agency,] we have to work under time and budget con-straints, so we must do the best work for the least amount of money. This is ef-ficiency in a capitalist system. For the moment, I find this efficiency to be more important than boat rides and little flowers, even if I like boat rides and little flowers. (TRC.23.10)

This employee also complained that the time-consuming process of opening project designs to the public hindered his organization's ability to meet the strict time constraints imposed on the Water Treatment Agency by its primary funding sources, the Walloon and EU governments.

This more economistic perspective contrasted sharply with the standpoint taken by the environmental NGOs involved in the TRC partnership. These groups tended to prioritize environmental factors over all others. Moreover, they seldom restricted their environmental objectives to the limits called for in exist-ing standards. They pushed instead for more stringent regulations and continual improvements in every area of environmental quality. Their comments hardly ever focused, however, on the time, cost, and political constraints also involved.

The different prioritization of variables involved in the environmental prob-lem-solving process is further exemplified in the two camps' views of the TRC initiative. Most of the environmental organizations evaluated the partnership in terms of its environmental potential. They were primarily concerned with its ability to preserve wetlands, safeguard riverbeds, protect the landscape, or en-sure that future decisions taken with regard to the river would be environmen-tally benign. The Water Treatment Agency, on the other hand, assessed the value of the TRC partnership in terms of its efficiency. As one employee noted:

> If [the TRC partnership] is there to slow down work, this doesn't help [my agency.] If it is there to work, then it must work as fast as us or even faster. What I am hoping for is an intermediary organization which helps us but does not obstruct us. . . . [The Water Treatment Agency] is not against things like the [TRC partnership]. We just want it to be more efficient. Because we are in the train, and the train is moving, and we know that it is moving quickly. We would like to stop at as few stations as possible along the way. At the present, I'm not sure that the station called [the TRC partnership] is helping us. (TRC.23.8-9)

This contrasting treatment of economic and environmental variables was accompanied by additional differences in each camp's prioritization of a macro-

level approach to environmental action. While both sides emphasized the importance of taking a macro view, they varied in their interpretations of what this
meant. The environmental community's conventional approach was to advocate
for an "ecosystem" view of environmental problems. TRC participants from the
NGO sector often argued that air, soil, and water should not be treated independently of one another. Some NGO participants took this argument a step
further, calling for a more "global" approach. These participants contended that
social, cultural, and economic factors needed to be integrated as well. They applied this global perspective to the Toupin River, stating that the river must be
dealt with in its entirety. They considered it absurd to address the river's problems in a piecemeal fashion, such as would be the case if only some of the
communes through which it ran were involved. They perceived the environment
as transcending boundaries, so they believed that political frontiers must be
crossed to deal most effectively with environmental problems.

For the Water Treatment Agency and the Provincial Waterway Service, the
macro view had less to do with integratedness than it did with practicality and
feasibility. Waterway Service representatives, for instance, were quite aware of
the very real political boundaries dividing up the landscape. In their discussions,
they countered environmental NGOs' complaints regarding the absurdity of
dealing with flooding problems one commune at a time by stating that storm
water basins could only be built in communes willing to approve and pay for
them. Likewise, Water Treatment Agency officials often noted that their actions
were ultimately driven not by small-scale concerns but by societal necessity.
This view was captured by a Water Treatment Agency representative's description of how he went about constructing a water treatment facility:

> Imagine that we need to build a water treatment facility. The first thing we
> must do is choose a location. The options are always limited, because water pu-
> rification plants are always found along waterways. By definition, they are not
> found on top of valleys. So, we already have limited decision possibilities, be-
> cause we are obliged to locate on the valley floor. I then take note of the vari-
> ous opinions being put forward—some of which are positive, and some of
> which are negative. I look at which opinions I can take into account, given the
> feasibility of the project, and then we make a decision and commence building,
> even if there are opponents. . . . It is evident that . . . all of the water treatment
> facilities that have been built are in environmentally protected zones. Why?
> Because valley floors are protected. So, if we want to purify the [water in the]
> valley, well then we have to install ourselves somewhere in the valley.
> (TRC.17.8)

For these governmental agency officials, top priority in environmental action
was given not to what *should* be done but to what *could* be done and what really
needed to be done.

The third area of sociohistoric distinction characterizing the opposing
camps' views on how environmental action proceeds concerns a difference in
their basic strategies for addressing environmental problems. In particular, the

governmental agencies assumed an approach that was primarily reactive and curative in orientation, while the environmental NGOs espoused one that was more proactive and preventive. This distinction was evident from the different ways that these organizations expressed their environmental goals. Representatives of the Water Treatment Agency, in the interviews and in their annual report, described the agency's work as focused on "purifying" and "controlling" the quality of surface waters and "treating" and "disposing" of wastes. This revealed an "end-of-pipe" mentality that has historically been the purview of industry and government throughout the West.

Representatives of environmental groups, on the other hand, more commonly described their goals in terms of "protecting," "conserving," and "preserving" the environment. To this, many of them added the goals of "informing," "educating," and "sensitizing" the public with regard to environmental issues and human-environment relations. Some even spoke about "struggling" or "fighting" against those who pursue detrimental environmental practices. Collectively, these terms evoke an approach that goes beyond simply reacting to environmental problems as they arise. This approach is more concerned with actively preventing future damage by preserving specific ecological zones from future development, helping people become more aware of how their behaviors affect the environment, and helping industry and government make better environmental decisions.[12]

This distinction is also evidenced by differences in the two camps' approaches to protecting the Toupin River. Interestingly, participants from both sides of the conflict described their actions in this regard in terms of "managing" the environment. Provincial Waterway Service and Water Treatment Agency representatives portrayed themselves as "managers" of the river just as some environmentalists, especially those coming from larger conservation organizations, described themselves as working toward better "management" of the river basin. A disparity existed, however, in how each sector used the term "management." In particular, the two sides differed in their conceptualizations of both the *objective* and the *object* of management. The overall management objective for the Waterway Service and the Water Treatment Agency, for instance, was for the river to continue to flow and for the water quality to remain at an acceptable level. Management here was geared toward maintaining the status quo. This approach was expressed by a Waterway Service employee who described his role in managing the river as involving such tasks as supervising the use of the river, conducting inspections of it, policing major problems, and initiating projects when necessary. For the environmental NGOs, on the other hand, the primary objective of management was both to improve existing environmental conditions and to prevent future damage. With regard to the object of management, the Waterway Service and the Water Treatment Agency wanted to manage the river itself while the NGOs wanted to manage the polluters as well.

These divergent environmental problem-solving strategies are further illustrated by each camp's specific approach to the Toupin River Contract project. The NGO approach, for instance, was always proactive in this regard. These organizations initiated the project and were largely responsible for pushing it along. This orientation is evident in the following comments on the partnership by a particular NGO representative:

> We must take advantage of the possibilities that this contract, this concertation, brings us by being very active. [We must] use the few years during which the contract will be in operation as best as we can to get things going and to make good decisions. It requires much perseverance and courage to accomplish what we have set out to do. . . . The opportunity exists during a limited period of time to advance things by bringing everyone together, but it must be seized. (TRC.5.9)

This NGO approach may be contrasted with the decidedly reactive reasons given by some of the agency representatives for participating in the partnership. Water Treatment Agency employees asserted that their organization was participating because it was obliged by its corporate mission to support water quality initiatives having objectives similar to those of the TRC partnership. For their part, members of the Waterway Service stated that their participation was necessitated by their professional responsibilities as managers of the Toupin River.

What Is the Most Appropriate Form of Environmental Governance?

The final major sociohistoric difference marking the disputing parties in the TRC conflict under examination revolves around the issue of governance. In manifestations of this conflict, such as the technical committee dispute described previously, NGO participants strongly promoted environmental decision making built around the participatory process of concertation. Water Treatment Agency and Provincial Waterway Service officials, for their part, generally resisted this position. My argument in this section is that this opposition is explained by the parties' contrasting approaches to concertation. Two key distinctions are at play here. At a general level, the parties differed in their overall understandings of the concertation process. More particularly, they diverged in their conceptualizations of how concertation relates to democratic practice. The findings are summarized in table 4.5.

The first key distinction between the disputing parties' approaches to concertation stems from their differing understandings of the general process of concertation. For representatives of the Provincial Waterway Service and the Water Treatment Agency, this conceptualization derived in large part from past experiences with public participation. These experiences typically involved one-time meetings intended to secure public approval for large construction projects such as sewage treatment plants or storm water basins. When discussing these experiences, members from both agencies commonly portrayed concertation processes as oppositional in nature. Some described the context for concertation as inherently confrontational, as was the case with the following Water Treatment Agency employee:

**Table 4.5. Alternative TRC Partnership Approaches to Concertation
as a Foundation of Environmental Governance**

Sociohistoric Factors	Government Agencies	Environmental NGOs
Views on concertation	• Short-term, confrontational process for opposing public projects. • Consultative process where experts retain decision-making control. • Viewpoints of technical experts are privileged over others. • A process that cannot greatly affect the outcomes of projects.	• Multi-viewpoint process of information exchange and learning. • Collaborative process based on consensus and compromise. • Viewpoints of citizens seen to be as important as those of technical experts. • A process that can greatly improve current decision making.
Understandings of the relation between concertation and democracy	• Concertation viewed as a threat to present political regimes founded upon representative democracy. • Concertation allows the will of the few to trump the will of the many.	• Concertation viewed as a form of participatory democracy that permits democratic control over traditional authoritarian decision making. • Concertation allows for solutions to be produced by more people to the greater satisfaction of all.

My job means that I meet up with pressure groups all of the time. Here is the difficulty: when we do a concertation, the people whom we meet, who are present at the concertation, are usually people who are opposed to the project. The people who support it, they don't show up. So, frequently, when I defend a project in public, and this happens regularly, I find myself faced with an auditorium that is principally an audience of opponents. (TRC.17.6)

Others perceived the process of concertation itself to be conflict inducing. One Waterway Service representative noted:

The system of concertation is flawed, because it is undertaken in an inconsistent and unequal manner. One person will speak up and say stupid things, while someone else who has good ideas won't venture to speak. . . . But if someone has a good idea and doesn't express it, the idea is stifled; it doesn't exist. Here, concertation becomes contestation, because the person who had the good idea and never ventured to state it will later become a protester. He will say: "that's not how we should proceed," and he will have reason. Therein lies the difficulty. (TRC.14.7-8)

Complicating this dissatisfaction with the concertation process was the belief of some Waterway Service and Water Treatment Agency representatives that little room for negotiating or compromising actually exists in these public works projects. They saw project designs as being largely predetermined by both the technical constraints in play and the expertise brought by the agencies involved. Although these governmental agency officials were willing to make small changes to appease the public, such as planting new trees or flowers, they generally viewed such revisions as peripheral because they did not affect the actual sewage treatment or water runoff problem.

The Water Treatment Agency and Waterway Service officials also described the concertation decision-making process as ultimately hierarchical and nonegalitarian in nature. This was evidenced by some of the analogies that these participants drew upon in their depictions of concertation. A number of them, for instance, tended to conflate concertation proceedings with "public inquiries"—a distinctively consultative process in which political elites or technical experts solicit the opinions of individual members of the public and then take these opinions into account (or not) when making their decisions. One particular Water Treatment Agency official also compared concertation to the rather paternalistic manner in which decisions were made in his family. He described concertation as a way by which he could solicit the opinions of his family members before making decisions for them.

The NGO participants diverged from their governmental agency counterparts primarily by conceptualizing concertation as a multi-viewpoint process of information exchange and discovery. Rather than seeing concertation as a battle between those who want to build projects and those who want to prevent them, most of the NGO representatives portrayed concertation as a place for sharing and learning about each other's objectives and concerns. The goal was less confrontation than it was consensus and compromise. As described by a member of a communal-level environmental group,

> [concertation] is a round table, large or small, in which people who are concerned with the problems around them and who come from any point of view—whether this be social, economic, cultural, environmental protection, etc.—strive to achieve consensus solutions that take all factors into account. (TRC.13.6)

Implicit here are the assumptions that all of these different perspectives are necessary for making sound decisions and that the views of citizens are as valid as those of technical experts or agency officials.

The second key distinction marking the disputing parties' approaches to concertation concerns their diverging views of the relationship between concertation and democracy. For the NGOs involved in the TRC partnership, concertation was a fundamentally democratic process. As one NGO representative put it: "Concertation is democracy, plain and simple" (TRC.12.8). Moreover, these participants contrasted concertation with traditional, "authoritarian" decision making and related it instead to participatory forms of democracy.[13] As one NGO representative commented,

There is a whole new spirit [of participatory governance in Belgium], although this spirit still needs to be hammered into the heads of representatives of the old regime, who still believe that once elected they do not have to inform the public or pay attention to the public's needs. (TRC.13.5)

Several went so far as to characterize concertation as a means of public control over the political process that allows citizens to test the goodwill of public authorities. One participant stated,

[Concertation provides] control by the public, by civil society, over the way that public administrations function and especially over the way that they take their political decisions. It is a democratic control. It is essential. It is via concertation that we can have some reconciliation between civil society and its politicians. (TRC.5.5)

The assumption here was that without concertation, decisions would be made by a few people to the displeasure of many, while with concertation, solutions would be determined by more people to the greater satisfaction of all.

Although few of the Water Treatment Agency or Waterway Service representatives drew direct links between concertation and democracy in their comments, they did seem to perceive concertation as a threat of sorts to the current political regime. One problem with concertation for these participants was that it presented a means by which individual concerns could trump the collective or common interest. A second problem stemmed from the potential for concertation processes to become obstacles to political administrations. One of the Waterway Service representatives made this position clear when he complained about the increased use of participatory advisory committees in the domain of land-use planning:

I don't like [these advisory boards]. . . . I consider them to be a counter power. They are made up of people who were not successful in getting elected or who want to cause problems for elected officials. . . . People in [these advisory boards] are trying to walk in the flowerbeds of those in power. (TRC.14.4)

The Water Treatment Agency and Waterway Service members also differed from their NGO counterparts in that they favored a representative form of democracy over a participatory one. As summed up by one Water Treatment Agency employee:

In a democracy, we can't include every last inhabitant of a village in a discussion, allowing all of them to express themselves in any old way. This is called a "protest." Sometimes we mix up the two. (TRC.23.23)

The governmental agency participants generally supported the position that only publicly elected officials have the authority to make decisions that affect the population as a whole. They based this argument on the fact that only these elected officials can be held accountable for their actions to the public. This differed from the NGO view, which saw the primary duty of elected officials to be one of facilitating citizen involvement and participation rather than maintaining authoritative rule over the public.

Sociohistoric Explanations of the Practice of Conflict

Up to this point in the discussion, I have merely explored some of the sociohistorically based differences characterizing the contending parties in the TRC partnership conflict over the proper role of public participation in environmental decision making. The next step is to draw upon these differences in perception, interpretations, and meaning to more fully explain why the actors engaged in conflict as they did. In this section, I address several questions only partially answered by the interest-based analysis explored previously. These include why the conflict commonly played out as it did, why the NGOs were so adamant about increasing NGO involvement in environmental decision-making processes, why the NGOs targeted the Water Treatment Agency and the Provincial Waterway Service in particular, why the governmental agencies tended to resist environmental NGO influence in their project design decisions, and why they resisted participatory decision making in general. I also draw upon this sociohistoric-based analysis to explore why certain interests may have been prioritized over others, such as why governmental agency interests in resisting increased public participation may have outweighed their corresponding interests in exploiting potential benefits involved, and why NGO interests in public participation may have outweighed the risk of losing credibility from failing to participate effectively.

In the TRC conflict under examination, specific instances of disputes were typically instigated by the NGO community. This aggressiveness can be attributed to several sociohistorically based influences associated with their particular approach to environmental action. These include their general impression that the health of the Toupin River was in dire straights, their active and preventive approach to environmental issues that sought not only to maintain the state of the environment but also to improve it, and their understanding of the environmental problem-solving process as one that requires and ultimately depends on initiation and motivation from the environmental community. Their push for greater inclusion of the public, and of the NGO community in particular, in environmental decision-making processes may also be seen as a product of their historically based skepticism of the Water Treatment Agency's and the Provincial Waterway Service's commitments to addressing environmental concerns. This view is further informed by the biocentric-oriented and ecosystems-based approaches that the NGOs brought to environmental problem solving, their prioritization of environmental factors over economic or political ones, and their belief that actors such as the Water Treatment Agency and the Waterway Service, who are supposed to be resolving current environmental problems, are actually contributing to these problems for reasons of organizational self-interest.

In a similar fashion, the lack of attention that the Water Treatment Agency and the Waterway Service were placing on environmental concerns is explained by their general perception that the Toupin River and, indeed, the province's natural heritage in general were not in such bad shape, and by their tendency to prioritize economic efficiency and political feasibility over ecological concerns in their work. Also influencing this behavior was their narrower, more anthropocentric view of the environment, their conceptualization of pollution as a normal phenomenon, and their historical tendency to address environmental issues in an ad hoc fashion only after they become problematic. As for their tendency to resist environmentalist attempts to insert themselves more into the environmental decision-making process, this is clarified by their overall perceptions of NGOs. They viewed NGOs as single-issue focused, private-interest organizations whose willingness to delay or terminate projects at the expense of environmental remediation efforts made them a major part of the problem. In resisting the demands of environmental groups, the Water Treatment Agency and Waterway Service were merely acting out their self-perceived roles as the primary implementers of top-down policy decisions.

Also underlying the overall conflict are sociohistorically based differences associated with the concept of multistakeholder environmental collaboration. Environmental NGO attempts to be better informed of and involved in Water Treatment Agency and Waterway Service decisions, and the reluctance with which these governmental agencies responded to this pressure, become clearer when their particular approaches to environmental governance are taken into consideration. Here, the NGOs placed much greater value on participatory forms of governance. They viewed access to information regarding the plans of environmental policy makers and agency personnel to be necessary for ensuring the transparency of decisions and for maintaining some level of control over traditional, authoritative decision-making regimes. These NGOs promoted the concertation process in particular because they understood it to be one that naturally brings together all of the viewpoints and competencies necessary for addressing complex environmental issues. They took it for granted that the public has both a right and an obligation to participate in these types of decision-making processes, and they presumed the views of citizens to be as valid as those of technical experts or agency officials.

For the Waterway Service and Water Treatment Agency, however, concertation consisted of little more than confrontational encounters with citizen groups already predisposed against whatever actions were being proposed. Given that the Water Treatment Agency and Waterway Service tended to treat concertation as an advisory process and viewed project designs to be relatively fixed, these governmental agencies deemed it unlikely that concertation processes would result in any significant changes other than project delays. Their resistance to increased NGO participation is further explained by the emphasis that they placed on the technical dimensions of environmental action and the precedence that they gave to representative forms of democratic governance. They perceived the environmental problem-solving process to be composed, first, of policy making, which they saw as the proper purview of elected political representatives, and, second, of all the myriad steps involved in implementing these decisions, which they concomitantly viewed as the task and unique responsibility of bureaucrats and technocrats. This division of labor (and power), as they saw it, left little room for input from the lay public.

Conflict and Competing Discourses

Although the preceding discussion focuses on particular differences in stakeholder perceptions, interpretations, and meanings that led certain actors to view and act toward one another in conflictual ways, the conflict under examination may also be understood as a product of interacting and, in this case, competing discourses. As is discussed in the following paragraphs, this view, when combined with a practice-based approach, also helps to explain why the technical committee dispute under examination played out as it did.

In chapter 1, I describe how it is possible for a series of sociohistoric-based ideas, categorizations, and assumptions to be related to one another in a more or less coherent way. I refer to these broader frameworks for making sense of and giving meaning to the world as *discourses*. In the TRC partnership conflict, many of the sociohistoric differences tied together in this way. As it turned out, the representatives from the Water Treatment Agency and the Provincial Waterway Service drew heavily on one particular discourse, while the NGO participants drew on a combination of two others. All of these discourses shared the assumption that human interaction with the environment has produced a host of environmental problems that need to be addressed by human problem-solving measures. They differed, however, on the subject of *how* these problems should be resolved. The basic features of these three discourses are summarized in table 4.6.

Borrowing from terminology developed by John Dryzek, the discourse favored by the two governmental agencies was that of "administrative rationalism."[14] Administrative rationalism emphasizes the role of the technical or bureaucratic expert rather than the citizen or consumer in problem solving. It also emphasizes social relationships of hierarchy over those based on equality, with people at the top being seen as knowing more than the people at the bottom. Governing is about administration, not democracy. Governing is about rational management in the service of public interests, which are themselves determined by the best available expertise. Cost-benefit analyses tend to be one of the most favored tools. Finally, nature, as a subject of rational management, is subordinated to human problem solving.[15]

According to David Harvey, who refers to this same general discourse as the "standard view of environmental management," this perspective also promotes an after-the-event approach to environmental problems.[16] In other words, it presumes that problems need to be addressed only after they have become

Table 4.6. Key Features of the Competing Discourses in the TRC Conflict

Discourse	Key Features[1]
Government Agencies	
"Administrative Rationality" (or the "standard view of environmental management")	• Governing is about rational management relying on the best available expertise. • Emphasis is on technical/bureaucratic expert rather than citizen or consumer. • Hierarchical relationships favored over egalitarian ones. • Cost-benefit analyses are a preferred tool. • Nature is subordinated to human problem solving. • Environmental problems are treated as incidents resulting from errors or mistakes. • Approach to environmental problems is reactive and ad hoc. • Preference is given to curative, "end-of-pipe" measures. • Environmental problems are assumed to be reversible. • Scientific knowledge is assumed to exist to cope with any obstacles.
NGOs	
"Democratic Pragmatism"	• Governing requires citizen participation and cooperation among a diversity of perspectives. • Emphasis is on plurality. • Participating citizens are viewed as equals. • Problem solving requires compromises achieved through competition and cooperation.
"Green Rationalism"	• Nature is viewed as having intrinsic value. • Greater amounts of citizen power in decision making is promoted. • Consensus-based decision-making process are favored over the influence of political power and money. • Participants must strive to learn and understand each other's perspectives.

[1] These key features are derived from Dryzek (1997) and Harvey (1996).

distinctive and unavoidable.[17] This approach is predicated on the assumptions that (1) any after-the-event environmental difficulties can be effectively cleaned up if necessary, (2) environmental problems are not irreversible, and (3) scientific knowledge exists to cope with any obstacles that may arise. In the standard view of environmental management, environmental problems are treated as "incidents" resulting from "errors" or "mistakes" that should be dealt with on an ad hoc basis.[18] Preference is given to curative, "end-of-pipe" measures rather than proactive, preventive ones.

In the TRC partnership, the discourse of administrative rationality is illustrated by the great weight that employees of the Water Treatment Agency and the Provincial Waterway Service placed on "doing" things, taking "concrete" actions, addressing "real" problems, and committing only to "achievable" projects. It is evidenced by the priority that these governmental officials gave to pragmatic economic, political, and technical concerns, their reactive rather than proactive approach to environmental problem solving, and their tendency to favor people who have technical expertise over those who do not. Finally, among representatives of the Water Treatment Agency, it is demonstrated by the importance that they placed on time and cost efficiency in their work.

In the TRC conflict over the role of public participation in environmental decision making, the discourse of administrative rationalism came up against a combination of two other environmental discourses being forwarded by the environmental community. The first of these was the discourse of "democratic pragmatism."[19] Democratic pragmatism differs from its competing administrative rationalism counterpart primarily in its approach to government. Democratic pragmatism treats government not as a unitary, administrative state but as a "multiplicity of decision processes populated by citizens."[20] This perspective is driven by a need to secure legitimacy for environmental decisions via the involvement of broader publics in explicitly *interactive* problem-solving efforts. This discourse assumes that participating citizens are all equal and that problem-solving processes will proceed in a piecemeal fashion through a series of compromises achieved through competition and cooperation. The environmental NGO representatives participating in the TRC partnership expressed this discourse via their repeated calls for "concertation," "transparency," "civic responsibility," and "citizen participation." They favored these ideas over authoritarian rule and what they considered to be the ignominious tradition of secretive, closed-door decision making.

The second discourse that was being advocated by the environmental community was that which Dryzek has broadly termed "green radicalism."[21] The combination of these two discourses led the resulting discourse to depart from simple democratic pragmatism in three fundamental ways. The first concerns the emphasis that these environmentalists placed on nature as an important beneficiary of environmental action. Rather than subordinating nature to problem solving, as is the case for nature under democratic pragmatism, the NGO participants in the TRC took a more biocentric view that acknowledged the intrinsic value of the natural environment. The second difference concerns the degree to which democratic participation was privileged. In democratic pragmatism, problem solving requires multiple voices as well as cooperation across a plurality of perspectives. The emphasis, however, remains on achieving this plurality. NGO participants in the TRC partnership pushing for a shift toward a more participatory democracy endeavored to go beyond mere democratic pragmatism by promoting greater amounts of citizen participation and power in the actual decision-making process. The final difference concerns the manner by which decisions actually get made. Although democratic pragmatism fosters the production of compromise decisions via a competitive process, the NGO representatives in the TRC partnership called for a more consensus-based decision-making process where participants strive to learn and understand each other's positions and where political power and money play less of a role.

Participants drew upon all of these discourses in the technical committee dispute under examination. When the NGO committee representative presented his committee's comments on the proposed river regulation in front of the technical committee, his arguments that the regulation needed to allow for greater citizen involvement and to better account for ecological factors were direct expressions of the logic and assumptions embedded in the discourses of democratic pragmatism and green radicalism. Similarly, when the Provincial Waterway Service and Water Treatment Agency members of the technical committee resisted these arguments, promoting the need for efficiency and their own expertise, they did so following a line or reasoning and understanding that was the embodiment of the discourse of administrative rationalism. The divergent presumptions embedded in these discourses, however, made it difficult for them to coexist on an equal basis. Participants from each side of the dispute wanted their particular ways of interpreting the world to dominate. The result was conflict.

Why the conflict played out as it did in this particular setting is another important question that still needs to be addressed. Why did the lone NGO representative promote his democratic pragmatist and green rationalist ideas in such a bold fashion? And why did the governmental agency representatives, with their administrative rationalist arguments, resist him in such an uncompromising manner? Answering these questions demands greater consideration of some of the contextual forces at play.

In chapter 1, I describe *practice*, or what people actually do in particular contexts, as the product of the dialectical interaction between sociohistorically informed actors and the social or material constraints confronting them.[22] The practice of conflict in the technical committee example, then, may be seen as the product of alternative discourses being wielded in a nonneutral setting.

In general, different discourses tend to dominate in different contexts.[23] The discourses of democratic pragmatism and green radicalism, for instance, were dominant in the NGO committee meetings, just as the discourse of administrative rationalism prevailed in the technical committee setting. When the environmentalist discourses were transplanted into the technical committee setting, however, they carried much less weight. They did so because supporters of the dominant discourse resisted the impetus to alter their preferred ways of understanding the world. They also carried less weight because the technical committee members interpreted all of the NGO representative's statements through the filter of whether they made sense from an administrative rationalism point of view. This impeded the ability of the governmental agency members to hear, understand, and value ideas different from their own. The result was the near total rejection of the NGO suggestions for change.

Conclusion—On Conflict in Environmental Partnerships

Conflict is an important practice that occurs in every multistakeholder partnership. Competing interests are often at the source, but other factors are often involved as well.[24] This chapter examines a series of sociohistoric differences characterizing partnership participants that provide a more complete understanding of why particular conflicts emerged and played out as they did in the GBP and TRC partnerships.

The case examples explored also highlight particular areas of sociohistoric distinction that are suggested by this book to frequently underlie conflict in environmental partnerships. Two were examined in the GBP partnership example, including differences in stakeholder understandings of their partnership and interpretations of each other. Several others were investigated through the TRC partnership case. These included differences in stakeholder perspectives on the need for, the causes requiring, and the proper approach to environmental action. They also included differences in stakeholder views on the appropriateness of multistakeholder collaboration forms of environmental governance.

Sociohistoric differences can lead to conflict in multistakeholder partnership settings by encouraging different participants to interpret and then act upon particular ideas or events in incompatible ways. These differences can also make it difficult for participants to hear, understand, and value concepts different from their own, leading them to feel misunderstood at best or ignored at worst. Attending to sociohistoric differences is thus imperative for practitioners concerned with *managing* conflicts in the multistakeholder collaborative setting—a topic to which I turn in chapter 5.

Notes

1. Gulliver (1979), Ross (1993a).
2. Daniels and Walker (2001).
3. Winslade and Monk (2000). See Roy (1994) and Ross (1993a) for other sociohistoric or meaning-based approaches to the study of conflict.
4. This is as opposed to societal-level analyses of conflict that examine broader large-scale conflicts—e.g., see Pearce and Littlejohn (1997) and Ross (1993a).
5. Ross (1993a).
6. Ross (1993a).
7. Winslade and Monk (2000).
8. My strategy for quoting is described in appendix C.
9. I am not making the argument here that the environmental deputy had no interest at all in resisting participation in the GBP partnership. Indeed, one might contend that, as a member of the new ruling political coalition in the commune, he had little to gain and perhaps even something to lose by promoting projects from the previous administration. New administrations inevitably have their own programs to implement and their own

political agendas to satisfy. My point is that, even if such alternate interests are taken into consideration, an interest-based approach alone does not adequately explain the practice of conflict in this instance.

10. Though I do not describe them here, the communal governments, in their capacities as managers of the smaller rivers in the province, also played an important role in this debate. They have been excluded for the sake of narrowing the scope of discussion.

11. For this Water Treatment Agency participant, waste and pollution were equivalent in this case, because the waste that his organization was responsible for treating was the same waste being dumped directly into and thus polluting the river.

12. To the extent that the NIMBY philosophy may be characterized as a reactive rather than a proactive approach to environmental problems, it was also frowned upon by some of the environmental NGO participants.

13. This strong connection between concertation and participatory democracy owes its source in part to a new politics of participatory democracy in Belgium. This new politics was institutionalized in the early 1990s in the form of a governmental "Decree of Decentralization and Participation."

14. Dryzek (1997, 63-83).

15. Dryzek (1997) describes "administrative rationalism" as the most dominant discourse in the domains of environmental economics, environmental engineering, environmental law, and planning and policy analysis.

16. Harvey (1996).

17. Harvey's (1996) description of this discourse differs from Dryzek's (1997) in that Harvey does not privilege the role of government in environmental management quite to the extent that Dryzek does. Harvey is also interested in how this discourse plays out in the private sector.

18. Harvey (1996, 373-376).

19. Dryzek (1997, 84-101).

20. Dryzek (1997, 95).

21. Dryzek (1997, 153-193).

22. Bourdieu (1977, 1990).

23. Bourdieu (1982).

24. Ross (1993a), Schwarz and Thompson (1990), Winslade and Monk (2000).

Chapter 5

Conflict Management

For a long moment, the room was utterly quiet. It was one of those uncomfortable silences that accompanies the collective uncertainty following a moment of extraordinary emotional tension. Two men were squared off in the meeting room. One, named Laurent, was from a large and powerful multinational corporation. The other, named Stephan, represented an influential environmental NGO in Europe. Both were red faced, and although they were seated only a couple of chairs from one another, they appeared to be light-years apart.

This incident took place in a European Union Partnership for Environmental Cooperation (EUPEC) expert group meeting tasked with exploring possible reforms to the EU's Environmental Management and Auditing Scheme (EMAS) regulation.[1] Group members had spent the day looking for ways to have the regulation better contribute to sustainability in Europe. During the debate, several participants, led by Stephan, pushed for a stronger overall regulation. In particular, they argued for the addition of stricter measures to ensure greater stakeholder participation in these processes. Others responded negatively to these propositions, however, and they did so along a number of fronts. Some criticized the prescriptive quality of the EMAS regulation and complained of its cost ineffectiveness. Others pointed to the pragmatic constraints inherent in augmenting stakeholder involvement in the EMAS process, contending that it would be impossible to ensure adequate stakeholder representation in every EMAS certification procedure. Still others, including Laurent, went a step further, questioning whether the EMAS regulation was in fact necessary to ensure continuous environmental improvement on the part of the corporate sector.

It was late in the meeting when one of these critics of the EMAS regulation suggested that the regulation might achieve better participation from the industrial sector if it were weakened. This comment really upset Stephan. He quickly denounced the option of lowering existing EMAS standards, but he did not stop there. Abruptly broadening the debate, he went on to charge that the real problem with EMAS and its International Standards Organization counterpart, ISO 14001, was that the rules were being made by large multinational corporations for the purpose of improving their market positions relative to those of small and medium-sized companies. Laurent adamantly denied this, but Stephan continued, warning even more vehemently that if corporations refused to follow EMAS, environmental advocacy groups would pressure local governmental authorities to restrict public procurement to only those firms that were EMAS certified. Laurent began shouting now as well and angrily accused Stephan of resorting to the typical NGO technique of using threats to force corporations to change their behaviors.

This furious interchange left the rest of the group in stunned amazement. The moderator of the meeting, himself one of the expert group members, sat there speechless. After a long pause, and realizing that he had to do something, he awkwardly proposed that the group move on to the next agenda item. Another participant, however, ignored this rather overt attempt to change the topic and instead admonished the two combatants for their behavior. He stated that he found it unlikely that the two of them could ever be in a partnership together. This comment had the rather remarkable effect of causing both of the antagonists to swiftly shift their attention away from each other and toward this last speaker. In a nearly simultaneous manner, both strongly defended their status as partners. Stephan stated that dialogue is the first step to partnering, and Laurent added that he and Stephan see each other all of the time. They seemed put off that someone would question the quality of their relationship within the partnership.

Like the examples presented in chapter 4, this narrative illustrates a type of behavior that proved to be prevalent in the multistakeholder partnerships studied. It involved not just conflict, however, but also efforts made by partnership participants and third-party neutrals to actively manage and limit the conflict present. I refer to this behavior as the *practice of conflict management.*[2]

The practice of conflict management is significant because of the frequency with which it occurred in the partnerships studied. Given the diverse stakeholder interests and the histories of contentious sectorial relations present in the case studies examined, I expected to see a fair amount of antagonistic and hostile behavior. What I did not anticipate was that such overt expressions of conflict would turn out to be the exception rather than the norm. This chapter examines the general retreat from confrontation observed in these partnerships and explores why efforts to manage conflict prevailed as they did.

Modes of Conflict Management

In their interactions, participants from the four case studies adopted a variety of methods of conflict management. Some they used alone, while others they employed in combination. All were encouraged or at least modeled by third-party facilitators when present. The most common of these included what I am calling the practices of civility, argument minimization, nonengagement, conflict diffusion, and reconciliation. These are summarized in table 5.1.

The Practice of Civility

A first main manner by which participants in the four case studies attempted to manage conflict was via their civil comportment in the collaborative setting. Participants expressed this civility in various ways. First, they generally treated one another politely and interacted in an amicable and congenial manner. This was evident, for instance, in the courteous welcomes that participants exchanged at the beginning of meetings. In the Toupin River Contract (TRC) and Gascoigne Biodiversity Project (GBP) partnerships in particular, participants would enter the meeting rooms by greeting and shaking the hands of all of the participants present. In addition, participants would almost always take time before or after the meetings to exchange pleasantries. This commonly included discussions of personal or professional affairs ranging beyond the focus of their partnerships.

Another important way by which participants demonstrated civility was via the respect that they conventionally showed one another. Participants respected, for example, each other's right to speak and be heard. They typically waited their turns to talk and made efforts to refrain from interrupting. In addition, participants generally avoided attacking or criticizing one another personally. They almost never used inflammatory language or resorted to name-calling. Even when actors found their counterparts to be acting inappropriately—for instance, speaking too long, being judgmental, or failing to move the discussion forward—they would withhold making criticisms during the meetings themselves. In fact, participants seldom acted in an openly hostile fashion in the partnerships studied. It was a rare event when stakeholders raised their voices or expressed strong emotions in front of others.

A final way by which participants exhibited this civility was by showing humility in the collaborative process. Participants typically acted modestly when sharing their views and expertise and generally refrained from grandstanding. Although some stakeholders may have felt more entitled or qualified to participate than others or more critical to the partnership's success, open displays of arrogance along these lines were infrequent.

Table 5.1. Primary Forms of the Practice of Conflict Management

Type of Practice	Description	Case Examples Explored
Civility	Participants treat each other politely, respect each other's right to speak and be heard, and show humility in the face of others.	• General
Argument minimization	Participants minimize the adversarial quality of their communication by prefacing their statements in ways that make them less threatening and by attempting to avoid polarizing, debate-oriented interaction.	• CIMNR case-study examples
Nonengagement	Participants keep private those opinions that might initiate open conflict with others. This also includes participants withholding their views for the purpose of preventing an existing conflict from being perpetuated or exacerbated.	• EUPEC conflict over executive directorship • CIMNR conflicts over environmental justice and free-market environmentalism issues
Conflict diffusion	Participants terminate conflict once it becomes manifest. This typically involves third parties acting to dissolve particular disputes by placating the opposing factions.	• EUPEC expert group conflict over proposed EMAS revisions • TRC conflict over the "trouble spots" report
Reconciliation	Participants reconcile openly expressed and contending views by finding common ground.	• EUPEC business plan conflict • CIMNR "stewardship" conflict • CIMNR conflict between mitigation and prevention working groups

The Practice of Argument Minimization

A second related method by which participants attempted to manage conflict in the partnership setting was by minimizing the adversarial quality of their discursive interactions. Rather than making their points in an argumentative or challenging fashion, participants commonly attempted to advance their ideas or respond to each other's comments in a manner that was not overly threatening. Participants employed two main strategies to achieve this end, both of which were encouraged by partnership facilitators when present. First, they would preface their statements in ways intended to keep other stakeholders from feeling attacked or becoming defensive. Second, they would make efforts to minimize the debate-style (i.e., back-and-forth, point-counterpoint) quality of the discussions. Partnership facilitators encouraged both of these modes of interaction.

Although present in all of the partnerships studied, the practice of argument minimization was most pronounced in the CIMNR initiative. I therefore draw on examples from this partnership to illustrate.

Prefatory Comments

Participants in the CIMNR partnership prefaced their statements in a variety of ways that all had the effect of decreasing the confrontational tone of their discussions. These are summarized in table 5.2.

First, participants often prefaced their statements by indicating that they were offering their ideas or propositions without any great sense of attachment, ownership, or commitment. For instance, participants would begin their comments by describing them as "a work in progress," "straw proposals," or "something to shoot at." Participants would also start by acknowledging in advance that the group might elect not to use their comments or by stating that they did not really care whether their ideas were ultimately adopted.

Second, participants often preceded their statements with compliments directed toward either the contributions of other stakeholders, the quality of the discussion, or the overall work of the group. In the meetings observed, I heard participants note how they were "enjoying all of the comments" and how they "really liked" the ideas being put forward. I heard them describe the discussion as "great," "robust," or "a good step forward." I also heard them "congratulate the group for doing very good work," state that they were "happy with the way the group is going," and "toast" the group's overall efforts.

A third type of preface involved participants apologizing in advance for what might be perceived by others as less than useful or helpful contributions to the discussion. This was an act of humility that signaled to other stakeholders that the speaker was neither infallible nor fixed in his or her positions. Participants preceded their comments with such statements as "Forgive me if this is off track," "I'm sorry to be so small minded," and "Maybe you guys already know about this, but. . . ." This technique was especially common when participants were returning to points that they or others had made earlier. Here, I heard such phrases as "I apologize for belaboring this point," "I'm sorry if I'm drawing us

Table 5.2. Types of Prefatory Comments Contributing to Argument Minimization

---

- Relinquishing ownership, attachment, and commitment to one's ideas.
- Complimenting others and the group's efforts.
- Apologizing in advance for inadequacies.
- Integrating others' comments into one's own presentation.
- Incorporating humor into one's presentation.
- Presenting comments in a relativistic manner.
- Reframing the intent of one's comments as nonoppositional.

---

back," or "I apologize for failing to communicate better." Participants also pursued this technique by adding apologetic phrases at the end of their statements. Finishing their comments by saying "but I don't know" or "but this may not be useful" was especially common.

A fourth type of preface consisted of participants introducing an idea or making a point by explicitly integrating it with past comments. This strategy had the effect of making the speaker appear to be both less exclusive and less positional. In the CIMNR partnership, this technique often appeared when the discussion turned to topics around which considerable opposition already existed. It was used in a specific discussion on the merits of strengthening natural resource regulations, for instance, when an environmental NGO representative interested in more substantial "sticks" was careful to first repeat the argument made earlier by several business representatives regarding the importance of retaining significant "carrots." This technique also appeared frequently in CIMNR debates over the relative merits of approaching natural resource management issues from a "bottom-up" versus a "top-down" perspective. Top-down-oriented participants would often pay homage to past comments made regarding the benefits of a bottom-up approach prior to making their own points, and vice versa.

A fifth method of prefacing that had the effect of lessening the adversarial quality of the ensuing discussion involved the incorporation of humor. One typical way by which CIMNR participants accomplished this was by mocking the supposed seriousness of their disagreements. This was particularly true for debates that pitted stakeholders from one sector against those from another. In these cases, participants would exaggerate the fact that they were disagreeing with one another. One illustrative exchange between two stakeholders—one from the business sector (Darcelle) and the other from the environmental NGO sector (Cathy)—proceeded as follows:

Cathy: In the interest of dialogue, I want to disagree slightly with the previous comments made.
Darcelle: [Laughing] Please feel free to disagree fully! [Laughter follows.]
[Other comments made.]
Cathy: Since I was being disagreeable before, I will be agreeable now. . . .
Darcelle: I am happy to say that I now disagree fundamentally with [Cathy]. [More laughter.]

This tactic had the effect of lessening the threat implied by conflicting points of view.

A sixth method of prefacing involved participants qualifying their comments in a relativistic manner. Rather than forcefully advancing their ideas as absolute givens, obvious to all, or as plain fact, participants would instead present them more as personal opinion. The most common way by which CIMNR participants did this was to note that their views did not necessarily represent those of their organizations, their constituents, or their sector. The partnership's facilitators encouraged this practice as well by specifically asking participants every so often to speak as individuals. This overall technique had the effect of shifting the context of any particular disagreement from the level of societal conflict to the level of individual difference. Participants appeared to be much less intimidated by the latter.

A seventh and final method used to diminish up front the level of threat that might be perceived by a participant's statements involved the tactic of reframing the discussion as distinctly nonadversarial or nonoppositional. In particular, participants often characterized their statements as emerging from overarching efforts to "learn" rather than fight. They did so by beginning their comments with phrases such as "In the spirit of furthering our understandings" and by portraying their comments as arising out of efforts at "brainstorming" or to "get our hands around the issue." The partnership's facilitators endorsed this technique as well by frequently encouraging participants to avoid speaking out of what they termed "advocacy," "judgment," or "assessment" modes.

Debate Curtailment

The second main strategy used in the practice of argument minimization involved lessening the back-and-forth, point-counterpoint, formal debate-style quality of the participants' discursive interactions. This was accomplished in two major ways in the CIMNR partnership: through the adoption of a discontinuous form of linguistic turn taking in the discussions, and through the temporal removal of contentious ideas from the immediate discussion.

In the CIMNR meetings, facilitators employed the convention of placing participants who wanted to speak into a queue and addressing their comments in turn. In addition, facilitators would also at times solicit discussion by going around the room and asking participants to present their thoughts one at a time. These techniques often led to rather disjointed discussions, as participants found themselves referring to points made by speakers several turns earlier. These techniques did have the effect, however, of helping prevent disagreements from escalating into more sustained and conflictual arguments.

Of importance to this discussion, participants generally adhered to this convention of linguistic turn taking even without the guidance of facilitators. When disagreements began dissolving into one-on-one, tit-for-tat bickering, individual participants would often interrupt the interaction and admonish both the speakers and the facilitators for letting the discussion run loose.

The second manner by which participants acted to limit the debate-style quality of their discussions was by introducing potentially volatile ideas in ways other than through face-to-face interaction. One approach was to postpone potentially disruptive debates until after the partnership meetings had ended. Another way was to introduce potentially offensive ideas in written rather than verbal form for consideration at a later time. This technique afforded participants a way of having their ideas heard without risking provocation of a reactive, defensive, or hostile response.

The Practice of Nonengagement

A third main way actors attempted to manage conflict in the partnerships studied was via the practice of nonengagement. This practice took two forms. The first involved participants striving to keep private those thoughts or opinions that might incite open conflict with others. This technique had the effect of keeping conflicts hidden or latent. The second form involved the act of holding back one's views for the purpose of preventing an existing conflict from being perpetuated or exacerbated.

Withholding Opinions to Keep Conflict from Occurring:
An Example from the EUPEC Initiative
  The existence of the first of these two forms of nonengagement was evidenced by a discrepancy between how participants behaved in the interview versus the partnership setting. In the interviews, participants often expressed strong views that were fundamentally at odds with the views of others, while in the meetings themselves, these participants would remain silent on these issues, even when the topics were directly addressed.
  An example of this comes from the EUPEC initiative. The situation involved the partnership's inaugural elections of its executive committee officers. In private conversations and in the confidential interviews, members of the environmental NGO sector expressed great anger toward the business representative who had been elected as the partnership's first president. They were upset with him for dividing another of the officer positions—that of the executive director—into two separate positions to be filled by members from the governmental and NGO sectors. These NGO participants claimed that a prior agreement had been reached whereby the position would be kept whole and assigned to an environmentalist to serve as a counterbalance to the power of the presidency. When the actual voting for the two executive director positions took place, however, not a single word of dissatisfaction was articulated, despite the fact that these NGO participants continued to express resentment among themselves for months afterward.

Withholding Opinions to Keep Conflict from Escalating:
Examples from the CIMNR Partnership
  The second form of the practice of nonengagement involved the act of withholding one's views for the purpose of preventing an existing conflict from being perpetuated or exacerbated. In the CIMNR partnership, this technique was illustrated in two separate examples involving stakeholders from opposite ends of the political spectrum.
  In its earlier work on the topic of regulatory flexibility, the CIMNR partnership sought the participation of representatives from the environmental justice community.[3] These stakeholders were concerned with protecting the interests of the many socioeconomically disfranchised segments of society currently being forced to accept a disproportionately large share of the burden of environmental

degradation. They were also troubled by the underlying inequities inherent in the prevailing political and economic systems that were driving this dynamic.

In their initial meetings with the partnership, most of these environmental justice participants adopted the decidedly conflictual approach of repeatedly demanding that the group more seriously address these basic environmental justice concerns. At first, the remaining participants from industry, government, and mainstream environmental groups did engage these issues, at least somewhat. After a while, however, the majority of the partnership's members began responding to these continual provocations by ignoring them. This led to great frustration among the environmental justice participants and caused most of them to either stop trying or to quit the partnership altogether.

A second example of this form of the practice of nonengagement involved a CIMNR participant interested in advocating the ideals of "free market environmentalism"—a provocative ideology promoting the wholesale privatization of natural resources and a severe retreat from all regulatory control.[4] This individual also made repeated attempts to engage the rest of the CIMNR partnership on the merits of this approach, but as in the environmental justice case, most of the other participants elected to avoid these potentially contentious issues by not responding to them in anything more than a cursory fashion. Over time, this lack of responsiveness led this actor to drop the issue and eventually to terminate his participation in the partnership.

The Practice of Conflict Diffusion

A fourth main manner by which participants managed conflict in the case-study partnerships involved the practice of diffusing conflict once it became manifest. This typically involved third-party individuals acting to dissolve particular disputes and to placate the contending factions. This role was often played by meeting facilitators when present, but it was commonly played by stakeholder participants as well.

This is precisely what occurred in the EUPEC expert group example presented at the beginning of this chapter. Here, a disagreement between representatives of the environmental NGO and business sectors over the EMAS regulation escalated to the point that the opposing parties began shouting at and threatening one another. What happened next was that a third-party individual—in this case, simply another of the expert group participants—stepped in to reestablish peace and order. He did so by questioning the disputants' commitment to the collaborative process. This caused the two disputants to come together to reject this implication. The result was the near total diffusion of the earlier conflict.

Case Example: TRC Partnership Conflict over the "Trouble Spots" Report
A second example comes from the TRC partnership. At one of the NGO committee meetings, the participants undertook the task of reviewing a report

evaluating the state of the Toupin River as part of their preparations for an upcoming river committee meeting. The report drew upon survey data collected by
TRC volunteers and established some of the specific trouble spots plaguing the
river.

During the NGO committee's discussion, Charles, one of the project coordinators, took a moment to describe the Walloon Region's system of environmental enforcement. He noted that although the Walloon government is ultimately responsible for going after people or organizations causing damage to
rivers, it generally lacks the staffing or the resources to do this. Consequently,
many violations of existing environmental laws go unprosecuted. This comment
incited an emotional response from Pauline, an active member from a communal-level environmental organization. Pauline complained of recent problems
that she had encountered along one of the Toupin River tributaries during her
own survey work for the trouble spots report. She described the damage to the
river and riverbed as "horrendous" and demanded that more people be made
aware of this desperate situation.

Michel, another of the project coordinators and the partnership's lead facilitator, responded to this outcry by suggesting that the NGO committee attempt to
develop a strategy to get public authorities to do more. Pauline protested again,
lamenting the difficulties in getting communal governments involved in these
types of issues. Michel replied that the most important thing is to establish a
dialogue. Here, Michel was strongly seconded by an influential representative
from a large and prestigious nature conservation organization in Belgium. Michel then went on to suggest that the NGO committee present a few examples of
current, successful multistakeholder collaborations at the upcoming river committee meeting. The purpose would be to highlight some of the benefits that had
come out of the process of dialogue. After some discussion of possible case examples, Pauline reentered the conversation in a much more subdued tone, recommending that it might not be wise to complain about issues and problems for
which the NGOs lack the competence to resolve.

Later in this same meeting, Charles described the purpose of the trouble
spots report as a means of getting all of the TRC partners to agree on the state of
the river. This would then pave the way for the production of collectively agreed
upon, concrete projects. Yvette, a member of another local environmental organization, intervened here, arguing testily instead that they use this report to
pressure public authorities to do something about the problems. She suggested
showing them the report and saying: "OK, here are the problems; what are you
going to do about them?" She even proposed that the results of the trouble spots
report be published in the press as a means of further coercing the communal
governments. Michel, the lead facilitator, stepped in again here and recommended that this action not stop at provocation alone. He suggested that the
press article also announce that a follow-up story would be done in a year's time
to see what progress had been made. Another participant, in this case representing a farmer's union, ended the discussion by warning even more forcefully that

consensus-based collaboration, and not provocation, is the key to the TRC partnership and should always remain its primary goal.

At the ensuing river committee meeting, neither the crisis-oriented complaint expressed by Pauline nor the proposal for antagonistic practice made by Yvette were submitted before the plenary by the environmental NGO representatives present.

The Practice of Reconciliation

A final way by which actors managed conflict in the partnership setting, and one of the most important for this discussion, was for opposing parties to attempt to reconcile openly expressed and contending views. The primary manner by which actors accomplished this was by finding common ground around which they could all be in agreement. Three case examples, one from the EUPEC initiative and two from the CIMNR partnership, serve to illustrate.

Case Example: EUPEC Initiative Conflict over a Business Plan

A first example illustrating this practice of reconciling conflicts once manifested comes from the EUPEC initiative. The context was an executive committee meeting in which the committee members were attempting to develop a business plan. The purpose of the business plan was to help the EUPEC initiative clarify and hone its mission and intended benefits as part of its efforts to expand membership.

Prior to this meeting, representatives from the business sector had produced a preliminary version of a business plan and circulated this to other EUPEC members for review. In response, two participants from the NGO sector—Stephan, a leader in the European environmental community, and Marcus, a representative from a prominent think tank—proposed a series of revisions to the original. In this executive committee meeting, both of these contending documents were on the table for review.

Over the course of the discussion, a dispute arose over specific sections of the competing business plans. Although the business and NGO sector authors held fairly similar views of the partnership's mission, they differed more markedly in their characterizations of the partnership's "unique contribution" and its intended "end product." Key sections of the original business version and the NGO suggested replacement are reproduced in table 5.3.

The primary author of the business plan presented both the original business plan and the proposed NGO revisions. Afterward, he initiated the discussion with the following statement:

> [With regard to EUPEC's unique contribution,] there is a difference there between what I am proposing and what is written here [in the NGO version]. . . .
> The document that [Stephan] proposes has a "reinvented economy" and ways

Table 5.3. Comparison of Business and NGO Sector Proposals for a EUPEC Business Plan

Business Version	NGO Version
Mission	
To jointly establish among sectors of society priority issues that will benefit from a *partnership approach*.	To execute clearly defined environmental projects, within the framework of the EU's Environmental Action Program, which will help society *move toward sustainability* (emphasis mine).
To execute in partnership selected projects that address priority environmental issues.	
The selected projects will help society *move toward sustainability* in a socially attractive manner (e.g., create employment) (emphasis mine).	
EUPEC's Unique Contribution	
[EUPEC] brings sectors of the European society (NGOs, business, legislators, unions, academia, etc.) together in a very practical setting and provides the know-how, conditions, and *trust* to innovate together.	By successfully implementing innovative and *fundamental changes* (i.e., executing the projects) gradually a unique network of individuals and organizations will shape itself, with a mutual fascination for *breakthrough innovations* that lead to a "*reinvented economy*" (the way we consume, produce, work, manage, etc.).
The deadlock of perceived conflicting interests between sectors of society transforms into the challenge of *sharing responsibilities* and creating commitment for the effective implementation of *innovations toward sustainability* in a socially attractive manner (emphasis mine).	And with a feeling of being part of a fascinating—not formalized—alliance, which [sic] virtual bonds were created by shared intense learning experiences (emphasis mine).
The End Product	
[EUPEC]'s efforts will lead to actions supported by the [EUPEC] membership with a *measurably positive environmental effect*.	[EUPEC]'s efforts will lead to projects supported by the [EUPEC] membership to build a *new European development model*, to help make *breakthrough innovations* in business practice, consumer behavior, NGOs, public authorities, trade unions, institute approaches (emphasis mine).
This can take the form of recommendations to the EU administration on regulatory matters, campaigns to educate consumers, jointly run experiments on business practice, etc. (emphasis mine).	

we consume, produce, etc., as an end result that to me sounds a bit like revolution. . . and that loses sight of the objective, which is: we want to have a sustainable Europe, not how we want to get to a sustainable Europe by creating a revolution, but we want to get to a sustainable Europe. The difference here is that I'm trying to define the end result. Here, this document that recommends the change tries to define the way to get to that end result, particularly the last sentence: "And with a feeling of being a part of a fascinating—not formalized—alliance." I consider that to be a side effect, a very important side effect, but not an end result to base the existence of [the EUPEC initiative] on. . . . And the same comments essentially apply to the proposed recommendation for the end product. It concentrates on a "new European development model" to help break up . . . whatever exists and replace it with something else. . . . But I leave it up to you of course. I'm much more in favor of defining the end result than in defining the way toward the end result.

At this point, Dieter, an influential representative from the government sector, added:

The end product: I think there could be said something more, in the line of what [Stephan] has put, but not necessarily in revolutionary terms. It could say something more about sustainability or what is meant by "measurably positive environmental effect."

David, another leading representative from the business sector in the environmental arena, concluded the conversation with the following:

I can [identify] with some of the comments from [Stephan and Marcus]. I would like to see some more ambition of a benefit to society and then a benefit to membership in the vision. And I think it's almost all there. It's just a matter of putting sustainable development and the Fifth Environment Action Programme rather up front. That is what should energize us to do something. And reveal in the mission [statement] the key process by which we do it, which is to create partnership on priorities we decide together. And I think that in the definition of the end product, I wouldn't go as far as to commit to build a "new European development model," as we can have at least twelve alternatives probably proposed. . . . I think it's not business as usual. It's true innovation. I would push it to be ambitious and exciting.

Stephan, one of the coauthors of the NGO version of the business plan, was offered the opportunity to react to these criticisms. Rather than respond negatively, however, he accepted the comments and simply stated that he had nothing else to add. This lack of antagonistic response was all the more meaningful because Stephan, as an active leader within the European environmental community, was speaking and writing passionately in other venues about the imperative of transforming Europe's economic system.

The disputants were able to reconcile their differences in this case by retreating to core ideas that they all shared. These ideas were present in their respective "mission" statements and involved the beliefs that the partnership's primary value lay in its multistakeholder collaborative qualities and that its primary goal was the realization of sustainable development.

Evidence of this reconciliation appeared in some of the documents that the partnership later produced to describe itself to potential new members. In a subsequent newsletter, and again in website descriptions that followed, the partnership defined its unique contribution to be the "multistakeholder model of partnership" that it provided and the "cooperative action" and "strategic environmental alliances" that it brought to the European environmental and economic arenas. It defined its intended product as "movement toward sustainable development." The partnership dropped, however, any broader references to a desire to bring about more revolutionary, system-level changes in the form of a "reinvented economy" or a "new European development model."

Case Example: CIMNR Partnership Conflict over the Role of "Stewardship"

A second example illustrating the practice of reconciliation comes from the CIMNR case study. The conflict here was over the utility of the concept of stewardship as a means for improving natural resource management in the United States. A particular manifestation of this conflict involved a dispute that occurred between two individuals in a working group meeting. One was Darcelle, an environmental manager from a large corporation in the energy sector, and the other was Kirk, a representative of an international environmental organization. Darcelle initiated the debate when she stated that if her corporation does good stewardship, it should be able to receive some competitive advantage in return. Her point was that given the current regulatory and economic incentive systems, her company is all too often penalized for attempting to be a good steward. Kirk was visibly disturbed by this statement and asked Darcelle what kind of compensation her firm wanted. Was it just public recognition? Darcelle answered that it was broader than that. She wanted Wall Street to value her corporation accordingly. Kirk responded somewhat derisively that this was purely an economic motivation.

The meeting facilitator, sensing a brewing conflict, stepped in at this juncture and pointed out that Kirk and Darcelle have different understandings of stewardship. The facilitator noted that Kirk sees stewardship as an *ethic*—that is, as something people do voluntarily because of its intrinsic value. For Kirk, the idea of receiving economic compensation for doing the right thing goes against this ethic. Darcelle, on the other hand, sees stewardship more along the lines of a *practice*. She has no problem reconciling profit-driven behavior and stewardship so long as the behavior accomplishes the natural resource conservation goals of stewardship.

Shortly after this interlude Darcelle picked up the argument again, contending that people need to be more creative in their attempts to promote stewardship. She described how her organization, in collaboration with a prominent environmental group, developed an energy efficiency program that had the end effect of decreasing resource consumption while at the same time earning a profit. At this point, Ken, a representative from a federal regulatory agency, objected to Darcelle's position, stating that the partnership's goal is not to defend corporate bottom lines but to protect the environment. Another environmental NGO member, Cathy, supported Ken's comment, declaring that she too did not share Darcelle's definition of stewardship. Echoing Kirk's position, Cathy contended that stewardship stems from enlightened self-interest, proceeding in the form of short-term sacrifices for long-term gain.

Eric, a representative of the environmental NGO that had worked with Darcelle's company on the energy efficiency project, came to Darcelle's defense here, cautioning against Ken and Cathy's line of reasoning. He stressed that the group needs to break through what he called "this trade-off paradigm." Instead of asking for environmental benefits in exchange for economic sacrifice, the group should be asking itself: How can more effective and more profitable stewardship of resources *both* be achieved? Kirk and Cathy continued to resist this line of reasoning, however, replying that the energy efficiency project was not about stewardship but about perverse incentives and regulatory barriers. Kirk, in particular, was still irked by the idea that corporations will only do the right thing if they are compensated financially for doing so.

Darcelle reentered the debate here. Picking up from Eric's comments, she replied that for her, being a good steward means that the impact of her company on nature is not "negative" but "sustainable." She also felt that society should value such actions by her company, and not only economically. At this point, Mark, an influential representative of a state governmental administration, closed the discussion by stating that in the context of sustainability, stewardship includes not only resources but human beings and livelihoods. It would therefore be hard to eliminate the economic component even if people wanted to do so.

The following day, several representatives from both sides of the conflict gathered together in a subgroup with the goal of producing a common understanding of stewardship. At the end of their meeting, they concluded that stewardship needs to be understood as being influenced not only by individual and group moral responsibilities but by economic and environmental policies as well. They recommended to the larger group that stewardship be understood as both an ethic and a practice, because only in this way could it be prioritized to achieve win-win success factors.

CaseExample: CIMNR Partnership Conflict between Mitigation and Prevention Working Groups

A final example illustrating the practice of reconciliation comes from the CIMNR case study as well. The conflict in this case involved tension that developed between the partnership's two main working groups. Each of the working groups was focusing on a key path toward achieving the partnership's primary goal—improving natural resource management in the United States. Participants were free to participate in the working group of their choice. They were also free to move from one group to the other as they wished.

The first of these two groups had charged itself with the task of addressing some of the limitations of the existing regulatory regime. In particular, this group sought to envision ways by which natural resource management rules might be reformulated to make the regulatory process more efficient and cost-effective. The group comprised primarily representatives of large firms already embroiled in a host of mitigation issues. Also present were several environmentalists generally opposed to any relaxation of existing regulatory standards as well as a few federal regulators responsible for writing and implementing such rules. This group named itself the "mitigation group" and focused its work on the relationship between federal mitigation laws and big business.

The second working group started out by looking at some of the land and water conservation issues facing different geographical regions of the United States. Although its overall goal, like that of the mitigation group, was to improve the tools that exist for making natural resource management decisions, this group assumed a much broader focus. The participants were interested in examining decision making at the level of both the individual and the large firm. They also hoped to address economic and cultural as well as political and legal barriers to effective natural resource management. A major goal here was to come up with innovative ways for reforming existing economic practices and institutions—such as in the areas of tax, trade, and fiscal policy—that promote destructive environmental behaviors. This working group comprised a broad mix of representatives from the industrial, agricultural, and land development segments of the business sector; an assortment of large and small environmental NGOs; and a range of state and federal governmental officials. They began by calling themselves the "land and water group."

Over time, a certain degree of animosity developed between the two groups. The land and water group criticized the mitigation group as being much too narrowly focused in its approach to natural resource management. The mitigation group, for its part, deemed the land and water group to be rather unfocused and indeed unrealistic in its aims given the time and expertise constraints of the partnership. The mitigation group also considered its counterpart to be too top-down oriented in its desire to search for large-scale changes. Both groups began to take on the attitude that their focus was of greater importance to the partnership.

In the meetings that followed, the mitigation group continued to work on improving the use of mitigation as a means for protecting natural resource systems. The land and water group, on the other hand, redefined its focus, and it did so in counterposition to the mitigation group. The land and water group came to the conclusion that its primary interest was really "prevention"—that is, the changes that need to be instituted so as to avoid having to mitigate in the first place. The land and water group defined such preventive actions in terms of stewardship, which it characterized as per the previous case example above, and officially renamed itself the "path to excellence for enterprise stewardship of natural resources working group." Most participants simply referred to it as the "prevention working group."

The tension between these two working groups remained for another couple of meetings. During this time, several participants began to express concern over whether the two working groups would be able to reconcile their differences and reunite. Directed attempts to do so finally came in the partnership's next to last meeting. The lead came from the prevention group, which proposed using stewardship as a unifying concept for the two working groups and indeed as the key path by which to achieve the partnership's overall objective of sustainable natural resource systems.

Initially, members of the mitigation group resisted this suggestion. Some objected to the nonregulatory nature of the concept of stewardship, arguing that voluntarism is not enough to change people's behaviors and that a stewardship ethic alone offers no guarantee that people will manage natural resources appropriately. Others claimed that the concept of stewardship was simply too vague, intangible, and difficult to implement.

Members of the prevention working group defended their proposition in several ways. First, they argued that laws and regulations, while valuable, are not enough to ensure natural resource sustainability. What needs to be added, they stated, is an ethic of individual responsibility and caring, both at the level of the citizen and at that of the enterprise. Second, as was described in the previous case example, these participants reasoned that stewardship, in addition to being an ethic, is also a practice. As a practice, it can therefore be operationalized. In particular, stewardship behaviors can be fostered both politically, via policies and regulations, as well as economically, via the use of economic incentives. They contended that it was especially important here that stewardship behaviors be aligned with the profit motive. Finally, these members of the prevention group noted that although the notion of stewardship might be somewhat idealized, it can be promoted through education. They added, moreover, that stewardship has the extra benefit of addressing certain key issues that the traditional regulatory approach has not handled very effectively in the past. Primary among these is the natural resource management that takes place on private lands.

Consensus over how to unite the two working groups was achieved in the meeting when leading members of the mitigation working group finally embraced the value of a stewardship-based approach to natural resource management. Further evidence of this reconciliation appeared in the language adopted in the partnership's final report. In this document, the partnership officially defined prevention and mitigation as "action agendas that apply the stewardship approach to the task of reconciling economic development and natural resource management." The partnership did differentiate between these two action agendas, however, recommending that prevention be treated as the first course of action. Finally, the partners advocated pursuing a "stewardship path" toward sustainable natural resource management, which they defined as:

> Built upon explicit recognition that the current set of environmental laws and regulations is necessary but not sufficient to achieve sustainable natural systems. We recognize that our existing rules and regulations will continue to provide enforceable safeguards to protect the environment. But, to be successful, any stewardship path must go beyond basic compliance with existing laws by encouraging innovation and cooperation among the public and private sectors, individuals and communities. We believe these efforts have considerable untapped potential to realize a stewardship path to sustainability—a path that will draw on a common cooperative approach to secure healthy natural systems.

A Sociohistoric Perspective

A variety of reasons exist for why practices of conflict management were prominent in the environmental partnerships studied. To be sure, there are potential political and economic advantages to be gained through such behavior. Participants benefiting from the specific goals or objectives of a partnership, for instance, would find it to be in their best interest to avoid or at least limit conflictual situations capable of undermining the partnership's success. It is also possible that the interests at stake extend beyond the partnerships themselves to encompass broader sectorial relations. By acting in a conflictual manner, representatives from high-visibility industries, for instance, might end up unnecessarily antagonizing the NGOs present, thus inviting potentially damaging protest actions, or causing governmental regulators to lose trust, thereby attracting greater regulatory scrutiny. Similarly, adversarial practices by governmental representatives might result in the loss of business cooperation in matters of regulatory compliance and in diminished respect and credibility in the eyes of the public. Finally, contentious practices on the part of environmental NGOs might jeopardize their place at the table as well as the possibility of participating in future collaborative processes.

Despite the obvious significance of such an interest-based approach, however, it can provide only a partial explanation for the conflict management behaviors observed, in part because it does little to explain the prevalence of these practices. Here, we may look instead to the role played by sociohistoric factors. In the sections that follow, two such factors are examined in detail. The first concerns the existence of particular shared understandings of what environmental partnerships are supposed to be like, and the second involves the presence of a privileged discourse by which many of the partnership participants conceptualized and talked about the environmental concerns at issue.

A Cultural Model for Partnership

Evidence collected from all four of the case studies suggests that many of the participants, regardless of sectorial affiliation, shared a *cultural model* for how multistakeholder partnerships are supposed to work. Cultural models are presupposed, taken-for-granted models of the world that are widely shared by the members of a society.[5] They constitute the horizon of meaning against which events are interpreted and evaluated. In guiding people's expectations, they also influence behavior. In the partnerships studied, the particular cultural model at issue conceptualized partnerships as ideally nonconfrontational.[6] In other words, conflict is viewed as something to be avoided.

While distinct, cultural models do not necessarily remain consistent or stable over time. Indeed, they are better seen as being created and re-created in practice.[7] Some people come to hold cultural models by deriving them on their own. With regard to the cultural model in focus here, it is likely that some individuals simply came to the recognition, via their own life experiences, that the key to resolving environmental problems is for diverse stakeholders to come together to work with rather than against one another. Other people learn cultural models from others. In the multistakeholder partnerships studied, the model of partnerships as ideally nonconfrontational was being taught by some of the professional facilitators involved.

Numerous examples reveal the existence of this particular cultural model in the case studies examined. A GBP participant from the environmental NGO sector demonstrated it when he stated:

> [In partnership,] we have learned a new mode of operating . . . that is rather simply: Why not achieve results in ways other than by conflict? (GBP.20.18)

A EUPEC governmental representative echoed this perspective when he described the EUPEC initiative as having the goal of:

> Creat[ing] a network or fora for dialogue and nonconfrontational reflection on the environment and other problems that society has to face. (EUPEC.4.1)

Some participants expressed the model by portraying the partnership process as one that aids in circumventing or overcoming conflict. A EUPEC representative from a trade union federation described the partnership process as follows:

> Partnership . . . allows all the participating people to know [each other's] standpoints. It allows us to come closer in the discussion points. It allows us to come to compromises. It allows us to go away from confrontation. (EUPEC.15.10)

A representative from a local environmental group participating in the TRC partnership depicted concertation, the basic process of partnership action, in a similar fashion.

> Concertation must permit the resolution of . . . conflicts, avoiding them as much as possible, and when they present themselves, finding a way of action or different modes of reasoning that permit the resolution of these conflicts, thereby arriving at a solution that takes [everyone's] needs into account. (TRC.12.5)

Other participants displayed this model when they contrasted collaboration-based partnership processes with other adversary-oriented decision-making modes. An influential CIMNR participant from the environmental NGO sector noted that in partnerships:

> People actually do assemble for the purpose of attempting to cooperate. And that often is very different [from the typical] context [in which] we see a lot of

representatives of these institutions. When we are before the [regulatory] agency in traditional rule making, we're usually not cooperating with one another. We're trying to knock each other's arguments and trying to do so in the most skilled, adversarial fashion. When we're in court, we're certainly doing that. . . . So, it's helpful to have a forum for discussing even some of these same issues in a process where the ground rules are that you are not supposed to just be trying to score points but you're supposed to be seeing whether you can reach through the apparent differences and find some points of agreement. . . . It's good to be out there in a nonadversarial process interacting with people whose daily lives are spent doing things in very different institutions. (CIMNR.20.9-10, 13)

The EUPEC coordinators also promoted this general idea. In an article entitled "Replacing Conflict with Cooperation" that appeared in the EUPEC newsletter, the EUPEC president wrote:

> The challenges at hand are daunting. No group of social actors can make it happen in isolation. Nor will conflict and contention accelerate the necessary changes of behaviour, consumption, and production.
>
> New forms of dialogue and cooperation are fundamental to successful change: dialogue that engages the daily and immediate concerns of citizens, consumers, and employees as well as the larger ethical and global issues; dialogue that leads to solutions, new models of success and new opportunities; dialogue that facilitates a transition to better legislative rules and instruments; dialogue with no losers.

For these participants, the partnership approach stands out in stark distinction from advocacy-based processes and the us-versus-them and winner-versus-loser mentalities embedded in them.

Supporting Metaphors

In their descriptions and definitions of partnerships, participants from the four case studies also made certain analogies and used certain metaphors that supported the dominant model of partnerships as ideally nonconfrontational.[8] A number of participants, for example, contrasted partnering with the antagonism-based processes of "fighting," "struggling," "battling," or being at "war." A governmental official participating in the EUPEC initiative illustrated this when he stated:

> Partnership could mean, or should mean, people coming together from different groups with a common goal and agreeing on the objectives and strategy to achieve these objectives. But it shouldn't be a fight or a power struggle. This should be done in a way that nobody feels strong or weak. (EUPEC.13.4-5)

A second type of metaphor compared partnerships with other cooperation-based activities in which conflictual behavior was seen to be detrimental. Some participants, for instance, likened partnerships to teams. A business representative from the TRC partnership was comparing partnerships to soccer teams in particular when he explained:

> When a soccer team wins, the person who scored the goal always says that, even if he played well, he scored the goal because he received a good pass from a teammate, and he always thanks the goalkeeper for saving the last shot. (TRC.19.27)

His point was that partnerships, like any team effort, can succeed only if everyone works together and in a selfless manner. Other participants discussed partnerships along the lines of a boat. They described partnerships here as collaborative processes in which everyone either succeeds together or fails together. As related by an NGO representative from the GBP partnership:

> I also believe that once we engage officially [in partnership], we must carry out the project. We have to finish it. It is unacceptable to quit mid-stream or to rely solely upon the work of the other partners. We're all in the same boat. We have to bring things to a successful conclusion. (GBP.11.7)

They also depicted partnerships as boats in which everyone must row together and in the same direction if they want to get anywhere.

A third example of a cooperation-based metaphor comes with the analogy drawn between partnership and marriage. One participant, a business representative from the TRC partnership, compared the concertation process to a marriage, asserting that,

> in a couple, the man is not more important than the woman and the woman is not more important than the man. (TRC.19.27)

A EUPEC representative from a national-level environmental group expounded further on this idea, stating:

> [Partnership] is the recognition first of the weaknesses and strengths that exist, and then the ability to marry the expertise and the willingness . . . to give the information, to give the time, to give the monetary commitment in a way that benefits all. I think that partnership has to be without selfishness; otherwise it doesn't work. . . . Self-interest of one group cannot override all the others. . . . [Participating in partnerships] has really been a giving and a taking situation where both have gained. (EUPEC.17.6-7)

These and other comments point toward an understanding of partnerships as a process where generosity and equality rather than self-interest and dominance are critical, and where concerted effort rather than antagonism pays off in the end.

A fourth such metaphor that was particularly prevalent in the TRC partnership concerns the frequent comments made referring to the consensus-based concertation process as a game. More specifically, participants viewed the success of concertation to be dependent on whether, or how well, people "play the game." For these actors, this idea of playing the game demands a level of goodwill on the part of the participants. This is illustrated by the following comments made by a member of a communal-level environmental group:

> I believe [concertation] is good because it is based on the goodwill of all of the parties. If one of the parties stops playing the game and starts doing things in secret, I believe that it is over at that point. It will never work again. Given that [concertation] doesn't have any legal or obligatory basis, it really rests upon people's goodwill. (TRC.9.5)

Also incorporated in this notion of goodwill is the idea that people should be motivated to participate, willing to abide by the decisions taken in the process, and dedicated to play until the end. One does not quit the game just because one does not like the results. To "play the game," people must be honest. They should play fairly, by the rules, honorably, and without ulterior motives or cheating. It is interesting that if we compare the game metaphor with the fight or struggle metaphors discussed above, it appears that the actors who use these analogies find the partnership process to be more fun and perhaps less dangerous than traditional, adversary-based decision-making processes.

A final cooperation-based metaphor to be explored comes from the EUPEC case study and was prominent among certain representatives from the business sector. In particular, these participants conceived of the partnership process as a "commercial dynamic" and viewed the other partners as "customers" or "consumers" with needs to be satisfied. An influential business representative described the commercial dynamic as follows:

> You go to somebody who is purchasing products from you and he wants it faster, better. He's going to complain about not getting enough service. So he's going to demand that you change and do things more. You know, he's going to demand stretch from you all the time. When I listen to environmental leaders [in partnerships], I understand that they demand change and stretch from me—to stop doing this or to do this better, etc. And when you are a commercial person, you never tell your customers "Go to hell; you are demanding too much," because if you do this, you will wonder who is going to pay your salary. . . . So, instead of fighting back or not looking, which I wouldn't do with a customer, why should I not talk to them? (EUPEC.16.6-7)

In a parallel fashion, a top environmental official from another large corporation explained his approach to environmental partnerships as being similar to his corporation's strategic approach to consumer research.

> The concept of sitting down and talking with people about what we're doing and why we're doing it, understanding their reaction to it, is second nature to us. . . . [My company] is driven by understanding what people need and devel-

oping the technology that can deliver the needs. Needs include: people need companies to be environmentally responsible. (EUPEC.28.12-13)

As with these other metaphors, the "customer is always right" ethic embedded in the commercial dynamic metaphor constitutes a retreat from hostility and a movement toward accommodating the other partners whenever possible.

The Privileged Discourse of Ecological Modernization

A second major sociohistorically based factor influencing the practice of conflict management in the environmental partnerships studied concerns the existence of a *privileged discourse*. I found this discourse to be more favored and persuasive than any other within the partnership meetings.[9] This was the discourse of *ecological modernization*.[10]

Since the late 1980s, the discourse of ecological modernization has existed as a prominent way of conceptualizing and talking about issues in the environmental policy arena. Although the discourse is by no means perfectly bounded or coherent,[11] several important premises underlie it that are important to this discussion. These are summarized in table 5.4.[12]

The first premise concerns the supposition that the resolution of today's complex environmental problems requires collective rather than individual or isolated action. Ecological modernization recognizes a broader range of legitimate environmental stakeholders and promotes the greater use of collaboration in decision-making processes. The assumption is that an environmentally sound organization of society can be achieved if only every individual, firm, and governmental body would participate.

A second critical premise underlying the discourse of ecological modernization is the presumption that environmental protection is a precondition of long-term economic development. In particular, ecological modernization rejects any assumed fundamental opposition between economy and ecology. It portrays environmental protection as a positive-sum, rather than a zero-sum, game. Eco-

Table 5.4. Key Premises of the Discourse of Ecological Modernization

---

- Resolving today's environmental problems requires active participation by and collaboration among society's diverse interests.
- No fundamental opposition exists between economy and ecology. Environmental protection is seen as a positive-sum rather than a zero-sum game.
- An anticipatory, preventive approach to environmental problem solving is more appropriate than a reactive, curative strategy.
- Although the prevailing economic system of liberal capitalism is at the root of many of today's environmental problems, this is still the most appropriate system from which to address these problems.

---

logical modernization substantiates this view by adopting an economistic approach to environmental degradation. It defines ecological problems from a position of scientific rationality and frames them in monetary terms, thereby providing a common basis via which the costs and benefits of pollution can be taken into account. The catchphrases that best represent the ideology here are "sustainable development"[13] and "pollution prevention pays."[14]

A third important premise underpinning ecological modernization is the belief that it is better to address environmental issues before they become problematic rather than afterward. Ecological modernization favors anticipatory, preventive approaches to environmental action over more traditional reactive and curative strategies.

Finally, attached to these three premises is a particular understanding of the relationship between current environmental problems and the prevailing economic system of liberal capitalism in the industrialized West. Although ecological modernization recognizes that this system of production and consumption is at the root of many current environmental dilemmas, this acknowledgment is not accompanied by calls for this system to be replaced. On the contrary, ecological modernization views existing political, economic, and social institutions as the most appropriate structures for addressing current issues of environmental protection.

Evidence of Ecological Modernization: The Discourse of Collaboration

In the research conducted, I found ecological modernization, more than any other discourse, to permeate the texts, discussions, and individual understandings concerning current environmental problems. This was particularly true for the element of the discourse that promotes the indispensability of multisectorial collaboration in environmental problem-solving efforts. Statements emphasizing the need for dialogue and collective action were so profuse that they may be viewed as comprising a subdiscourse of, or discourse embedded within, ecological modernization. I refer to this as the *discourse of collaboration.*[15]

Participants from the four case studies demonstrated the discourse of collaboration in a variety of ways. Some illustrated it in their comments claiming partnerships, and collaborative action in general, to be a superior approach to solving problems, achieving goals, and doing work, especially when compared with individually based or isolated actions. When asked to discuss the drawbacks of the concertation process, a communal-level governmental official participating in the TRC partnership responded:

> Disadvantages? None. None. Without a good concertation, nothing is possible. It's not possible to do good work. . . . With concertation, we can accomplish many projects and improve many situations. (TRC.11.5)

An industrialist from the EUPEC initiative stated:

Partnership is a way . . . is a tool for getting to a better end result faster. . . . It reduces waste [in the form of] time and money and effort. (EUPEC.1.4-5)

A member of a local environmental group participating in the GBP partnership asserted:

For me, you can't get away from partnership. If we work individually, we will not succeed. . . . We must use partnerships in order to do good work. (GBP.8.9)

Many other participants took this point a step further, claiming that partnerships and collaborative action are required for resolving environmental problems and integral, in particular, to achieving sustainable development. An environmental consultant participating in the EUPEC initiative expressed this conviction when he stated:

I can't see sustainable development happening without very unlike people drawn from very different parts of society, sectors of industry, and all the rest of it learning to work together in a fundamentally different way. And I think these partnerships at a very small scale give people the experience of working with strange allies. (EUPEC.22.8)

In a similar fashion, a governmental regulator from the CIMNR initiative declared:

I passionately believe that these are big issues and have to be dealt with by a broader public from a positive perspective—that if we are to advance as a society, and if we are to be in any way sustainable into the next millennium, we've got to think in different ways. . . . Collaborative ventures play a major role because they bring people together. I honestly do not understand how [these changes] can happen without some sort of organizing arena [like partnerships] in which these [issues can play out]. They don't play out in the general body politic. They don't play out in the economic arena. Nowhere do these issues arise other than in a disciplined, organized collaborative. (CIMNR.4.24)

All of the partnerships explicitly fostered this idea in their own publications as well. The EUPEC coordinators, for instance, wrote the following in a document intended to introduce and promote the partnership to prospective members:

[The EUPEC initiative] is not a group to lobby or defend positions. Its only bias is a firm belief that partnership actions will be more effective in the long run to ensure the conditions of Sustainable Development.

Within the EUPEC initiative, one of the most pronounced ways in which this idea was expressed was via the privileging of the notion of "shared responsibility," a phrase borrowed from the European Commission's Fifth Environmental Action Programme. Although different participants in the EUPEC initiative had varying understandings of the exact meaning of shared responsibility,[16] most agreed that this term was critical to the resolution of pressing environmental issues. A participant from an environmental consulting firm expressed this general sentiment when he commented:

> For society and our economies to become sustainable, people have to work together on a shared vision, and a set of objectives, and performance measures, and practical projects, processes, and all the rest of it, and in doing so, accept a degree of shared responsibility. (EUPEC.22.8-9)

These participants also believed that multistakeholder partnerships were an excellent way of manifesting shared responsibility. This was voiced by a governmental official participating in the initiative:

> If you postulate the idea of "to make things happen you need a shared responsibility," then you have to find mechanisms to ensure that shared responsibility can be effective. And a partnership approach is probably the most effective means of doing that. (EUPEC.12.7)

Yet another manner by which participants demonstrated the use of the discourse of collaboration was via comments professing the advantages of partnership processes over more traditional, adversary-based decision-making approaches. A CIMNR business representative clearly exemplified this with his assertion that

> there is a general agreement that the traditional command-and-control regulatory system, with the stakeholders participating in legal hearings or court-like procedures, is just not going to work in the future, and that collaboration, partnership, [and] stakeholder types of common efforts [are] going to be a major element of a better way of doing things in the future. (CIMNR.6.7)

Similarly, a TRC participant from the business sector stated:

> There is an expression in French that says: it is better to have a bad agreement . . . than a good legal proceeding. . . . This is a good expression because we are never certain of the results of a legal proceeding. . . . Concertation in the environmental domain is the same thing. It is better that people, that humans, come to agreement amongst themselves rather than having laws imposed on them by politicians who don't always know the situation. Laws are made to be twisted. . . . So laws are not always that attractive. It is better to have the other person's heart than his reason or his law. It's more durable if you have the heart of others. In five or ten years, the law may no longer be valid. But in ten years, the other person's heart still will be. This appears to me to be a real foundation of concertation. (TRC.19.18)

All of these illustrations of the discourse of collaboration are tied to a general conviction that one of the major problems facing society today is the omnipresent lack of communication, information, and trust among actors in the environmental domain. This discourse contains the assumption that the very act of engaging in multistakeholder cooperation will permit such problems to be resolved.

Evidence of Ecological Modernization: The Premise of Economic-Ecological Integration

Further evidence of the prominence of the discourse of ecological modernization comes with the frequent expression of a particular view on the relationship between economy and environment. This view saw the need for better integrating economic and environmental factors and perceived a positive-sum relationship to exist between these two domains.

Participants made comments to this effect when talking about their various approaches to the environment. A TRC representative from a national-level environmental organization used the discourse when he described his own personal philosophy of environmental protection:

> The protection of and research for a better environment is in agreement with the pursuit of economic activities—economic activities done with better attention to the environment. (TRC.5.6)

Others demonstrated this aspect of the ideology in their descriptions of their organizations' approaches to the environment. Such comments were especially prevalent among representatives of large corporations. An environmental manager from a multinational consumer products company participating in the EUPEC initiative asserted:

> Doing the right thing by the environment is as important as doing the right thing financially for our shareholders. (EUPEC.28.5)

Similarly, a CIMNR representative from the energy industry described his firm's most important goal to be that of

> integrating environmental considerations into business planning so that when strategic business plans are made, environmental considerations are brought in up front into them with the idea that you can actually use environmental performance or excellence as a competitive factor. (CIMNR.6.2)

Such comments came from the other sectors as well. An NGO representative participating in the GBP partnership described his organization's goal to be that of working toward improvements in both agricultural production and nature conservation:

> We are trying to integrate the two, and I don't believe that there are fundamental contradictions to doing this. (GBP.23.5)

In the same vein, a public official from the CIMNR partnership described the major questions facing his state governmental agency as follows:

> How can we as government affect the economic situation that will produce better natural resource management? . . . [And how can we] produce better environmental outcomes that can be more efficiently implemented by the private sector and by government so that it's better for business and better for the environment at the same time? (CIMNR.3.11)

The most frequent demonstration of this economic-environmental integration aspect of the discourse of ecological modernization, however, came when participants were discussing their own partnerships. A EUPEC member from a national-level environmental NGO commented:

> From the standpoint of environmental groups, I think the benefits [of participating in EUPEC] lie in . . . better managing the economic-environmental ties, in integrating the economic dimension into environmental concerns. I believe that only by forcing the environment to leave its narrow preoccupations and integrating it into the economic machine will the environment reach fulfillment. (EUPEC.7.14)

Another environmental NGO representative went into greater detail describing the CIMNR partnership's objective as one of

> coming up with specific proposals for tax changes, trade policy changes, fiscal policy changes, [and] institutional changes to better ensure that desirable environmental behavior [is] compatible with the private sector's built-in behavioral incentives to act in ways that [are] rewarded economically. . . . You align the economic policies so that to succeed economically you've got to perform environmentally. (CIMNR.15.17)

In the introduction to their biodiversity charter, the membership of the GBP wrote:

> The essential task of this partnership is to place into operation a genuine policy of protection and development of biological diversity, in accordance with the economic and social realities of the commune.

An especially common formulation of this notion of economic-environmental integration came with comments alluding to the necessity of finding win-win solutions to current environmental problems and, in particular, to the importance of achieving the preeminently valued objective of sustainable development. This idea was evident in participants' discussions on the topic of how best to address current environmental issues, as when an environmentalist from the EUPEC initiative declared:

To not have sustainable development today as an objective when we want to be on the front lines of environmental struggles is . . . unacceptable. (EUPEC.7.14-15)

It was also evident in the published writings of the four case studies, all of which labeled sustainable development as a major goal. The EUPEC coordinators exhibited this particular component of the ecological modernization discourse when they wrote in one of their brochures advertising a EUPEC seminar on partnership:

Partners will succeed together and the objectives of Sustainable Development will come to fruition when investments are directed to business opportunities that create jobs and measurably improve environmental quality. The triple win of environmental quality, business opportunities and job creation will be the challenge of the participants in the [EUPEC] programme and initiatives.

Evidence of Ecological Modernization: The Promotion of Prevention

Final evidence demonstrating the existence of the discourse of ecological modernization in the partnerships studied comes from comments made regarding the importance of pursuing anticipatory and preventive rather than reactive and curative approaches to environmental problem solving.

Participants from the business sector frequently expressed this idea in their discussions of their organizational approaches to environmental management. For business representatives from the EUPEC initiative, for instance, taking care of the environment was no longer something to be done only after problems arise. Instead, they spoke often about the importance of taking environmental considerations up front into all of their decision-making processes. They described how environmental quality now held an important position in their corporate mission statements. They also explained their corporate approaches to the environment by saying such things as: "we will be as environmentally conscious, aware, and sensitive as we possibly can be" (EUPEC.14.4), or "all aspects of our business are done with attempts at absolute minimum impact on the environment" (EUPEC.28.5).

Another way by which partnership participants, and especially those from the NGO community, expressed this preference for prevention-based approaches was via their comments on the need for better education on environmental matters. For some participants, this meant educating members of the public regarding the effects of their actions on the environment. One TRC partnership NGO representative stated that a key to cleaning up the Toupin River is to

educate all of the inhabitants of the province regarding the water issues that they are facing. [We need to] help them to understand that we are all polluters, from the smallest household to the largest industry, including agriculture. If we all make efforts to change our behaviors so as to decrease our impact on water and the environment in general, I think this would already be a good thing. (TRC.9.8)

For other environmentalists, this also meant educating people as to how they are being affected by the environmental actions of others.

Among members of government, this element of the discourse of ecological modernization commonly appeared in their accounts of how their own approaches to environmental management have changed over time. This is illustrated by a GBP partnership participant's account of recent changes that had occurred in the Gascoigne communal government. She recounted that before the 1990s, environmental problems had seldom been recognized, let alone addressed, by local officials. It was only in 1990 that the commune added the environment as an official area of governmental responsibility. She noted that with the creation of the commune's first environmental deputy, people increasingly began approaching the communal government with their particular environmental concerns. Typically, they complained about isolated incidents, such as pollution in the streams behind their homes or pesticides from near-by farms being blown into their yards. At first, the communal government responded to each of these problems individually as they arose. Over time, however, the officials involved came to the understanding that there was a better way. As the governmental representative participating in the partnership put it:

> We finally came to realize that we needed to start taking measures to prevent these little problems from happening in the first place. (GBP.5.9)

While all of the partnerships made statements in their published materials as to the importance of taking a proactive approach to addressing environmental problems, the CIMNR case study was the most explicit in its promotion of this element of the ecological modernization ideology. This was demonstrated by the CIMNR participants' decision to make prevention one of the centerpieces of their alternative approach to natural resource management. It was also evidenced in the statements made in the partnership's final report, such as when they wrote:

> We believe that, wherever possible, environmental impacts should be prevented before they arise. For this reason, we recommend that prevention be considered the first course of action.

The Role of Sociohistoric Factors

Given this description of the sociohistoric factors at play in the environmental partnerships studied, I now turn to the role that these factors play in the efforts to manage conflict. This section explores the influence that the cultural model characterizing partnerships as ideally nonconfrontational and the favored discourse of ecological modernization have on the practices of civility, argument minimization, nonengagement, conflict diffusion, and reconciliation.

The Role of a Cultural Model of Partnership Interaction

The existence of a prominent belief on the part of partnership participants that multistakeholder collaboration processes are supposed to be nonconfrontational helps to explain all five main modes of nonconfrontational practice. The presence of this belief drove participants to behave in specific ways that had the effect of preventing conflict when possible.

By itself, this cultural model was a primary determinant of the first three of these conflict management practices. Participants generally entered into these partnerships knowing that, given the competing interests involved, conflict was a distinct possibility. To diminish the risk of such conflict occurring, then, participants would act in an overtly polite manner. Treating each other with civility, respect, and humility was viewed as a way of keeping conflict—a state viewed as detrimental to the success of partnerships—from arising in the first place.

Similarly, participants wary of inciting unwanted conflict adopted the strategy of framing their opinions, ideas, or proposals in distinctly nonantagonistic ways. By disassociating themselves and their interests from the ideas being presented, by integrating their contributions with those of potential antagonists, by diminishing the seriousness of the debate with humor or apologies, by limiting the possibility that general disagreements might quickly escalate into bilateral arguments, or by otherwise presenting their comments in nonthreatening ways, participants helped ensure that inevitable differences of opinion did not evolve into full-blown dissension.

Finally, although conflicting views and interests were present in all of the case-study partnerships, participants did have the choice of whether to openly engage in these conflicts in the meetings themselves. When participants viewed conflict to be harmful to the partnership process, they acted to keep latent conflicts from exploding into full-blown open confrontation. Participants did so by keeping private those opinions that might incite hostility in the first place, as was the case when the NGO representatives in the EUPEC initiative concealed their anger over the splitting up of the executive director position. They also did so by withholding views that might perpetuate or exacerbate already existing antagonism. Such was the case when the majority of the CIMNR partnership participants elected not to respond to the repeated pressure and polarizing ideas put forward by proponents of the environmental justice and free-market environmentalism viewpoints.

The Role of the Discourse of Ecological Modernization

For the final two conflict management practices, however, more than just the cultural model is at work. Here, the discourse of ecological modernization also plays a significant role. To illustrate, each of the case examples explored in the sections on conflict diffusion and reconciliation are revisited in turn.

EMAS Expert Group Conflict in the EUPEC Initiative

The EUPEC initiative EMAS expert group conflict that I used to open this chapter constitutes a situation in which a third-party participant attempted to diffuse an example of open, antagonistic conflict. The third party did so by appealing to a shared understanding of the way partnerships are supposed to work. In particular, when the environmental representative (Stephan) and his industrial counterpart (Laurent) began shouting at each other in such an uncharacteristic way, this individual called upon the cultural model of partnerships as nonconfrontational to admonish the two antagonists for not behaving as proper "partners." Interestingly, Stephan and Laurent quickly countered this rebuke by drawing on the discourse of collaboration in their self-defense. Stephan reinterpreted the heated exchange by stating that they were just participating in "dialogue," while Laurent redefined their relationship as cooperative by noting that they work together often in the partnership. Not only did this maneuver on the part of the third-party participant diffuse the conflict, but the two main actors abruptly shifted from antagonists debating the topic of deregulation to fellow protagonists—or partners—in the cause of partnership.

"Trouble Spots" Report Conflict in the TRC Partnership

The case example involving the TRC partnership conflict over a trouble spots report involves two separate instances in which a mounting conflict gets diffused. Early on in the NGO committee meeting, a local environmental activist, Pauline, became increasingly agitated as she described in very crisis-oriented terms the deteriorating state of the Toupin River. She complained of the difficulties in getting local public authorities to do anything about this and demanded instead that some sort of campaign be organized to inform the general public of this dire situation. At this point, the TRC facilitator, seconded by an influential participant from a prestigious environmental group, responded to this call for confrontation with the discourse of collaboration. The two gently reminded Pauline that the partnership needed to work with, rather than against, the communal authorities to resolve these problems and that the best way to do this was by establishing a dialogue with them.

Later on in the meeting, a similar pattern ensued when Yvette, another environmental activist from a communal-level NGO, aggressively argued that the partnership should publicize the trouble spots report in the media as a way of pressuring public authorities to do something about the degraded state of the river. This confrontational demeanor led the TRC facilitator to invoke the cultural model of partnerships as nonconfrontational. He did so by suggesting that the partnership's actions not be limited to "provocation" alone. A participant from the business sector also responded by drawing upon the discourse of collaboration to warn that collaboration and not provocation is the key to accomplishing the partnership's goals.

In both of these instances, the use of this particular cultural model and discourse led belligerent actors to temper their contentious conduct. In addition, these sociohistoric factors induced these aggressors to withdraw from their antagonistic propositions, as neither of the two environmental activists pursued their arguments at the ensuing river committee meeting.

Business Plan Conflict in the EUPEC Initiative

The EUPEC business plan conflict constitutes an example of the practice where actors reconcile a dispute by seeking common ground. One way by which we can explain the practice of conflict management here is to reconceptualize the entire event as an interaction between two competing discourses where one discourse is privileged over the other.

At the heart of this conflict was a difference in opinion over what should constitute the partnership's final contribution to society. On one side of the conflict were representatives from the NGO sector, who described these intended contributions as involving "fundamental changes" and "breakthrough innovations" that would lead toward a "reinvented economy" and a "new European development model." These ideas are firmly grounded in the beliefs and assumptions subsumed under what John Dryzek has termed "green rationalism."[17] Green rationalism is one of several diverse discourses found within the environmental community and a subset of the broader discourse of "green radicalism" introduced in chapter 3. As with many of these other environmentalist discourses, green rationalism operates from a standpoint that considers the earth to have limits regarding the extent to which its resources may be exploited or its environment degraded. Where green rationalism differs from other such discourses is in regard to its proposed solutions to current environmental crises. Growing out of an underlying critique of instrumental reason and a firm belief in the equality of all people, green rationalism assumes that the resolution to the multifaceted social and economic problems underlying these environmental crises lies in radical political action and structural change. It calls for the establishment of more egalitarian political structures while invoking the possible replacement of the dominant liberal capitalist system.

On the other side were representatives from the business and governmental sectors to whom such ideas sounded too "revolutionary." These participants argued that the ultimate contribution of the partnership should be a "sustainable Europe" and that the way to get there should be via the "key process" of "creating partnership." These notions are firmly rooted in the ideology of ecological modernization. While ecological modernization accepts the notion that current environmental problems are fundamentally a product of our capitalistic system of production and consumption, it departs from green rationalism in that this acknowledgment is not accompanied by the concurrent conviction that the prevailing system therefore must be supplanted. Indeed, ecological modernization looks to these very extant economic and political structures for solutions.

When the ideas composing ecological modernization and green rationalism collided in the discussion, the contending parties were able to find common ground in the former. In particular, when the business and governmental representatives drew upon ecological modernization and its associated discourse of collaboration to respond to Stephan and Marcus's green rationalist calls for a "reinvented economy" and a "new European development model," they shifted the debate from the disagreement over the contributions of contemporary European economic structures to Europe's environmental problems toward a goal shared by everyone in the EUPEC initiative, including Stephan and Michel. This was the goal of a "sustainable Europe" effectuated by partnership action.

Stewardship Conflict in the CIMNR Partnership

As with the EUPEC business plan case example, the CIMNR partnership conflict over the role of stewardship in natural resource management can also be interpreted as a radical green discourse being trumped by the more privileged discourse of ecological modernization. On one side of this conflict were environmental NGO and governmental representatives who used the green rationalist critique of the instrumental reason and anthropocentric arrogance underlying assumptions of unlimited economic growth to object to what they perceived as the profit-oriented nearsightedness of the business sector. This argument was countered by an amalgamation of actors from all three major sectors employing the discourse of ecological modernization. They used this discourse to criticize the economic-environmental trade-off paradigm assumed by the first side and to call instead for actions that, rather than simply penalizing business, encourage the development of solutions to natural resource problems that have both environmental and economic benefits. These actors then attempted to further reconcile the dispute over the utility of stewardship in natural resource management by promoting sustainability as stewardship's true goal.

In the end, this second group succeeded in wielding the discourse of ecological modernization to carve out common ground for the CIMNR participants. This is reflected in the recommendations drawn up by the bipartisan subgroup tasked with producing a final definition of stewardship. The subgroup reconciled the differences between the two sides by redefining it as an "ethic" influenced by environmental values and morals *and* as a "practice" driven by economic and political constraints. In this way, both the economy and the environment could be integrated into a new win-win conceptualization of the term.

Mitigation versus Prevention Working Group Conflict in the CIMNR Partnership

Like the previous two case examples, the CIMNR partnership conflict between the mitigation and prevention working groups can be interpreted as an interaction between two competing discourses. In this case, however, the discourses involved were those of ecological modernization and administrative rationalism. The prevention group operated from the privileged perspective of the former, while the mitigation group adopted the discursive logic of the latter.

As introduced in chapter 4, administrative rationalism is a problem-solving-oriented discourse stressing the rational management of public interests. It emphasizes technical expertise, professional administration, and economic efficiency in the resolution of environmental problems. The discourse is also characterized by a reactive, curative, and after-the-event approach to environmental problems that treats these problems as something to be dealt with only once they arise. The mitigation working group expressed this logic via its emphasis on the technical dimensions of natural resource management, in its attempts to improve rather than obviate existing regulations governing mitigation practices, in its pursuit of cost-effectiveness, and in its willingness to address natural resource issues after they have already become problematic.

The prevention working group, on the other hand, operated much more clearly from the perspective of ecological modernization. This was evident in its emphasis on prevention as the first line of environmental defense and in its desire to modify some of the economic constraints driving natural resource use so that economic and environmental factors work with rather than against one another. The use of this discourse was also apparent in the prevention group's advancement of stewardship as the primary means by which to improve current management of natural resource systems. Stewardship, as the group defined it, is a distinctively ecologically modernistic concept, as evidenced by its promotion of uncoerced, collective, and cooperative forms of action and by its implicit support for conventional economic and political structures.

Despite the two working groups' divergent approaches to improving natural resource management, both were able to find common ground in some of the ideas subsumed under the discourse of ecological modernization. In particular, the mitigation working group was able to find accord with ecological modernization's attention to economic performance, its support for fixes that involve modifications to rather than complete transformations of current policies, and its promotion of collaborative processes. The mitigation group was also able to agree on the priority of a "stewardship path" because, in the end, this path did not greatly threaten key administrative rationalist ideals. Despite its support for voluntary measures, the stewardship path does not involve the dismantlement or termination of prevailing regulatory regimes. In fact, this path counts on such regimes to help ensure overall environmental performance. Moreover, although the stewardship path opens environmental decision making to nontechnical stakeholders, it still values the technical and especially the economistic aspects of environmental problem solving. Prevention can be managed just as mitigation can, and prevention can have very tangible results.

Conclusion—On Conflict Management Practices and Privileged Discourses

In all of the case studies examined, practices of conflict management were a major component of partnership action. One important factor behind the prevalence of such practices was the existence of a prevailing cultural model that portrayed partnerships as ideally nonconfrontational. Another contributing factor involved the privileging of a particular discourse—that of ecological modernization. This discourse was particularly effective in conflict management efforts because it meshed nicely with the cultural model and it, more so than any other discourse, provided common ground around which disputes could at least temporarily be reconciled. Ecological modernization was often able to serve as the basis for consensus because it was broad enough to encapsulate many of the ideals and premises of its competitors. We saw this to be the case with the discourse of green rationalism just as we did with the discourse of administrative rationalism.

This privileging of ecological modernization illustrates the presence of discourse hierarchies in environmental partnership settings. As participants communicate, they do not always give equal weight to all opinions or arguments put forward. More commonly, they tend to treat certain sets of ideas as being more appropriate, valid, or effective than others. In the environmental partnerships studied, the ideas that were able to hold the greatest sway were those promoting multistakeholder collaborative forms of problem solving, win-win economic-environmental solutions, and prevention-based approaches.

The existence of this particular discourse hierarchy in these and perhaps other partnerships, however, has certain ramifications for individuals or organizations wishing to pursue partnership approaches to environmental management. I return to these in greater detail in chapter 7.

Notes

1. Adopted in 1993, the EMAS regulation established a "voluntary" program involving third-party certification of environmental management and auditing systems implemented by major industrial facilities. For more on EMAS, see Taschner (1998).

2. Ross (1993b, 80) defines "conflict management" as "the steps disputants or third parties take in order to direct disputes toward certain outcomes which may or may not produce an end to the conflict and may or may not be peaceful, positive, creative, conciliatory, or aggressive."

3. See Newton (1996) for more on the concerns of the environmental justice movement.

4. For a description of free-market environmentalism, see Anderson and Leal (1991) and Anderson (1997).

5. Quinn and Holland (1987).

6. This finding supports the claim of Dukes et al. (2000, 20) that an "expectation" often exists within collaborative processes that "conflict is bad and . . . is therefore to be avoided."

7. Holland et al. (1998).

8. See Lakoff (1984) for a discussion on the capacity for analogies and metaphors to affect cognitive modeling.

9. In making this claim, I am not asserting that the discourse of ecological modernization was dominant in every partnership setting. Indeed, there were some meetings, such as the TRC partnership's technical committee meetings discussed in chapter 4,

where other discourses were dominant. I am merely stating that ecological modernization tended to be the most privileged on the whole. It was, for instance, the most prominent discourse in the TRC partnership's guiding River Committee meetings.

10. In this exposition, I treat ecological modernization not as a technologically oriented policy orientation but rather as an ideology that has become prominent in the environmental policy arena. See Christoff (1996) for an analysis of the different ways that policy analysts have been treating the concept.

11. Weale (1992) and Hajer (1995), among others, note that the ideology of ecological modernization does not exist as a consistent, well-formulated document or discourse on which there is collective agreement. Rather, it should be viewed more as a collection of central propositions capable of great elaboration and having components that are stressed more or less by different social actors.

12. In my description of ecological modernization, I draw varyingly upon the writings of Blowers (1998), Christoff (1996), Dryzek (1997), Hajer (1995), Harvey (1996), Mol (1996), and Weale (1992).

13. The notion of "sustainable development" here emphasizes the economic and ecological components of this concept over its social and equity-related connotations.

14. Hajer (1995).

15. The participatory quality of the discourse of collaboration overlaps to some extent with the discourse of democratic pragmatism that was described as being championed by members of the environmental NGO sector in the TRC case-study example in chapter 4. These two discourses differ, however, in one crucial respect. Although the discourse of democratic pragmatism was largely devoted toward increasing the participation of the public (i.e., of citizens) in decision-making processes, the discourse of ecological modernization promotes the necessary participation and cooperation of all of the "stakeholders" in society. This difference is one reason why TRC members from the governmental and business sectors privileged ecological modernization even though they did not espouse the discourse of democratic pragmatism.

16. See Poncelet (2003) for a more detailed analysis of these diverging interpretations of "shared responsibility."

17. Dryzek (1997).

Chapter 6

Personal Transformation

The mood was one of reverence as, one by one, the people in the dining hall rose to tell their stories. Some did so eagerly, while others had to be cajoled into participating. By the end of the evening, all had spoken, and all had done so with a spirit of gratitude and honor for the people seated around them.

The setting was a farewell dinner hosted by the CIMNR partnership to commemorate the work accomplished over the past two years. During the meal, the participants shared some of the experiences gained while participating in the partnership. Among these speakers was a manager from a large resource extraction company who confessed how he had expected, due to the rather primitive reputation of his industry, to be treated as a major culprit of environmental degradation by the other participants. He announced to the group that he had been quite surprised to find that rather than being vilified, he and his organization had been respected for what they were trying to do on behalf of the environment. There was also an environmentalist who, over the course of his participation in the partnership, had left his position representing a small, activist-oriented NGO to take on a job in government. This actor told how he had shifted during this period from an adamant defender of the environment to a committed proponent of collaborative processes, unattached to any specific environmental point of view. There was a bureaucrat from a state governmental administration who came to tears as she professed that the relationships she had developed in the partnership had become the most exciting and important part of her professional life. She lamented the rarity of this type of process and hoped that she had been worthy of it. There was a story told about one of the business sector participants who initially had resisted many of the partnership's ideas only to later become their greatest champion back in his own company. Finally, there was one of the partnership initiators who spoke in amazement of how much the partnership had changed since its inception. He compared the early days of the initiative, when representatives of NGOs, government, and industry used to meet in separate rooms, to the present situation, where it was becoming increasingly difficult to keep certain members from the different sectors apart.

At the conclusion of these testimonials, several of the participants began to share their artistic talents as well. Some recited poetry, while others told bawdy tales. A few, some with better voices than others, sang songs of love and longing. When the evening came to a close, more than one of these performers admitted to never before having revealed themselves in such a manner, even in front of family and friends at home.

These displays of openness, friendship, and respect were not uncommon in the environmental partnerships studied. This was in spite of the fact that some of the very individuals involved were actively lobbying or litigating against one another in other venues. The goal of this chapter is to explore some of the reasons behind this particular quality of multistakeholder collaboration. To accomplish this, I explore the capacity of environmental partnerships such as the case studies examined to encourage experiences of individual or subjective change among the participating actors. These *personal transformations*, as I call them, consist of changes to the sociohistoric predispositions that the actors bring with them to partnerships. In the partnerships studied, these personal transformations came in a variety of forms. In particular, participants developed new understandings of the issues at stake, themselves, and each other; they embraced new group processes, especially in the form of new relationships with others; and they adopted new practices with regard to environmental problem solving or decision making.

This chapter proceeds in three main sections. It starts by briefly exploring some of the structural and organizational features of the multistakeholder partnerships studied that were conducive to such forms of change. Next, it moves on to examine a cultural model held by many partnership participants regarding how multistakeholder partnerships are supposed to proceed. Then the main section of the chapter analyzes at greater length three primary ways by which personal transformations actually occurred in practice. These include social learning, the process of cultural production, and the formation of new or altered identities.

All three of these processes are introduced in chapter 1. To recap, social learning and cultural production take place at the interpersonal level. Social learning is a process in which actors come to alter their own thinking, understanding, and behavior by virtue of being exposed to new ideas, views, and practices while interacting with others.[1] Social learning takes two basic forms. First, there is single-loop learning, where actors use new information acquired to modify and make more effective their approaches to particular issues or objectives.[2] Second, there is double-loop learning. This type of learning involves critical self-reflection that leads to changes in a person's underlying values, beliefs, or assumptions.[3]

Actors do more, however, than simply learn from one another in situations of social interaction. At times, they also come together to produce new ways of knowing things, acting, or getting along. Cultural production is the process by which actors generate novel cultural forms in the shape of new meaning systems, practices, and group processes.[4]

The third process of personal transformation occurs at the intrapersonal level and involves the formation of new or altered identities. To make themselves understood in the multistakeholder partnership setting, actors must constantly choose from among the words, ideas, and behaviors that they each use for giving meaning to and acting in the world. Social identities are attached to particular words, ideas, and behaviors, however, so when actors selectively adopt certain ways of knowing, talking, and acting, this may lead them to perceive themselves in different ways.

Structures for Change

A first characteristic of the multistakeholder environmental partnerships studied that contributed toward experiences of personal transformation concerned the structural forms and operating procedures by which these initiatives were organized. All of the case studies, for instance, brought together a diverse assortment of societal interests, experiences, and perspectives. They were structured to do so by requiring adequate representation from, minimally, the environmental NGO, governmental, and business sectors. In addition, the partnerships strove to represent some of the diversity that existed within each of these sectors. They did so by encouraging the participation of organizations having disparate focal interests, operating at varying political levels, and having different amounts of influence in the environmental arena. All of the case-study partnerships thus exposed their participants to an array of ways of thinking and knowing that commonly exceeded what these people typically encountered in their daily lives.

At an operational level, all of the case-study partnerships encouraged cooperative interaction among their diverse participants, inciting these actors to explore each other's interests and points of view. The partnerships institutionalized intersectorial interaction by requiring balanced representation among the sectors in most working group activities, by promoting consensus-based decision-making processes, and, in some cases, by using professional facilitators to assist in these processes. The partnerships also encouraged social interaction and relationship formation in informal settings outside of the meetings by scheduling communal meals, receptions, or group recreational activities for the partnership participants.

Together, these basic structural and operational features provided a rich context in which social learning, cultural production, and identity change—the elements that lie at the root of personal transformation—could occur.

Expectations of Change: A Cultural Model

A second finding supporting the contention that the case-study partnerships were conducive to altering individual subjectivities comes with the discovery that many of the participants shared a cultural model conceptualizing multistakeholder partnerships as inherently transformative processes. Two main assumptions composed this cultural model. The first was the shared belief that partnership processes are capable of, and indeed predisposed toward, producing innovative decisions and generating creative, unforeseen outcomes. This aspect of the model was evidenced by some of the words used by participants to describe partnerships in general. Several people, for instance, referred to the partnership process as "magical." Here, they were alluding to what they perceived as the rather remarkable capacity of partnerships, especially in the face of conflicting interests and disparate perspectives, to generate shared understandings and consensus decisions.

A nice illustration of this belief in the magical quality of partnerships comes from a CIMNR environmental NGO participant who, during the farewell dinner described previously, compared his experiences with the partnership to the making of "stone soup." In the stone soup parable to which he was alluding, a weary traveler entered a poor village requesting something to eat. As this occurred during a time of famine when people were jealously hoarding whatever food they had, the traveler was brusquely refused by the suspicious villagers. Not to be discouraged, the traveler pulled a large stone out of his bag and set about making stone soup, which he announced he would share with the rest of the village. One by one, all of the villagers eventually offered to contribute some ingredients of their own, turning the soup into a delicious, memorable feast. This allegory, and its focus on the transformation of a stone into a meal of unparalleled quality, was frequently alluded to by other participants in subsequent CIMNR discussions. It demonstrated their belief in the capacity of partnerships to produce superior results among unlikely collaborators and in unforeseen ways.

Another way participants expressed this first assumption was via their comparisons of multistakeholder partnerships to the process of synergy. Many participants believed that partnerships were capable of producing ideas and actions that were greater than the sum of what individual partners could accomplish alone. This was expressed by a business representative from the EUPEC initiative:

> [In partnerships], you have an objective, and you decide to work together. And why should you decide to work together? Because your partner has skills, competencies, access to data, information you don't have, and it would take you a long time to get it. And he has it. And you have, of course, . . . capabilities, competencies, information he doesn't have. So, the sum of the two with a clear goal is more than two. That is partnership. (EUPEC.16.10)

It is presumed that the very process of searching for solutions among actors of diverse knowledge, expertise, perspectives, and resources engenders the production of original, inventive solutions to environmental problems that would not be discovered otherwise.

The second main assumption composing the cultural model of environmental partnerships as transformative concerns the commonly held presumption that participants are themselves *supposed* to be altered via their interactions in multistakeholder proceedings. Some participants expressed this aspect of the model by describing the partnership process as one that invites change. Along these lines, a TRC representative from a communal-level environmental NGO stated:

> I have found my few experiences with concertation to be enriching, largely because it is a dialogue with other parties and because one can change one's own position, . . . since one now knows the opinions and interests of others and all of the consequences that are at stake. (TRC.9.7)

Other actors clearly expected to be changed via their involvement in partnerships, as is evidenced by the comments of a business representative from the CIMNR partnership:

> [In partnerships,] you are impressed by the people you meet and their arguments for you to do more in the way of environmental protection. So one impact is that if you keep your mind relatively open on this, you may change your views and point [your organization] in a different, and one would hope better, direction. [On the other hand,] we would hope that the people we talk with can see from their perspective our view of things, and maybe it will influence them to come up with better solutions that are more cost-effective. So I hope to get both of those out of the process. (CIMNR.7.6)

This presumption of multistakeholder partnerships leading to mutual change is perhaps most clearly explicated in the allegorical comments of a TRC business representative, who compared the process of concertation in the environmental arena to an encounter between two men seeking to know the time:

> Two men meet. The first asks the second for the time. The second says 9:00. The second then asks the first what time he has. The first replies 9:30. They argue over who has the right time. Then they leave. Once they are alone, the guy who had 9:00 changes his watch to 9:30, and the guy who had 9:30 changes his to 9:00. This is a good example of how concertation can unblock things. We have the impression that we don't speak the same language or have the same interests, but in the end, we try to make things meet. (TRC.26.7)

This belief that partnership participants must be willing and able to change was strongly supported by the coordinators and facilitators of the four case-study partnerships. They did so by portraying transformations as normal and beneficial and by actively promoting these types of experiences. Such was the case in one of the EUPEC initiative workshops directed toward the topic of multistakeholder collaboration. In one exercise, participants were asked to change five aspects of their appearance. Most participants responded by making small changes on their own—for example, unbuttoning a collar or removing eyeglasses. Next, they were asked to quickly make ten additional changes. After a few seconds of panic, many realized that they had run out of small adjustments. Consequently, they turned to their neighbors and cooperated. In these efforts, they often made big, radical, and even comical changes, such as exchanging apparel. Interestingly, as the participants regained their seats, some had changed back to the way they had been before, whereas others adopted the changes as a new balance. In an editorial in the EUPEC newsletter, one of the project coordinators reiterated the importance of this transformative process:

> It will take more than just a day and a half to realize the triple win. It will take radical changes and new mind-sets. It will mean more than merely changing appearances. It will be more difficult than taking off your socks. It will take courage and perseverance in building real partnership initiatives. It will take the sort of dialogue, cooperation, and even fun in working together that emerged during this [EUPEC] Workshop.

Altered Subjectivities

The most compelling finding that the multistakeholder environmental partnerships studied contributed to personal transformation comes with evidence that participants actually did change via their participation in these collaborative processes. These changes occurred interpersonally, via social learning and cultural production, as well as intrapersonally, via identity formation. They involved transformations in participants' subjective understandings of and relationships to each other, themselves, and environmental action. A summary of the personal transformations to be examined is shown in table 6.1.

The Process of Social Learning

The case-study partnerships provided numerous examples of social learning, where participants gained new knowledge and understandings by virtue of their contact and interactions with other actors in the partnerships, whether fellow stakeholders, coordinators, or professional facilitators.

Single-Loop Learning

Many of these instances fell into the category of single-loop learning. This included cases where participants became better informed of the environmental issues around which they were acting. In the GBP and TRC partnerships, for

Table 6.1. Types of Personal Transformation

Type of Personal Transformation	Examples of Changes Experienced
Social learning	
Single-loop learning	• Learning about environmental issues at stake and existing policies for addressing them. • Learning about other stakeholders involved (e.g., their goals, interests, and the constraints that they face).
Double-loop learning	• Fundamental reevaluation of other stakeholders in the environmental realm. • Fundamental shift in approach to environmental problem solving.
Cultural production	• The production of new meaning systems (e.g., new conceptualizations of the concepts of stewardship and biodiversity). • The production of new practices (e.g., good partnership behaviors). • The production of new group processes (e.g., partnership-based friendships).
Altered Identities	• Associated with social learning. • Associated with the production of new cultural forms.

instance, participants were presented with new data on the status of local environmental conditions. GBP participants learned of the locations of the remaining focal areas of biodiversity within the commune, while TRC participants learned of the specific trouble spots facing the Toupin River. Similarly, in the EUPEC and CIMNR partnerships, participants learned more about the regulatory frameworks guiding environmental action in the European Union and the United States. EUPEC participants, for instance, gained specific knowledge about the EMAS regulation, while CIMNR members were informed of the complexities of existing federal mitigation policies.

A second common example of single-loop learning involved participants gaining knowledge and understanding of each other. As one EUPEC environmental NGO representative described it,

> partnership . . . is a learning process. By talking to people from other social sectors, you learn more about how they are organized, what their goals are, what they think. It enables you to function on a more intelligent level. (EUPEC.25.12)

From the CIMNR partnership, examples of this form of single-loop learning included environmentalists coming to better comprehend the constraints impeding proactive environmental action by the mining industry, federal policy makers gaining insight into how ranchers and developers approach environmental impediments, and business executives acquiring better understandings of how federal regulators in the natural resource domain think.

In most single-loop cases, participants applied this learning directly back to their partnerships, using the information gained to better inform their suggestions for specific environmental management projects or policies. In some instances, however, participants also took this learning back to their own organizations. Evidence comes from a EUPEC environmental NGO participant, who exclaimed:

> What I have gotten from partnerships is that I've met some people from industry, trade unions, and some [governmental] administration people who are highly interesting personalities. I have gotten some insight into their ways of thinking. I better understood the way business is thinking and developing, and [this will help] with the development of future [environmental] campaigns, to identify the points where our influence might make a difference. . . . I learned some things. I do have a better understanding of how some industrial mechanisms work. (EUPEC.26.15)

Double-Loop Learning

In addition to the single-loop variety, personal transformations in the form of double-loop learning also were present in all of the case-study partnerships. Participants typically described this type of learning in terms of increases that they had experienced in "awareness," "consciousness," or "sensitivity." These cases, which involved changes to some of the underlying assumptions driving people's behavior in the environmental arena, had an even more profound effect on the participants involved.

Double-loop learning in the partnerships studied was evident in two main types of cases: those where participants were led to fundamentally reconsider the value or worth of other environmental stakeholders, and those where participants came to significantly rethink their strategies for environmental action.

The first of these two types of double-loop learning grows out of the single-loop learning case involving participants increasing their knowledge of other stakeholders. In certain instances, such single-loop learning led to fundamental reevaluations of other actors in the environmental decision-making arena. One case involved a TRC partnership representative from the agricultural sector whose participation in environmental partnerships like the TRC initiative caused him to expand his understandings of environmental groups. This individual described how he used to treat the NGO sector as a homogeneous and, indeed, irritating block not worthy of his time and consideration. After his experience in several collaborative stakeholder processes, however, he began to differentiate between types of organizations within the NGO sector. In particular, he began to distinguish between what he called "environmental associations," on one hand, and "neighborhood groups," on the other. He described the former as productive, formally organized environmental protection NGOs. He depicted the latter as reactionary, citizen action groups made up primarily of "neo-rurals"—i.e., people who had recently moved to the province for its greenery and rural character but who also tended to be much less willing to tolerate its agricultural nuisances. He further contrasted the two types of organizations as follows:

> [Environmental associations] are serious because if they want to have credibility and importance, they cannot be NIMBY, because you cannot just reject everything. They have to dialogue. They have to have a politics, a standard of conduct, which means that when they say "yes" here, they cannot say "no" [there], and when they say "no" today, they cannot say "yes" tomorrow. The problem with . . . neighborhood groups is that they dump everything out on the neighborhood next door. They don't have a politics. This is the real NIMBY—not near me. The serious associations, on the other hand, they are well obliged to find solutions, whereas the neighborhood groups are egoists and nothing more. They are people who oppose things without thinking. For example, they will oppose a pork farm, but they eat pork. With the environmental associations, there will be a discussion, and corrective measures will be sought, such as deciding to eat less meat. (TRC.19.8)

He went on to add that, unlike neighborhood groups,

> [environmental associations] will have a discourse that is ecological and economical. They have understood that the two must be linked. The neighborhood groups, on the other hand, are ready to sacrifice the economy for the ecology, but without a politics, and that is the worst of all. . . . There are serious people who one finds in environmental associations, and there are nonserious people who one finds in neighborhood groups. I am happy to dialogue with people in serious associations, but with neighborhood groups, dialogue is impossible, discussion is not possible. Everything is "no," "no," and "no," whereas the environmental associations are in favor of searching for compromises and solutions. With these people, things can move forward. (TRC.19.8)

Over the course of his participation in the partnership, this agricultural representative revised his basic understanding of the environmental NGO sector. Whereas he initially saw the sector as having little value, he later came to view certain components of it as being worthy of contact, communication, and engagement on issues of environmental concern.

Another case of double-loop learning involving altered understandings of other stakeholders comes with a CIMNR representative from a small environmental group who experienced a shift in her conceptualizations of representatives of the business sector. She described how her understandings of them changed over the course of her participation in the partnership.

> [Meeting people from different sectors of industry helped me] to understand that these are not bad people. Their industries may have bad environmental impacts sometimes, but the people aren't bad. I'm sure there are a few malicious people, there are everywhere, but . . . fundamentally, [these] people are good people, and they care about the environment too. That's a basis from which to work for improvement. (CIMNR.13.15)

This learning experience led her to temper her advocacy-oriented stances relative to the business community.

A second type of personal transformation induced by double-loop learning involved participants altering their approaches to environmental action. One way this type of learning manifested itself was when participants, upon being exposed to new environmental information or to the perspectives of different stakeholders, adopted a more comprehensive or holistic perspective. These participants came to see their former approaches to particular environmental concerns as limited in that these approaches reflected only a fraction of the issues at stake, the interests involved, the points of view present, the experiences gained, or the ideas available. A nice illustration of this comes with a GBP participant representing a regional governmental agency. In his case, his particular experiences in the partnership caused him to expand his institutional approach to issues of biodiversity and nature conservation. He exclaimed:

> [Partnerships constitute] an opening up toward other groups of people that [my agency has] never experienced before. They [necessitate] taking into account the demands of people concerned about matters of nature conservation and natural heritage. [Partnerships] require taking these and other groups into account and better understanding their problems. To date, [my agency] has limited its nature conservation focus to forests and nature preserves. Thanks to the [GBP] partnership and its charter, we now recognize that we must address ourselves toward the totality of problems facing the entire area of the commune in question, whether these be school grounds, roadsides, or church steeples. So we are moving beyond the classic avenues by which we took care of things in the past. . . . If you wish, we have broadened our field of work. We have broadened our vision. (GBP.4.6)

Participation in the GBP partnership afforded this governmental official and, perhaps, his entire agency a wider view of the problems present and of the possibilities for improving and restoring biodiversity.

Even more prevalent were cases of double-loop learning involving the ideology of ecological modernization as a basic approach to environmental action. As discussed in chapter 5, numerous participants from all four of the case-study partnerships espoused this logic, and many of them learned these ideas in the partnerships themselves. Exposure to this ideology led some of these participants to fundamentally reevaluate their former approaches to the environment. In some cases, this involved people reconsidering their previous assumptions about economic-environmental trade-offs. A EUPEC participant from the business sector, for instance, stated that participating in multistakeholder environmental partnerships helped him to learn that

> [my company] needs to use the environment more as a tool for creating new jobs and for inventing new technologies. . . . We need to avoid treating the environment as misfortune and begin treating it more as something useful for the company that can contribute to its economic development. (EUPEC.11.16)

Similarly, an environmental NGO representative from the CIMNR partnership explained that for him, participating in the initiative has

> reinforced my general sense that, gosh, there are better ways to do things. There are win-wins out there, but you've got to find them, and you have to work to get them. (CIMNR.14.18)

He later added:

> I do believe in the multiple benefits, win-win logic. I do think that it's important to get the economic gains in addition to the environmental gains. I do see them coupled, because I think it builds the strength. (CIMNR.14.20)

In even more cases, however, this learning involved replacing the traditional assumption that environmental problems can best be resolved via unilateral, authoritarian action with the belief in the superiority of multistakeholder collaborative approaches. A governmental official participating in the TRC partnership noted that her experience with partnerships has reinforced her conviction that

> it is better to work slowly but with many people on environmental issues than to go forth alone. We need to change people's mentalities in the struggle over the environment, and concertation permits this. (TRC.22.9)

Similarly, drawing upon his own experiences in multistakeholder proceedings, a EUPEC business representative stated that for his organization

> the necessity of [participating in multistakeholder environmental partnerships] is becoming more and more evident. Even if we didn't want to [participate in them], they are still a necessity. . . . Early on, people from industry felt that their opinion was the only one worth hearing. But now, [we acknowledge] that industry represents only one part of the experts, only one of the interlocutors. (EUPEC.11.9)

Finally, a CIMNR environmental NGO representative demonstrated this same transformation when she exclaimed that via participation in the partnership

> I've learned the value of having different voices involved in determining policies or frameworks or paths, because you get very different perspectives. You know, a group of environmentalists could sit down and say: "these are the rules that we think should govern industry and mitigation of projects." But it's much more valuable to have industry folks who have actually been there and done it involved in that process, . . . and the governmental people [as well]. (CIMNR.13.25-26)

This learning experience led this participant to develop a more nuanced understanding of environmental issues that was, to use her own words, much less "black and white" than her previous assumptions. Coming up with solutions to environmental problems was no longer a matter of simply imposing one's view and getting one's way. As she put it:

> [People without partnership experience take the attitude,] "We have the right answer; if you only understood that we have the right answer, you would embrace it." You see it very differently when you participate in the partnership process. You are offering your idea, but it is only one idea. It is one of many ideas to a complicated problem. . . . [Participating in partnerships] sort of infuses what you are doing with reality [and the recognition that] it's not simple, and it's not quickly done, and the end product is not going to be what you want alone because other people have points of view and ideas. (CIMNR.13.26-27)

This double-loop learning led this particular participant to shift toward a mode of environmental action that was more inclusive of other stakeholders than it had been before.

Participants used these forms of double-loop learning in different ways. Many applied the learning directly to their own partnerships. They did so by proposing projects or policy recommendations that took a more global approach to the specific environmental problem at issue, that were more encompassing of a greater variety of interests and perspectives, and that were directed toward achieving both environmental and economic benefit. Some took the learning back to their places of work and used it to suggest changes in the ways that their agencies, firms, or organizations operated. Still others employed this learning by initiating or agreeing to participate in grass-roots multistakeholder environmental processes in their own communities. In all of these cases, this learning caused these individuals to redefine for themselves the proper way by which environmental issues should be addressed.

The Process of Cultural Production

The second main way by which personal transformation transpired in the case-study partnerships was via the process of cultural production. These were cases involving not the learning of preexisting material but the production of new cultural forms. These cultural forms came primarily in the way of new meaning systems (or ways of knowing things), new practices (or ways of doing things), and new group processes (or ways of being together).

The Production of New Meanings

All of the partnerships studied provide instances in which participants collectively generated novel conceptualizations of the environmental issues under consideration. In the CIMNR partnership, for example, new meaning was produced around the concept of stewardship. Midway through the two-year tenure of the partnership, several participants began to champion the idea of stewardship as a key step toward improving natural resource management practices in the United States. A debate ensued among various participants regarding the exact meaning of this term. To recap, one side contended that improved natural resource management required the development of a societal ethic that valued and respected healthy natural systems in their own right. These participants argued that a sense of individual and social moral responsibility was necessary to help overcome some of the wasteful and shortsighted natural resource management strategies currently in use. The other side of the debate stressed that stewardship went beyond simply caring about the environment. These participants portrayed the term more as a behavior, contending that what people actually do in relation to the environment is just as important as what they think or feel about it. They reasoned that good stewardship actions are good stewardship actions, regardless of the underlying incentives that help to bring them about.

The CIMNR partnership was able to reach consensus on the role of stewardship by conceptualizing it in a new way: as an ethic *and* as a practice, both of which are deemed necessary to ensure a treatment of natural resources capable of sustaining their benefits for future generations and neither of which is seen as precluding the other. The participants redefined stewardship as being a function not only of moral values but of economic policies and environmental regulations as well. In this way, the partnership felt that it could promote a stewardship ethic without threatening prevailing modes of economic production or undermining existing regulatory structures. The CIMNR participants adopted this new meaning of stewardship in their final report and made this term the centerpiece of their policy recommendations for improving the management of natural resources.

A second example of the production of new meanings comes from the GBP initiative and involves the partnership's guiding concept of biodiversity. Prior to the formation of the GBP partnership, the term *biodiversity* was not a part of the general lexicon of most of the local inhabitants. According to one GBP member, it was a term that, if employed at all, was used to refer to the lush plant and animal life of the Brazilian rain forest. The GBP partnership introduced the term to many of its participants, where it came to take on its own particular meaning.

In the introduction to the partnership's charter detailing the specific projects to be undertaken, the partnership presented a rather broad definition of biodiversity, defining it as "the ensemble of all living things found within a milieu, in all of their manifestations and relations." The increasingly frequent association of the term with the partnership itself, however, led many participants to attach additional meanings to it. First, they came to understand biodiversity as something that was present not only in the Amazon Basin but in their very own commune as well. Second, they represented this biodiversity as something that was presently endangered. In the case of their agriculture-based commune, it was primarily threatened by the prevailing practices of monoculture and real estate development. Third, they took an action-oriented approach to the term. When asked to describe what biodiversity meant to them, many respondents defined it via the use of verbs rather than as a noun. For these participants, biodiversity was understood as something that needed to be "promoted," "respected," "brought back into equilibrium," "restored," "saved," "re-created," "maintained," "ameliorated," "conserved," "preserved," and most of all "managed." Along these lines, one of the participants even noted that the term *biodiversity* was beginning to replace the idea of "nature conservation" within the commune. Finally, these participants described biodiversity as something that could be managed only via collective, collaborative efforts on the part of all of the affected societal interests.

The Production of New Practices

The active, collective creation of new practices constitutes a second type of cultural production that took place in the environmental partnerships studied. An illustrative example of this process that comes from all four case studies involved the generation of what I call *good partnership behaviors.*[5] This particular cultural form is founded on a cultural model that many participants shared regarding how ideal partners are supposed to act in the partnership setting. This model was itself a product of social learning in the partnerships, deriving from both the instructions given by the project coordinators and facilitators for how best to operate in multistakeholder partnerships and the knowledge and convictions that participants brought with them from past collaborative experiences. This cultural model, which can be seen as an extension of the model depicting partnerships as nonconfrontational that is discussed in chapter 4, was primarily discernable from the distinctions that participants drew between what they commonly labeled as "good" versus "bad" partnership behaviors.

Participants revealed this model in their discussions on the topic of partnership. Summarizing this model, good partners privilege listening over speaking and take responsibility for the success of their communication. They try to understand the views of others, search for shared understanding, and forward the discussion whenever possible. They talk *to* rather than *at* one another. Good partners are humble, trustful, respectful, and show confidence in the capabilities of others. Good partners express rather than hide their own opinions and do so in an honest and candid manner. They avoid negative, argumentative roles, opting to confront disagreements more positively via a search for common ground. Good partners are willing to change their minds, suspend individual interests, compromise in the search for consensus, and serve the interests of the group without necessarily needing to control its direction. Finally, good partners treat each other as equals and demonstrate goodwill in their interactions.

Bad partners, conversely, are everything that good partners are not. They speak without listening. They are entrenched in their opinions and intolerant of others' views. They adopt an "us versus them" mentality and quickly resort to adversarial posturing. They withhold information and act not to advance the collaborative process but rather to check its progress. Bad partners do not operate with the best interest of the partnership in mind.

The production of good partnership practices occurred in the social interaction of the meetings themselves. Participants coproduced these practices in two main ways: by promoting good behaviors and by discouraging bad ones. Participants encouraged good behaviors by practicing these desired traits themselves and by calling positive attention to the adoption of such conduct by others. Leading by example, these participants made explicit efforts, for instance, to actively listen to the views of others, to acknowledge and praise each other's work, and to build on each other's ideas when possible. They expressly avoided taking self-interested, advocacy-oriented positions. When they did speak from a standpoint of organizational or sectorial self-interest, they did so explicitly, distinguishing it, when appropriate, from their own personal views. They prefaced critical, provocative, or potentially polarizing statements in ways, such as via the use of compliments or an apologetic tone, that diffused the potential for confrontational responses. Finally, they made efforts to diminish their own individual status and authority in the partnership by deflecting credit, openly admitting ignorance and mistakes when appropriate, and deferring ownership over ideas proposed or work accomplished.[6]

Participants discouraged bad behaviors in several ways as well. They castigated other participants for reverting to the traditional, but now unwelcome, modes of advocacy, negotiation, and entrenched pursuit of self-interest. They also actively worked to minimize conflictual conduct. As discussed in chapter 5, they did so in a variety of manners, such as avoiding topics likely to incite the ire of others, striving to find common ground when divisive disagreements presented themselves, and stepping in to diminish anger once expressed. They diffused conflictual situations through the use of humor and by reminding the hostile parties how good partners are supposed to behave.

The Production of New Group Processes

A final type of cultural production to be explored here involves the generation of new relations among partnership participants. For some participants, this involved the formation of new networks of professional contacts. For many others, such as the grateful governmental employee described in the opening section of this chapter, these relations also included the close, enduring, and trusting friendships that had been developed over the course of regular interaction with the same group of stakeholders.

Drawing from comments made by participants from all four of the case studies, two main features can be said to characterize these partnership-based friendships. The first concerns their distinctiveness from most of the participants' other relationships. In particular, these friendships stood out by the fact that they occurred among people of diverse backgrounds, experiences, and interests who normally did not come into contact with one another in everyday life. Many participants found this element of these friendships to be personally satisfying, as is evident from the comments of a EUPEC business representative:

[Partnership] brings a tremendous broadening of my field of experience and my field of personal contacts. . . . When I compare notes with some of my other colleagues within [my organization] or who have the same job with other companies, . . . they don't have that sort of interface. They meet customers to talk of products, they meet researchers and talk about development of the products, they meet the accountants to talk about results, . . . and then there is some time to go and play some golf. They have great fun. They are successful in business. But [participating in partnerships exposes me to more]. It brings me great fun—getting to meet [different people], even meeting you. This is great fun. It is not something that you would normally do on your normal business agenda. So, personally, because I am quite curious for experiences and I like to experiment a lot, from that sense, I get a lot of satisfaction. (EUPEC.16.12)

These friendships were also marked by the fact that they often united individuals who in other contexts might be standing in opposition to one another.

The second main feature characterizing these partnership-based friendships was a strong sense of group cohesion among the participating actors. This was evident from the terms that participants used to describe their experiences with other stakeholders in the partnership setting. They spoke, for instance, of the feelings of "integration," "solidarity," "comradeship," "togetherness," and "belonging" that they had experienced, the "bonding process" that they had undergone, and the "esprit de corps" that had been generated. Participants also used a number of integration-based metaphors to depict their partnership experiences. As mentioned in chapter 5, some described partnerships as a boat in which everyone is, by definition, together or as a team in which success is collectively achieved. Others compared partnerships to a club where actors can meet and where they know they have, as one respondent put it, a "place at the bar." A EUPEC participant even compared partnerships to kin groups, stating:

[Participating in partnerships involves] creating bonds where they would not exist naturally. . . . It's kind of like kinship, a cause-related kinship, where there's no preexisting reason for you to be together. . . . It gives you access to contacts with people who can help, and because you have this relationship of partnership, they are more willing to help you than if you just came up to them out of the blue. (EUPEC.18.10)

All of these metaphors indicate the production of relationships that tie the participants to one another beyond the scope of the partnership itself. In many cases, these partnership-based relationships involved a sense of communal connectivity. In the TRC and GBP partnerships, participants alluded to this by talking about how concertation-based partnerships had brought them closer to their own local communities. In the words of an Ixtoup Province resident participating in a TRC communal working group,

[Concertation brings me] rich personal contacts and the discovery of other people in my community. [Concertation] is also a strong integrating factor in life for entities such as [my commune]. It is a way of implicating oneself and getting involved in the life—the political, administrative, economic, and associative life—of a little commune. . . . You improve your quality of life at the human level. You create a fabric of relations that make it so that it becomes more enjoyable to live in one's environs. (TRC.24.17)

In the EUPEC and CIMNR partnerships, participants described this sense of communal integration in terms of the "harmony" that partnerships bring to society and the welcome role that partnerships play in helping to combat the prevailing sense of alienation currently confronting people in modern industrial societies. As expressed by a CIMNR environmental NGO member,

> [In partnerships,] you see the best sides of the best people. You experience real success and bitter defeat. It's genuine. It's not sham. It's larger than self. I get to use all of [my] skills . . . to help people achieve their particular goals, but I get a sense of greater connectedness and hopefulness, which I think is in short supply. My personal bias is that the greatest toxin in the country today is cynicism and an increasing sense of alienation and despair that will ultimately destroy the democratic experience if we don't figure out alternatives based on hopefulness. (CIMNR.16.9)

This sense of social cohesion underlying these partnership-based relationships derives from several sources. First, it comes from people discovering that others share their interests and sensibilities. An environmentalist participating in the EUPEC initiative described his experience in partnerships along these lines:

> I like meeting people who have the same mind-set as me. We become friends. It is always enriching to meet people who think as you do, whether they are in NGOs or corporations. It's good. It makes me happy. It's a warm feeling. I like meeting periodically with people who are on . . . the same wavelength as me. (EUPEC.23.13)

Similarly, an NGO participant from the GBP partnership stated:

> [Partnerships bring me] the pleasure of meeting people who think the same way as me and the opportunity to share my way of seeing things and to hear every once in a while: "Hey, you have a good idea." (GBP.22.7)

From the TRC partnership, a governmental agency official added:

> [The TRC partnership gives me] hope that what I do professionally and what interests me personally is . . . valued by many of my fellow citizens. (TRC.27.16)

All of these comments indicate the formation of a sense of integration that grows out of mutual acceptance, respect, and validation of self-worth.

A second source of social cohesion arises from participants' experiences of working together and producing consensus-based solutions to problems of common concern. As expressed by a CIMNR business representative,

> [Partnership-based] friendships can become really strong friendships because
> they are ultimately based on having worked together on what are sometimes
> very difficult issues and then breaking through on these issues and often finding
> ourselves at the leading edge of these things. (CIMNR.6.11)

This sense of collective unity comes from the process of collaborating with other
key societal actors for the public good rather than merely for organizational or
personal self-interest.

A final source of social cohesion stems from the sense of equality shared by
partnership participants. Although participants from the four case studies acknowledged the decidedly asymmetrical quality that marks environmental
stakeholder relations outside of the partnership setting, these participants also
maintained the belief that multistakeholder partnerships exist as a specific moment in space and time in which heterarchical rather than hierarchical relations
prevail. As summed up by a TRC representative from the business sector:

> Everyone is equal in concertation. This is a basic principle. I don't enter into a
> concertation saying that I am . . . more important than anyone else, or that
> someone else is less important than me. (TRC.19.20)

This notion of equality contributed to a general perception that while stakeholders from the same partnership may have unequal influence and opposing
interests on the outside, when in the same partnership, they are all valued participants working together on the same side of an issue.

The Formation of Altered Identities

When participants use each other's meanings, words, and behaviors to communicate among one another in multistakeholder partnership settings, they create
the possibility for a final means of personal transformation. This change occurs
at the intrapersonal level and involves alterations of people's self-perceptions
and self-conceptualizations. Such identity formation and change are linked to
processes of both social learning and cultural production.

Social Learning and Identity Change

Earlier in this chapter, I described several areas of social learning that
caused participants from the case-study partnerships to alter their thinking and
strategies for action in the environmental domain. In some instances, these experiences of social learning also led to shifts in people's notions of identity. One
area in which this was prevalent concerned participants' improved understandings of other stakeholders in the environmental arena. Such transformations
were experienced by participants from all three major sectors.

One example from the business sector involved the TRC agricultural representative described previously in the section on social learning. Over the course

of his interaction with the partnership, he began to distinguish more and more between different types of environmental groups—those he saw as serious "environmental associations," and those he viewed as insincere "neighborhood groups." This led him to adopt a more complex understanding of the environmental NGO sector and even to pursue contacts with several of these more serious "environmental associations." It also led him to alter his identity. In particular, he described in the interview how he had begun to think of himself less as a pure "defender" of agricultural interests and livelihoods and more as an "interlocutor" between the two sectors whom environmental associations could contact if they had any questions or concerns about agriculture in the province. He also came to embody this new identity as an interlocutor in the TRC partnership meetings. While he continued to defend the agricultural way of life, he also actively began networking with many of the other environmental NGO stakeholders for the purposes of making information available to concerned citizens or setting up meetings between agricultural and environmental interests.

From the NGO sector, an illustrative example involved an environmentalist from the CIMNR partnership. This participant described the process of meeting other stakeholders and becoming better informed of their desires and views as having brought about an increase in her own "maturity." When discussing what she had gained from her partnership experiences, she remarked:

> Part of it is just growing up. I am more attuned to trying to deal with people, especially people I don't agree with . . . and trying to listen fairly to what they are saying, which is the point of the whole thing. (CIMNR.1.7)

In conjunction with this altered self-conceptualization, this participant came to visibly temper her own positions in the CIMNR partnership and to approach the views of others with more openness and less disdain.

An example from the governmental sector concerned an identity shift that was shared by many of the governmental officials participating in the four case studies. In these instances, learning more about the aspirations and perspectives of different societal interests caused these officials to see themselves as being more in tune with the public and hence as being better public servants. One TRC communal-level governmental official described her participation in the TRC partnership as having permitted her to

> be as close to the population as possible and to adhere to the social reality that exists within the commune. . . . We are not here to bother the public but to serve them. (TRC.31.7)

Another TRC governmental official attributed this shift in self-perception to "not having to decide unilaterally without having heard the opinions of others" (TRC.32.7).

A second area involving identity changes instigated by social learning experiences involved participants who became transformed by what they learned about alternative approaches to environmental action. Many of the case-study participants, for instance, were changed by their exposure to the ideology of ecological modernization. One illustrative case involved a EUPEC member from a European-based multinational corporation. In the previous section on social learning, he was described as having learned the logic of economic-environmental win-wins via his participation in the partnership. In the interview, this individual characterized his company as having a long-standing tradition of taking defensive, reactive stances toward environmental issues. Correspondingly, he described his company as a "polluter" and indeed a "black sheep" in the environmental domain. As his job involved lobbying the European Commission so as to limit any detrimental impact of EU environmental policies on his firm, he, too, had adopted this identity over time. As he became more involved with the EUPEC initiative, however, he began to see himself less as a laggard and more as an environmental leader. This was evident in his comments on his changing role within his own company:

> Relative to my company and my group, I can [now] serve as a pioneer in order to attempt to change their mentalities vis-à-vis environmental problems. . . . I would say that now that I'm involved with [EUPEC], I am at the origin of things. I need to lobby my own organization now. In Brussels, I lobby [the EU]. But my most difficult lobbying now takes place within my own company, where I am trying to help change the mentalities of people who are still just beginning [to realize the importance of the environment] and who from the outset [have] thought solely of profit and improving technologies to reduce costs. (EUPEC.11.7-8)

Although this actor did not yet consider his corporation to have become an environmental leader among industrial firms, he did believe that it was improving. His perception of his role within his company did evolve, however, to the point where he began conceiving of himself as a "pioneer" whose task it was to enlighten other employees still caught up in a reactive approach to environmental factors in which economic success and environmental protection were seen to be at odds.

Cultural Production and Identity Change

In addition to identity changes associated with social learning experiences, the partnerships studied also provide several examples of participants altering their self-conceptualizations as a result of adopting some of the cultural forms produced. This section provides illustrations of people who developed new identities after embracing some of the newly produced meaning systems, practices, and group processes described in this chapter. Each of these three areas of identity formation is examined in turn.

Examples of identity shifts associated with the production of new meanings come from the CIMNR partnership, with its redefinition of the concept of stewardship, and the GBP partnership, with its reconceptualization of the concept of biodiversity. When the CIMNR partnership produced a novel meaning for the concept of stewardship, it created the possibility for participants to think about natural resource management in a different way. Certain participants began adopting the new understanding of the term in their thinking and discussions on environmental problem solving, and in some cases, this led to changes in their perceptions of self. One instance involved a representative from the business sector who noted in the interview that, over the course of participating in the partnership, he had come to increasingly use the term *stewardship* to describe his work in the mining industry. Although he did not believe that the new understanding of the term had caused him to become a better steward, he did claim that it had heightened his self-awareness of being a practitioner of stewardship. He also asserted that it had bolstered his self-opinion as an agent of positive environmental action. Accordingly, he described his participation in CIMNR as resulting in

> an enhanced awareness of my environmental ethics and how they stand with the environmental ethics of other individuals who come from an opposite perspective or point of view on life in terms of natural resource development and use. I became much more aware of the fact that I am every bit as focused on environmental protection, and I think my environmental ethics and standards showed me that I was every bit as strong minded as somebody who spends their life working for a nongovernmental organization. (CIMNR.11.11)

A related instance from the CIMNR case study involved a regulator from the federal government. In his case, adopting the partnership's prioritization of stewardship as the key to achieving sustainable natural resource systems led him to alter his view of his own regulatory agency. This involved a shift in his own organization-based identity away from his previously conceived role as a commander and controller of environmental action and toward a new role as a guide helping society to better interact with the environment. He described the particular effect of this new idea of stewardship on his organization as follows:

> [Stewardship] gives us a new basis upon which to build broad public consensus. It gives us a basis to move beyond regulation and enforcement into a whole new arena of private, voluntary, cooperative endeavors which are driven by an ethic of stewardship, which are driven by the alignment of economic signals that support that ethic. And it is kind of a tacit admission that for all of the tools that [my agency] has, we cannot achieve protection of our natural resources using regulation and enforcement alone. . . . I believe that [my agency] does what it does because it is required by the law, but [my agency] also has a leadership responsibility to take society to another level. (CIMNR.4.20)

Other examples of identity change associated with the cultural production of new meanings come with the GBP partnership's generation of its own conceptualization of biodiversity. When GBP participants began thinking and talking about their own locality in terms of biodiversity, this also helped to instigate the formation of a new communal identity that was experienced by these participants at a personal level. This communal identity was characterized by three broad features. First, it involved the depiction of the commune as rich in biological diversity and, indeed, as an environmentally attractive locale. This constituted a relative shift away from the former representation of the commune as a predominantly agricultural area. The partnership propagated this new conceptualization of Gascoigne in some of the announcements that it mailed out to the general public. In one such bulletin, the GBP coordinators wrote:

> Did you know that salamanders and triton newts are living in our marshes? That kingfishers, black woodpeckers, and other rare birds are nesting near our villages? Located in a humid region, apart from the big cities, the territory of [Gascoigne] supports numerous species of wild plants and animals. This BIO-DIVERSITY is an irreplaceable richness.

The partnership also promulgated this idea of a biodiversity-rich commune via its institutionalization of an annual "Biodiversity Day" festival. Intended to educate and sensitize the general public with regard to their local natural environment, the GBP partnership used lectures, poster presentations, and on-site visits to demonstrate elements of the commune's biodiversity as well as the manner by which the partnership was working to preserve and enhance this biodiversity. The festival highlighted several of the partnership's projects, such as those involving delaying the mowing of roadsides, replanting hedgerows in agricultural fields, and cultivating indigenous wildflowers in private gardens.

The second feature characterizing this new communal identity involved the portrayal of Gascoigne as a commune rich not only in natural heritage but in human resources as well. Participants who began to think about the commune in terms of biodiversity also began to redefine Gascoigne as a "dynamic" and "diverse" commune with a "motivated" and "interested" population, an "active" voluntary sector, and a strong capacity for "collective," "participatory" action. As summed up by one NGO participant:

> [Via the GBP partnership,] we rediscovered the richness of the commune, including the variety of nature, the territory, the population, [or] the richness of the commune's NGO sector. (GBP.2.9)

The third feature of this new communal identity involved the characterization of the commune as an emerging environmental leader within the Walloon Region of Belgium. The shift toward this new collective self-conceptualization was evident in the different adjectives that some of the participants used to describe Gascoigne and its population in the periods before and after the onset of the partnership. These participants portrayed the commune beforehand as generally lacking in environmental awareness. Conversely, they described the commune after the creation of the biodiversity project as a veritable "pilot" of good environmental planning and management and as an "example" for other Belgian communes to emulate. For evidence, they noted that Gascoigne was one of only five communes in all of Wallonia selected to receive funding to create a biodiversity contract, that Gascoigne was becoming increasingly successful in winning environmental grant money from the regional government, and that more and more environmentally related businesses were being created in the commune. This image of Gascoigne as an environmental leader was further advanced by the many complimentary press articles written about the GBP initiative and the frequent requests made of the partnership to present its work to other communes.

For these participants, the loss of identity as a rural, agricultural commune that Gascoigne was experiencing due to the great influx of residents from nearby cities was being replaced by a new self-representation that portrayed the commune as an environmentally rich and socially dynamic locale. Moreover, the nostalgia with which these participants had viewed their commune in the past was being replaced by a sense of pride in where the commune was heading in the future.

A second general area in which identity formation occurred involved the cultural production of new practices. Illustrations come from cases where partnership actors altered their self-perceptions as a result of assuming the aforementioned good participant behaviors. Some participants, in their discussions of what they had gotten out of the partnership process, spoke of how they had become better "listeners" or "communicators" in their professional and personal lives. Others described how they had become better at participating in multistakeholder processes in general. One particular instance illustrating this adoption of a "good partner" identity came from the CIMNR partnership and involved the environmentalist from a small, advocacy-oriented NGO described at the opening of this chapter. This individual related how he had entered the partnership as a radical environmental activist strongly aligned with issues of social equity, environmental justice, and grass-roots environmental protest and how he had been prepared to resist efforts at co-optation by the other business, governmental, and environmental NGO actors. Over the course of his participation in the CIMNR partnership as well as other collaborative initiatives, he increasingly began to adopt good partner behaviors, becoming during the latter phases of the partnership one of the most vocal champions of multistakeholder collaboration and one of the participants most attentive to *how* the partnership was proceeding rather than *what* the partnership was producing. This shift was evident from his self-descriptions. Whereas he described himself early in the partnership as an "advocate" of environmental interests and the "politics of resistance," he portrayed himself later as an "assistant to the process." This transformation led this actor to leave his job in the environmental NGO sector for a position in government, where he assumed responsibility for coordinating similar types of multistakeholder collaborative proceedings at the federal level.

The third and final area of identity change to be explored is tied to the creation of novel group processes and, in particular, the production of partnership-based friendships in the case-study partnerships. Some of the participants who experienced the sense of social cohesion and integration composing these relationships also went on to adopt new identities associated with these experiences.

Two general types of identity change were evident here. The first type was characterized by the development of a sense of heightened authority and status. This feeling of personal empowerment derived from participants perceiving themselves as part of a large, diverse, yet univocal group and from being able to say that their partnership actions stemmed from the democratic processes of public participation and consensus decision making. For representatives of small, local-level NGOs, this empowered self-perception arose from several other sources as well. It came from the experiences of being on the same side (for a change) as some of the more powerful decision makers from government and business, of having increased influence at higher policy levels, of gaining greater access to material resources, and simply, as one GBP environmentalist put it, of "being taken more seriously." For governmental and business decision makers, this empowerment also derived from being able to speak with greater authority from the position of local-level constituents. In all of these cases, this identity shift led these participants to see themselves as holding positions of elevated importance in the environmental domain.

The second type of identity change associated with the production of partnership-based relations involved the formation of a civic-oriented notion of self. In particular, experiencing these close ties led many of the case-study participants to perceive themselves as more a part of, involved in, and contributing toward their greater communities. Some of these participants demonstrated this particular self-conceptualization by referring to themselves as "citizens" in these collaborative processes. One TRC public authority exclaimed:

> When we are in a concertation, there are no more deputies, there are no more directors, there are no burgomasters, no titles. In a concertation, there are only ordinary citizens expressing themselves. (TRC.30.11)

Similarly, a GBP governmental official declared that in a partnership,

> it may start out as a deputy mayor and a complaining citizen, but over time it becomes two citizens talking about the same thing. (GBP.9.9)

The assumption here was that the very process of multistakeholder collaboration has the effect of producing a more active citizenry. As expressed by another TRC governmental representative,

> [With concertation], society comes to life again. Without it, society is inert, and things fall apart. If we hold a discussion on the topic of the river valley or the city, for example, citizens become interested in their own affairs. They take their own evolution, at least in part, in hand. (TRC.28.18)

Other participants revealed this civic identity by describing how their experiences with partnership-based relations induced both a sense of social responsibility and a propensity to look beyond one's personal interests toward the greater public good. A CIMNR business representative displayed this identity when he stated:

> [In partnerships,] there is a satisfaction, just human satisfaction, of working with other people from other walks of life. You get a feeling that you are working outside of just your company or even your own industry or even the whole issue of environmental stuff. You get a feeling that you're just helping society move forward in a small way. (CIMNR.6.11)

More generally, an environmentalist participating in the EUPEC initiative declared:

> [Partnership] is citizenship. Partnership is doing things beyond one's immediate affairs that lead to the betterment of society. It is taking care of society instead of taking care only of oneself. (EUPEC.23.6)

These participants described multistakeholder environmental partnerships as having the capacity to increase democratic participation, rebuild public trust, and combat the disaffection that many people feel toward society. By virtue of their participation in such partnerships, these actors thus came to see themselves anew as valuable contributors toward societal well-being.

Conclusion—On Partnership-Induced Personal Transformation

This chapter presents multistakeholder environmental partnerships as dynamic processes that serve to encourage experiences of personal transformation among the participating actors. This capacity is supported by the structures and organizational procedures by which these partnerships operate as well as by an expectation held by many participants that they are in fact supposed to be transformed by their participation in these processes.

As we have seen, these personal transformations come in a variety of forms. Some participants develop new understandings of the issues at stake or each other. Others adopt new practices with regard to environmental problem solving and decision making. Still others experience novel group processes, especially in the form of new relationships with other partners. Some of these transformations involve changes in personal identity, such as when participants start thinking of themselves as stewards of the environmental or as interlocutors between the sectors. Others involve participants beginning to identify themselves more closely with particular collectivities, such as their own partnerships or even their local communities. In all of these cases, the personal transformations involved include changes to some of the sociohistoric predispositions that participating actors bring with them to these collaborative processes.

It is important to recognize, however, that these sorts of changes are not unidirectional or predetermined. People both change others and are themselves changed in these processes, and this may occur in unintentional or unforeseen ways. Nor are these transformations confined or relegated to stakeholders from any one particular sector. We have explored examples of social learning, cultural production, and identity formation that involved participants from business, government, and environmental groups. Finally, we must remember that not all actors will experience the same level of personal transformation in multistakeholder partnerships. Although some will be greatly affected by their participation in these processes, others may barely change at all.

The fact that some participants do change, however, is significant because this affects both the capacity of these processes to produce consensus decisions and the specific types of solutions that these stakeholders will entertain. This, then, has important implications for the future of environmental problem solving and conflict resolution. It is toward these issues that I turn in the final chapter.

Notes

1. Daniels and Walker (2001), Forester (1996), Friedmann (1987), Glasbergen (1996a), Innes (1999), Maarleveld and Dangbégnon (1999), Woodhill and Röling (1998).
2. Argyris and Schön (1996).
3. Argyris and Schön (1996), Woodhill and Röling (1998).
4. Johnson (1987), Willis (1977, 1981). In the literature on collaboration, Bush and Folger (1994), Cobb (1993), Daniels and Walker (2001), Dukes (1996), Dukes et al. (2000), Littlejohn and Domenici (2001), and Ross (1993b) also write about this generative component of collaborative processes.
5. The characteristics of "good partnership behavior" discussed here share similarities with the qualities of effective dialogue described by Dukes (1996), the features of "new value partnerships" described by Sagawa and Segal (2000), and some of the productive behaviors described by Dukes et al. (2000) that allow groups to "reach for higher ground."
6. Many of these behaviors fall under the category of the "practice of conflict management" discussed in chapter 5.

Chapter 7

Implications

Multistakeholder environmental partnerships, such as those examined in this book, exemplify an approach to environmental problem solving that has gained acceptance and credibility in regions such as Europe and North America since the 1980s. These partnerships have arisen out of a context of enduring conflicts among actors in the environmental arena. These conflicts stem from a variety of sources, including perceived opposition between economic and environmental interests and competing views on the rightful relationship between humans and nature, the suitability of capitalism as a guiding force for society (and for environmental action, in particular), and the primacy of private versus common interests.

Such competing standpoints helped fuel the rise in the 1960s and 1970s of the modern environmental movement in the industrialized West. The modern environmental movement, in turn, catalyzed the development of a broad array of environmental laws and regulations that have had a marked impact on environmental conditions in North America and Europe. The establishment of regulatory regimes, however, prompted significant resistance from stakeholders believing that the environment might be better protected in other ways. The outcome of this tension has been the development and, indeed, institutionalization of a complex arena of conflictual relations. NGO and business interest groups have lined up against one another, and both have pitted themselves against government.

In the 1980s and 1990s, neoliberal policies gained prominence, leading to deregulatory pressures and the increased promotion of market incentives and voluntary approaches to environmental management. Within this broader context, governmental actors began taking on a more facilitative and participatory approach to environmental governance, large firms became more involved in the environmental policy development process, and the environmental movement began to diversify, with a number of groups advocating market-based approaches to environmental protection. Perhaps most important, participants from all three of these sectors began calling for increased levels of intersectorial cooperation, including the formation of multistakeholder environmental partnerships.

In the early twenty-first century, the number of multistakeholder partnerships in operation continues to be on the rise, as evidenced by the approximately sixty partnership initiatives launched in conjunction with the 2002 United Nations World Summit on Sustainable Development in Johannesburg.[1] Despite the importance attributed to these types of partnerships, the processes by which they and other multistakeholder collaboration-based initiatives operate remain less than adequately understood. This book addresses this need by bringing clarity to the role that *sociohistoric factors* play in these processes. In particular, it highlights the influence that people's socially, culturally, and historically based perceptions, conceptualizations, and expectations can have on partnership *practices*—i.e., on the ways participants think, speak, and act in partnership settings. The book examines three prevailing practices in particular: those of conflict, conflict management, and personal transformation.

Demonstrating the influence of such sociohistoric factors, however, is but one of my goals. Investigating the broader consequences of this inquiry is another. This chapter explores the implications that my research and its findings have for the study of environmental partnerships, the practice of multistakeholder collaboration, and environmental problem solving in general.

The chapter starts by considering some of the academically related contributions that derive from my theoretical and methodological approaches to this topic. I then move on to examine the more practitioner-oriented implications that this study has both for multistakeholder partnerships as a form of environmental governance[2] and for the different sectors that participate in them. At this point, I draw upon these implications to comment on the appropriate role of partnerships as a decision-making tool and to suggest several ways by which the effectiveness of multistakeholder partnerships might be improved. I close the chapter by exploring the possible future of multistakeholder environmental partnerships.

Contributions to the Study of Multistakeholder Collaboration

This book contributes to the continuing study of multistakeholder environmental collaborative processes in two main ways: (1) via the analytical perspective and methodological approach that it forwards, and (2) via the specific research findings uncovered. This section reviews these two primary contributions in greater detail. It also explores some of the limitations that qualify the study.

Analytical Perspective and Methodological Approach

In the preceding chapters, I have presented an analysis of multistakeholder environmental partnerships that departs from conventional approaches to this topic. Rather than focusing on why such partnerships are initiated, the variety of forms that they take, the steps by which they proceed, or their actual impact on the environment, my primary objective has been to improve current understandings of how multistakeholder environmental partnerships—as socially interactive and communicative processes—work.

To achieve this objective, I have done two things. First, I have adopted an analytical perspective that highlights the actual practices of multistakeholder interaction, the sociohistoric forces that drive these practices, and the ways in which these sociohistoric factors, and the people who bear them, can and do change. Directing attention toward what people actually say and do in particular partnership contexts emphasizes the situatedness of partnership actions and helps avoid portraying these actions as simple products of rational, rule-based behavior. Emphasizing the sociohistoric factors at play helps focus attention beyond the instrumental influence of political and economic interests and toward the varied and oftentimes competing interpretive frameworks, discourses, and conventional practices that come into contact as diverse stakeholders attempt to communicate and cooperate on complex environmental issues. Finally, accentuating the dynamic nature of these sociohistoric attributes helps depict people's understandings, behaviors, and self-conceptualizations not as fixed, static structures but as dynamic elements undergoing continual production, reproduction, and revision.

Second, I have drawn upon ethnographic research of multistakeholder environmental partnerships. This research was conducted with four European and North American case studies to encapsulate the diversity that exists among these initiatives in terms of environment focus, stakeholder mix, sociopolitical level, and geographic location. Two primary benefits derive from an ethnographic approach to this topic. First, ethnography is better suited for studying micro-level social processes and the cultural factors that drive them than are more common survey-oriented or institutional approaches, which are directed more toward exploring structural factors.[3] In particular, ethnographic methods allow the researcher to distinguish between what people say in interviews or surveys and what they actually do in practice. Second, ethnographic research typically takes place over the course of months and years. This enables analysis of some of the changes that individual subjects might experience over time.

Main Finding—The Role of Sociohistoric Influences

The primary, overarching finding to be drawn from this book is that sociohistoric factors do play an important role in determining participant behavior and action in multistakeholder environmental partnerships. This finding stems from evidence presented in chapters 4-6 regarding the specific practices of conflict, conflict management, and personal transformation and supports the book's primary assertion that interest-based perspectives alone cannot bring full understanding of what transpires in these types of collaborative settings. This finding also confirms the claims made by other scholars that conflict, people's ability to manage conflict, and people's capacity to change their views and ideas all affect the ability of collaborative efforts to produce innovative, effective, consensus-based decisions.[4]

Sociohistoric Impact on Conflict

Chapter 4 demonstrated the influence that sociohistoric factors can have on the practice of conflict in the partnership setting. In particular, it showed how the existence of sociohistoric differences can lead participants to interpret and then act upon particular ideas or events in incompatible ways. It also showed how these differences can make it difficult for participants to hear, understand, and value concepts different from their own.

In this chapter, I drew illustrative examples from the Gascoigne Biodiversity Project (GBP) and Toupin River Contract (TRC) case-study partnerships.[5] The GBP case explored how different interpretations of the partnership itself led the new environmental deputy official to enter into a long and protracted conflict with other members of the GBP executive bureau. Similarly, the TRC case showed how different perceptions of the state of the environment, alternative approaches to environmental problem solving, and divergent views on the relationship between concertation (an ideally inclusive and consensus-based approach to decision making) and democracy resulted in antagonism between governmental agency representatives and members of environmental groups. Together, the case studies suggest that partnerships characterized by substantial differences in stakeholder perceptions of (1) each another, (2) their partnerships, (3) the need for environmental action, (4) the causes of environmental problems, (5) the most effective approaches to environmental problem solving, or (6) the appropriateness and value of collaborative forms of environmental governance might be especially prone to sociohistorically induced conflict.

The GBP and TRC conflicts examined turned out to have a direct impact on partnership outcomes. The GBP conflict between the new environmental deputy and other executive bureau members, for instance, had a debilitating effect on the partnership. The partnership had a difficult time recovering the sense of unity and enthusiasm that had existed under the former environmental deputy. Without the full support of the communal government, the partnership was unable in the period that followed to implement some of the projects laid out in its charter. The TRC conflict had a similar effect on the TRC partnership. It led the governmental officials concerned to entrench their resistance to NGO involvement in their decision-making processes. This had the effect of stymieing the partnership's progress toward accomplishing one of its original goals: increasing citizen participation in regional environmental governance.

Sociohistoric Impacts on Conflict Management

Chapter 5 focused on the effects that sociohistoric factors can have on efforts to manage conflict in the collaborative setting. Five main modes of conflict management were found to predominate in all four of the case-study partnerships. These included the practices of civility, argument minimization, nonengagement, conflict diffusion, and reconciliation. The analysis found two key sociohistoric factors to underlie these practices. The first was a cultural model held by many of the partnership participants specifying how people are supposed to behave in these types of collaborative processes. This model portrayed partnerships as rightly nonconfrontational and indeed conflict averting in nature. The second key sociohistoric factor concerned the presence of a privileged discourse in the four partnerships studied—the discourse of *ecological modernization*. The existence of such a dominant discourse made it possible for partnership participants to find common ground on contentious issues.

As was the case with the practice of conflict, the conflict management behaviors adopted had a marked impact on the products of the case-study partnerships. For instance, these practices had the general effect of encouraging participants to remain at the table, to maintain a constructive tone in their deliberations, and to persevere in working through personal and organizational differences. The main premises underlying the discourse of ecological modernization also had a profound influence on the particular decisions taken and, most notably, the partnerships' general promotion of collaboration-based, prevention-oriented, economic-ecological win-win centered solutions to the environmental problems at hand.

Sociohistoric Impact on Personal Transformation

Chapter 6 examined the influence that sociohistoric factors can have on personal transformation in partnerships. When entering these processes, stakeholders bring with them different conventions for understanding, talking about, and acting on the environmental issues of concern. By virtue of these sociohistoric differences, participants have the opportunity to learn new things, produce new ways of conceiving of and dealing with the issues, and alter their self-conceptualizations.

In the case studies examined, partnership participants shifted in their understandings of each other, the state of the environment, and appropriate methods for resolving environmental problems. They adopted new concepts for addressing these concerns, pursued new modes of acting in concert, and developed new ways of interrelating. They also developed new ways of thinking about themselves vis-à-vis the environment and their broader communities. Supporting these transformations was a commonly held cultural model presuming that participants are supposed to change via their participation in multistakeholder collaborative processes.

These types of personal transformation affected partnership outcomes in a variety of ways. Social learning that took place with regard to the issues and interests at stake led some participants to depart from their initial positions and arrive at solutions different from those originally sought or expected. At times, this learning resulted in the production of novel ideas that helped participants arrive at consensus-based decisions. In other instances, the exposure to other views and perspectives caused participants to begin seeing themselves differently and to alter their relationships with one another accordingly. These changes enabled participants to trust one another and deliberate more seriously. In cases where participants developed a strong sense of affiliation with their partnerships and fellow partners, the resulting collective identity often led to increased pride in and ownership over the products produced. This also had the effect of increasing the capacity of the partnerships to sustain themselves over time.

Other Key Findings

In addition to this main finding regarding the influence of sociohistoric forces in partnerships, the research also produced several other findings worthy of note. These concern the topics of conflict management, ecological modernization, and personal transformation.

The Prominence of the Practice of Conflict Management

Chapter 5 revealed that in the case-study partnerships examined, the tendency to engage in conflict was accompanied by even more prevalent efforts at conflict management. This was demonstrated by the predominance of the conflict management practices of civility, argument minimization, nonengagement, conflict diffusion, and reconciliation. This finding is significant, because it counters the presumption that multistakeholder interaction in the environmental domain will be dominated by contestation.

The Privileged Discourse of Ecological Modernization

The privileging within the case-study partnerships of the discourse of ecological modernization is itself another key finding that emerges from this research. This finding supports the claim that ecological modernization has been and continues to be one of the most prominent ways of "talking green" in Western environmental policy domains.[6]

The privileging of ecological modernization was evidenced by its capacity to generate consensus, especially in the face of conflict, around the major ideas subsumed under the discourse. Included are the ideas that economic development and environmental protection interests can be reconciled in win-win formulations and that proactive and prevention-oriented approaches to environmental problems are preferable to reactive, curative alternatives. Also included is the presumption that resolution of current environmental problems requires collective, collaborative action among a variety of societal interests. The prominence of this discourse lay beneath people's eagerness to pursue collaborative forms of environmental action and their willingness to rally around sustainable development as an overarching objective.

Partnership Contributions to Personal Transformation

A final finding worth highlighting concerns the topic of personal transformation. Underlying the finding that sociohistoric factors affect the types of personal transformation that occur in collaborative processes is a more fundamental finding suggesting that multistakeholder environmental partnerships are themselves effective inducers of personal transformation. Supporting this finding is the inherently multistakeholder structure of these partnerships and the fact that they are typically operated to encourage cross-sectorial interaction and exploration. Also supporting this finding is the presumption held by many of the case-study participants that personal transformation is supposed to occur in these settings.

Limitations of the Study

Despite the contributions that this research makes to the study of multistakeholder environmental partnerships, my particular approach does have certain limitations that bear consideration. Methodologically, two potential weaknesses stand out. The first concerns my reliance on a small number of case studies. This makes it difficult for me to draw sweeping conclusions about multistakeholder partnership practices in general, the sociohistoric factors that inform them, or the differences that exist between them (e.g., between partnerships situated in different countries or regions).[7] This limitation does not diminish the benefit, however, of using this type of "collective case study" approach[8] to pose questions, suggest trends, and explore implications that do extend beyond the particular case studies per se. The second weakness concerns the fact that the research was largely directed toward activities that went on in the partnerships themselves. The effects that participating had on the partnership members back in their professional or personal lives were left largely unexamined.[9]

Analytically, two potential weaknesses stand out as well.[10] First, while the proposed sociohistoric-based approach has significant *explanatory* value, especially with regard to its capacity to retrospectively elucidate why particular participants acted as they did, this type of approach tends to be less useful for *predicting* the practices that will emerge in collaborative processes.[11] Nor is it easy to discern in advance from my approach what particular sociohistoric characteristics will drive these practices or the degree to which they will do so. Second, my analysis of partnership processes is necessarily incomplete. In attempting to highlight the influence that sociohistoric factors have on the practices that predominate in these types of partnerships, I have emphasized these particular factors over others, such as interest-based influences. I have done so with the recognition that there are risks in promoting particular analytical models to the exclusion of others. The view that results from such a strategy is, and can only be, partial. I therefore believe that the real benefit of sociohistoric approaches lies not in their isolated use but in the way that they strengthen, and are strengthened by, other analytical approaches. Sociohistoric and interest-based approaches—when viewed as complementary or at least supplementary to one another—surely give a more complete picture of why multistakeholder collaborative efforts proceed and turn out as they do than when these analytical approaches are pursued alone.[12]

Implications of Multistakeholder Partnerships for Environmental Decision Making

Up to this point, my focus has been on the implications that this research has for the study of multistakeholder partnerships. I now turn toward broader issues that the major findings raise for multistakeholder partnerships as decision-making tools in society. In particular, I want to address the following questions: What are the potential benefits and limitations of multistakeholder partnerships as an approach to environmental problem solving? In what ways do these partnerships represent a possible reconfiguration of the long-term struggles that have characterized past action in the environmental arena? What is their significance for the different types of stakeholders who participate? In the sections that follow, I limit my discussion to those implications stemming specifically from the key findings considered previously.

Benefits of Multistakeholder Environmental Partnerships

The research findings presented here suggest three main ways by which multistakeholder environmental partnerships benefit environmental decision making. These are associated with the capacity of partnerships to (1) bring diverse interests together in a constructive manner, (2) increase the influence of stakeholders and their ideas, and (3) serve as crucibles for change.

Spaces of Interaction, Cooperation, and Constructive Conflict
The first potential contribution that multistakeholder partnerships make to environmental decision making concerns the role that they play bringing diverse stakeholders together. Such interaction may expose participants to new data, different experiences, and alternative ideas. This enables partnerships to enhance the information known with regard to particular environmental problems, spawn novel solutions, and impart greater legitimacy to decisions made. Without the availability of partnership settings, many of these stakeholders—with their different perspectives on, approaches to, and interests regarding particular environmental issues—might not come together otherwise. This simple act of gathering stakeholders from the different sectors of society to exchange thoughts or

share ideas is an unmistakable step toward overcoming the lack of face-to-face contact and harmful stereotyping that has plagued meaningful levels of concerted environmental action in the past.

Environmental partnerships do more, however, than merely assemble diverse stakeholders. They also strive to do so in a spirit of trust, respect, and cooperation. They constitute a space where stakeholders can find themselves on the same side of an issue, where participants must not always be on the defensive, and where the ethos is one of working for mutual gain. In this way, partnerships lay the foundation for the production of consensus-based decisions. Although the agreements themselves may be limited in scope by the competing interests and perspectives involved,[13] the very production of consensus can still have a positive impact in social arenas where public debate has produced little more than frustration and dissensus in the past.

This is not to say that partnerships do not produce disagreement as well. Multistakeholder partnerships, by definition, comprise competing interests, and contestation often arises out of this. As I note, additional conflict can also arise out of sociohistorically derived misunderstandings. My point here is that the conflict spawned in multistakeholder settings is not necessarily detrimental.[14] Several potential benefits can come from it. First, conflict can serve to encourage the active involvement of participating actors. One need only point toward the popularity of radio call-in shows to recognize that conflict can be very engaging. Second, conflict has a creative component. The attempted resolution of conflict can allow for the production of innovative solutions that might not arise otherwise. Finally, conflict can result in outcomes that, when viewed as acceptable by the contending parties, provide the basis for ongoing relationships. These may help pave the way for more constructive engagement among the same parties in the future.

Spaces of Influence

Environmental partnerships are also significant because they provide opportunities for stakeholders to exert influence in ways beyond the political power or economic resources that they wield in their professional or personal lives. First, participating in multistakeholder processes permits individual participants to express what Roger Fisher calls their "negotiating power."[15] In these settings, participants can directly influence the decisions being made via their knowledge of the issues involved, their skills as negotiators, their relations with the other negotiators, and their commitment to the collaborative process.

Second, as multistakeholder bodies, environmental partnerships inherently expand the audience that will be exposed to any one stakeholder's ideas. In their everyday lives, stakeholders generally spend most of their time working within their own sectors and preaching, so to speak, to the choir. Multistakeholder partnerships provide access to audiences from other sectors as well.

The existence of privileged ideas or actions within partnerships offers participants a third means of exerting power and legitimacy. Participants of all backgrounds can increase their standing and influence in their partnerships, and within the environmental domain more generally, simply by espousing privileged views or practices. In partnerships where ecological modernization is a dominant discourse, for instance, participants promoting actions that have simultaneous environmental and economic benefit will be taken more seriously and accorded more credibility than participants advocating for environmental or economic gain alone. In addition, participants who adopt some of the ideas or behaviors coproduced by partnership members will also find their contributions to be given more credence. Such was the case for the participants who assumed the good partnership behaviors described in chapter 6.

In addition to elevating the influence of participants espousing privileged ideas or practices, multistakeholder partnerships also provide a powerful means for transferring these ideas and practices both between and within sectors. Potential environmental problem-solving benefits thus reside in the particular ideas being propagated. Ecological modernization, for instance, poses several possible advantages to environmental problem solving. For starters, it fosters proactive rather than reactive environmental action, advocating the prevention of serious environmental problems before they arise. Moreover, ecological modernization sets as its goal the pursuit of both economic and ecological sustainability. Partnerships that promote such win-win solutions encourage new sets of environmental behaviors from actors who might have been able to see only economic-ecological trade-offs in the past. This may lead some industrialists to begin treating environmental protection less as an economic constraint and more as a means of making money. It may also lead some environmentalists and regulators to start treating corporations not just as the cause of pollution problems but also as part of the solution. Finally, ecological modernization advocates collaborative resolution of environmental problems. This may help ensure the inclusion of previously excluded environmental stakeholders as well as the retention of higher levels of public participation and involvement.

Spaces for Change

A third way in which multistakeholder environmental partnerships potentially benefit environmental decision making comes from their roles as fertile sites for personal transformation. Multistakeholder environmental partnerships present significant opportunities for stakeholders to learn new information, produce new ideas, initiate new behaviors, and develop new relationships with others. They also encourage participants to alter their own self-understandings.

The benefits of such changes for environmental problem solving lie both within and outside of the partnership setting. Within partnerships, one important advantage is that these types of personal transformation increase the probability that stakeholder differences can be reconciled and consensus-based decisions produced.[16] When people are willing and able to change their minds on an issue, the chances improve that common ground will be found. This permits the production of final agreements that not only satisfy a wider range of interests but also differ from what any of the participants might have been willing to commit to, or even imagine, at the onset. A second benefit within partnerships concerns the feasibility of partnership decisions. Personal transformations in the form of the production of group cohesion, shared responsibility, and good partnership behaviors, for instance, help increase the probability that the environmental decisions taken will be implemented and durable.

Beyond the collaborative setting, partnerships have the capacity to produce changes in individuals that extend to their professional or personal lives. For starters, participants may learn things about ecological conditions, environmental problem-solving approaches, or other stakeholders in the environmental realm that will lead them to alter the ways that they have been acting on the environment in the past. A second potential benefit is tied to the feelings of solidarity and integration that participants often experience by working together on the same side of an environmental issue. The resulting partnership-based friendships serve to create a network of actors in the environmental arena who remain connected even outside of the partnership. Such networks are significant, because they may be called upon to address new environmental problems in the future. A final advantage comes with the new identities produced. Some of these identities—such as those in which participants reconceptualize themselves as environmental leaders, as champions of multistakeholder collaborative processes, or simply as good citizens concerned with public welfare—have particular ramifications for the future of environmental governance. These new identities, for instance, may help produce a citizenry that is more active, involved, and committed to participate in environmental decision making and self-regulatory processes. Moreover, these citizens may be willing to do so in a more cooperative and nonconfrontational manner that may create possibilities for overcoming some of the gridlock that has hampered past environmental efforts.

Limitations of Multistakeholder Environmental Partnerships

Notwithstanding the above benefits, multistakeholder environmental partnerships such as the ones examined here also have distinguishing features that may restrict their contributions to environmental decision making. This section focuses on (1) the ramifications of prevailing practices of conflict management, (2) the shortcomings of ecological modernization as a privileged discourse, and (3) the limits and uncertain consequences of personal transformation.

The Consequences of Conflict Management
The first of these limitations is associated with the prominence of conflict management practices in partnership settings. One problem here is that if conflict management efforts result in the suppression of adversarial and contentious conduct, partnerships may lose out on the creative capacity of conflict to induce innovation and change. A perhaps more significant problem, however, is that the tendency to privilege or promote nonconfrontational styles of behavior may serve to delegitimize broader opposition-based approaches to environmental action. This is particularly detrimental for those stakeholders who tend to oper-

ate via conflict and contestation, whose primary expertise is in doing so, and who have achieved many of their past successes in this manner. These actors are placed at a distinct disadvantage within the partnership setting relative to other stakeholders, because their antagonistic style of discussion and negotiation may lead others to ignore the content of their arguments as well. This is precisely what happened to members from the environmental justice community in the CIMNR case study. Their pushy and confrontational style got them labeled as "bad partners," and over time their message began falling on deaf ears.

Outside of the partnership setting, the broader delegitimization of conflict-based environmental action poses other dilemmas as well. The main problem here is that the nonconfrontational tendencies of multistakeholder partnerships makes them vulnerable to co-optation by actors—especially the more powerful political and economic players in society—who may want to use these collaborative processes to build support for or manage opposition to their own policies or projects. Multistakeholder partnerships can thus serve these actors as pacification schemes for overcoming public resistance to their special interests.[17] Such acts of co-optation may benefit particular interests involved, but they do not necessarily profit the rest of society.

Ecological Modernization and Exclusion and the Reproduction of Prevailing Power Structures

A second potential constraint associated with multistakeholder environmental partnerships is specific to those partnerships that privilege the discourse of ecological modernization. This drawback takes the form of two distinct limitations. The first stems from the capacity of ecological modernization, especially when combined with the suppression of conflictual modes of environmental action, to reproduce the prevailing power structures around which the market economies of Western Europe and North America are based.[18] This becomes problematic if resolving today's complex environmental problems necessitates the critical reexamination and substantive reformulation of the systems of production and consumption that produced these problems in the first place.[19]

At issue is the relationship between ecological modernization and the system of liberal capitalism. On one hand, ecological modernization echoes certain radical green discourses by blaming specific elements of capitalism—e.g., capitalism's short-term profit approaches to both end-of-pipe pollution control measures and scarce natural resource exploitation—for many of industrialized society's current environmental dilemmas. On the other hand, ecological modernization also looks to this very system to help develop the expert knowledge and technologies deemed necessary to resolve these same environmental concerns. The problem with the dominance of this discourse is that it impedes the possibility for greater critical examination of some of these underlying impediments and contradictions. Although compelling critiques of such prevailing economic structures exist—such as the arguments that the market, alone, is incapable of protecting the environment,[20] or that liberal capitalism produces its own environmental barriers to production and is itself therefore not ecologically sustainable[21]—these types of arguments generally find little traction within the discourse of ecological modernization. To the extent that environmental partnerships privileging this discourse are reluctant to take a critical, reflexive look at some of the fundamental problems underlying modern industrial society, these tendencies function in a hegemonic[22] fashion to reproduce the status quo.[23]

The second limitation related to the privileging of ecological modernization in multistakeholder partnerships stems from the very presence of such a discourse hierarchy. What happens in these situations is that those who use or promote the predominant discourse gain in authority and credibility, while those who do not are similarly disadvantaged. The problem is that this dynamic may cause participants to stop listening to or promoting alternative perspectives.

This effective excluding of competing discourses takes place in three main ways. First, it occurs when participants in the collaborative process elect to stop talking. This is what happened in the EUPEC business plan conflict discussed in chapter 5 in which an influential environmental NGO representative attempted to introduce elements of the more radical green rationalism discourse into the debate. Pressure placed on him by other participants to relinquish his calls for a "reinvented economy" in favor of the more broadly accepted goal of "sustainable development" subsumed under the dominant discourse of ecological modernization resulted in some of his more out-of-the-box ideas fading from discussion.

A second way that this exclusion takes place is when stakeholders opt to terminate their participation in partnership processes. This was the case in the CIMNR initiative, when representatives of the environmental justice and free-market environmentalism perspectives elected to stop attending. In both of these cases, the participants involved expressed frustration that their ideas—especially those that directly contested basic ecological modernization beliefs—were being disregarded or ignored. For the environmental justice participants, this included their criticisms of the inequities embedded in capitalist political-economies. For the free-market environmentalist participant, this include his presumption that the world is facing a situation of resource abundance rather than resource scarcity. The departure of these participants left the CIMNR partnership even more entrenched in the mainstream middle.

A third and final way by which discourses may be silenced in collaborative processes occurs when legitimate stakeholders espousing alternative views choose not to participate in the first place. In the EUPEC initiative, this happened when a prominent environmental group with a reputation for being radical rejected EUPEC's invitation to join, stating in a decidedly nonecologically modernistic manner that it objected to both the concept of "sustainable development" and the idea of multistakeholder collaboration. As a result, the EUPEC initiative lost an important opportunity to expose itself to a broader range of environmentalist perspectives.

The Limits to and Consequences of Personal Transformation

A final limitation of environmental partnerships that may affect their contributions to environmental decision making is associated with the personal
transformations that they encouraged. Two potential problems stand out here.
The first has to do with the extent to which personal transformations will occur.
In short, there is nothing to guarantee that such changes will happen. To be sure,
some participants will be greatly affected by their experiences in multistakeholder partnerships, as was clear from the personal accounts explored at the beginning of chapter 6. Other actors, however, will be less affected, and some will
hardly change at all. Such was the case, for instance, for the new environmental
deputy official who participated in the GBP partnership (see chapter 4). Despite
the hopes of the other members of the GBP executive bureau that he would
evolve in his understanding of the project and come to embrace and lead the
partnership, this did not occur to any great extent in the research period that followed. In addition, there is also no certainty that any changes that do occur will
persist over time outside of the partnerships setting. Although the lives of some
participants—such as the CIMNR environmentalist whose collaborative experiences led him to leave his advocacy-oriented NGO for a governmental position
promoting partnerships—will be greatly affected by ideas learned or identities
formed, the day-to-day existence of others will not.

The second major problem facing the generation of personal transformation
in multistakeholder partnerships concerns the substance of the changes themselves. In short, there is no guarantee that the transformations produced in partnership processes will benefit the environment. Although many of the changes
engendered will help improve environmental protection and natural resource
management, some of these alterations may also have the effect of undermining
or at least delimiting such improvements. Take, for example, the partnership-
based friendships that were produced in all of the case studies. These friendships
were founded on feelings of social cohesion that were themselves based upon a
sense of equality experienced by participants while in the partnership setting.
Everyone thought that they had the same right to speak and be heard and that
everyone's perspective had value in itself. The problem in this case is that this
seemingly democratic quality of multistakeholder partnerships can also serve to
obfuscate the actual power relations involved. The reality of the situation is that
certain partnership participants will often hold substantial advantages over others in the areas of negotiation skills and experience, scientific and technical expertise, and time and material resources.[24] This means that it is unlikely that all
stakeholder interests will be equally served in a partnership process. This, in
itself, is not detrimental. What is potentially problematic for environmental decision making is that this assumption of egalitarianism and heterarchical relations
can be co-opted by particular interests and used to make the argument that the
decisions being produced benefit all of the stakeholders equally when in actual-
ity certain parties are benefiting more than others. Moreover, participants will be
less likely to resist these power imbalances within the partnership setting be-

cause partnership activities are based on the assumption that these imbalances do not exist.

Also implicated here is the role that partnerships are now playing in the evolution of environmental governance. As noted previously, partnerships can help to produce active, involved citizens who want to play an important role in the future of environmental decisions. Importantly, these new civic actors are willing to work in a collaborative rather than confrontational manner with other stakeholders in society and to share responsibility for environmental damage done.[25] They are also generally more supportive of voluntary measures for addressing environmental concerns. The point here is that such transformations are not neutral. In the policy realm, they conform more closely to and thus advance neoliberal ideals and agendas more so than they do the objectives of traditional regulatory regimes. This, in turn, will affect the types of actions that will be open for consideration to remedy the environmental ills of the future.

The Contradictions of Partnering for the Environment

One of the conclusions that can be drawn from this evaluative discussion is that multistakeholder environmental partnerships such as the ones explored here have somewhat contradictory implications for the future of environmental decision making and governance. In particular, they appear to simultaneously encourage and delimit possibilities for change in the environmental realm. This section examines three ways in which this contradiction is manifested. The first two affect the ability of multistakeholder partnerships to address environmental problems. The third affects the influence that these partnerships may have on enduring environmental struggles.

The first contradiction is associated with multistakeholder partnerships that propagate the view that partnering for the environment should ideally be nonconfrontational. The main incongruity here concerns the fact that although such partnerships enable the production of consensus-based solutions to environmental dilemmas, they also undermine other conflict- and opposition-based approaches to environmental change. This may be problematic if one heeds the claims by some scholars that the more radical wing of the environmental movement constitutes Western society's best hope of accomplishing significant, long-term environmental protection.[26] An additional incongruity arises, however, from the fact that by undermining such oppositional approaches, partnerships are also subverting those organizations that are instrumental in bringing about the impetus to collaborate in the first place. It is likely that powerful industrial corporations and public authorities would be much less interested in partnering with their environmental NGO counterparts without the threat of protest action or lawsuits hanging over them. Greenpeace's Brent Spar campaign against Royal Dutch/Shell is a good case in point, as several business representatives participating in the EUPEC initiative cited this campaign as something they hoped to use the partnership to avoid. Similarly, industrial firms would be less

compelled to sit down with government if it were not for the threat of regulations. To the extent that environmental partnerships serve to delegitimize such
oppositional approaches to environmental action, these partnerships are undermining the very forces that compel certain stakeholders to cooperate in the first
place. Partnerships may serve as effective "carrots," but they also obstruct the
utility of other valuable "sticks."

The second contradictory facet of multistakeholder environmental partnerships concerns the privileging of the discourse of ecological modernization in
these processes. On the one hand, partnerships that privilege this discourse promote an ideology that values and fosters win-win solutions to ecological problems in which both the environment and the economy derive benefit. On the
other hand, these partnerships also restrict what these win-win situations can
accomplish. For starters, they limit radically different proposals for action by
confining the topics of debate.[27] As mentioned previously, the argument that
liberal capitalism, with its supporting instrumentalist and anthropocentric ideologies, ultimately impedes the achievement of sustainability will not likely receive serious or critical consideration in these settings. In addition, the predominance of the discourse of ecological modernization may result in the exclusion
of alternative voices who self-select themselves out of these processes. Lost here
are the potentially innovative ideas and perspectives that might play a key role
in the pursuit of lasting environmental solutions. To the extent that long-term
sustainability necessitates large-scale societal changes in terms of resource consumption and waste production, stymieing public participation via the silencing
of such groups will only hinder democratic efforts made in this direction.[28]

The third and final way in which multistakeholder environmental partnerships both encourage and delimit change in the environmental realm concerns
their effect on enduring environmental struggles. Environmental partnerships
foster the transformation of ongoing conflicts in three main ways. First, they
bring to these struggles a new space of interaction and, indeed, of cooperation.
They are a place and a moment in time in which formerly or normally adversarial actors in society can come and be together in a fundamentally different way.
Second, environmental partnerships are also driven by a set of precepts that depart from past practices governing such struggles. These precepts deem that
while sitting at the table, each participant should be treated equally, each has his
or her own interests and perspectives that are valuable and worthy of respect in
their own right, and all action should grow out of mutual understanding of these
interests and perspectives rather than out of assumptions based upon ignorance
or fear. Finally, the generative quality inherent in multistakeholder partnerships
introduces *uncertainty* into the conduct of long-standing conflicts.[29] The social
learning, novel cultural forms, and identity shifts induced in these settings create
possibilities for changing the ways in which enduring environmental struggles
will play out in the future.

The flip side to this, however, is that just as environmental partnerships
make possible a reconfiguration of enduring environmental struggles, so too do
they maintain and reproduce them. For one thing, as tools of environmental

management, multistakeholder partnerships may serve less to *resolve* conflict than to *control* it.[30] For another, as both products and potential propagators of ecological modernization, these partnerships help to sustain the power structures and imbalances embedded in this ideology. In particular, they serve to promote the very anthropocentric values and self-interested capitalist formations that were described in chapter 2 as fueling many enduring environmental struggles in the first place.

Implications for Stakeholders

Linked to this analysis of multistakeholder partnerships and environmental decision making are additional implications that these collaborative processes pose for the different types of participating stakeholders. In this section, I examine some of the benefits and drawbacks that partnerships such as the case studies examined have specifically for the business, government, and NGO sectors.

The Business Sector

The main advantages that multistakeholder environmental partnerships present for the business sector are all associated with the role that partnerships play as a stakeholder management tool.[31] Certain benefits come in the realm of public relations. Voluntarily collaborating with a wide variety of societal interests on behalf of the natural environment provides a source of good publicity for participating firms. This, in turn, enables them to better manage public reaction to other existing or proposed corporate environmental actions.[32]

Other benefits derive simply from being in close, meaningful, cooperative contact with key stakeholders from government, environmental groups, and civil society. Corporations may gain competitive advantage, for instance, by being better informed of the latest developments in the legislative and regulatory arenas and by being in closer touch with the most recent trends in the environmental community.[33] In a related manner, corporations can protect themselves against uncertainties in the marketplace by using these partnerships to better anticipate how different stakeholders will react to specific corporate environmental actions—a benefit that Royal Dutch/Shell might greatly have appreciated in the case of the Brent Spar oil platform. In addition, corporations can use these consensus-based processes to better manage the production of more acceptable or tolerable environmental policies and public planning. The business sector is extremely well positioned in this regard, especially when the partnerships involved are dominated by the logic of ecological modernization, because these partnerships will place great value on the technical know-how and economistic perspective and tools (e.g., cost-benefit analyses) that these corporations inherently bring to the table.[34] Finally, for firms committed to becoming good corporate citizens, partnerships provide the opportunity to better respond to the needs of the greater communities in which they are situated and on which they ultimately depend.[35]

Along with these benefits, however, multistakeholder partnerships also present certain challenges for the business sector. Most important, they demand greater levels of transparency and information sharing on the part of corporate participants, although this will obviously be more problematic for firms with long histories of secrecy and exclusivity. In addition, companies will need to be able to defend themselves against charges of "greenwashing" and the claim that these partnerships constitute little more than business as usual with a slick green veneer.[36] In partnerships where ecological modernization is the dominant discourse and where certain topics—such as the reality of economic-environmental trade-offs and the prevalence of environmental injustice—rarely receive serious attention or critical discussion, it may be quite difficult for companies to convince a wary public otherwise. At risk is the legitimacy of any claims to good corporate citizenship.

The Governmental Sector

Multistakeholder environmental partnerships also afford government several distinct benefits. First, they provide the opportunity for public authorities to simultaneously fulfill three of their primary mandates. These include promoting economic growth, which is enhanced by giving business a greater voice in environmental decision making; protecting the public good, which is achieved by way of fostering a healthier natural environment; and governing in a public way, which is accomplished by opening decision-making processes to greater citizen input and involvement. Second, at a time when EU and U.S. citizens are calling for more efficient government, multistakeholder partnerships allow public authorities to do more with less. By creating access to the substantial resources and expertise stemming from the business sector, the environmental NGO sector, and the general public, these partnerships provide government with the opportunity to produce and implement environmental decisions all at a potentially lower cost to taxpayers. Finally, as was true for the business sector, multistakeholder partnerships provide governmental actors with a stakeholder management tool. Governmental officials can use partnerships to keep tabs on activities in the private and environmental NGO sectors. They can also use partnerships to test and manipulate private and public responses to proposed governmental actions.[37]

As was also the case for the business sector, however, participating in multistakeholder partnerships does demand that governmental participants be more transparent in their political decision making. When collaborating on projects with other stakeholders, it is more difficult for public authorities to conceal mistakes made or to justify special treatment given to one constituency over another. Moreover, being a partner in a collaborative endeavor also means that governmental actors must shift somewhat from their role of exclusive, authoritarian rulers to a new role of collaborative facilitators of environmental action. This may be difficult for some governmental actors to do, as it requires that they share power to a greater extent with the economic actors whom they are supposed to be regulating and the general public whom they are supposed to be representing.[38]

The NGO Sector

Of the three main participating sectors, the environmental community faces the most challenges from multistakeholder environmental partnerships. This is not to say, however, that significant benefits do not exist. Indeed, multistakeholder partnerships constitute what are still relatively rare opportunities for environmental groups to be included at the decision-making table with government and business. Having such a voice is the fulfillment of many an environmental NGO's longtime goals. Even partnerships in which the discourse of ecological modernization predominates pose certain advantages for environmental groups. This is especially true for those more moderate environmental groups that already share many of these same ideals. For these organizations, ecological modernization provides a common basis of understanding from which the advancement of many environmental causes may proceed.

Where multistakeholder partnerships are most troublesome for the environmental community is for those particular organizations whose actions are typically characterized by oppositional behaviors and hard-line stances. Several dilemmas stand out here. One grows out of the legitimacy that environmental NGOs bring to these partnerships—a legitimacy that stems from the relatively high levels of public trust that NGOs generally command in the arena of environmental affairs.[39] The problem is that if environmental NGOs become associated with multistakeholder partnership decisions that have the ultimate effect of harming the environment, these groups risk losing their primary source of capital in society—their very credibility.

A second dilemma stems from the mere act of sitting and conversing with sworn "enemies" from either the business or governmental sectors. By doing so, radical NGOs in particular risk falling out of touch with the grass-roots foundations and support that sustains them in the first place.

A third threat concerns the way by which institutionalized cooperation may be used as an instrument of control. As intimated earlier, it is much easier for businesses or governments to dominate citizens in cooperative processes than it is in adjudicative proceedings.[40] It is also much easier for the more powerful political and economic actors in society to manage environmental activists when they are sitting with them at the same table than when these activists are out protesting in the streets.

A final hazard that affects radical environmental groups in particular concerns the predominance of the discourse of ecological modernization in these settings. The manner in which this discourse adopts certain elements of modern environmentalism, such as its emphasis on pollution prevention or its condemnation of capitalist inefficiencies, while at the same time stripping them of their radical content has the potential to transform the environmental movement from a prominent opposer of prevailing power structures to yet another collective agent complicit with them.[41] Particularly problematic is the advancement of sustainable development, as this idea shifts priority away from the concept of "environment" as an autonomous subject meriting serious attention and action in its own right. In the pursuit of sustainable development, the environment can no longer be examined outside of its economic context. As the environment becomes further enmeshed within the economic domain, however, the environment risks becoming treated as just one of many factors influencing economic activity, and a relatively minor one at that. Multistakeholder partnerships can be dangerous for many environmental NGOs because they threaten the legitimacy of those radical green discourses, such as those promoting ecocentrism or the intrinsic value of nature, that exist outside of the economic sphere.

Implications for the Use of Multistakeholder Partnerships—A Partial Solution

Given the capacity of multistakeholder environmental partnerships to increase environmental knowledge, involve greater numbers of citizens in environmental problem solving, establish relations and encourage cooperation among key stakeholders, facilitate the production of consensus-based decisions, and instigate critical self-reflection and transformation on the part of their participants, it is clear that these processes have the potential to play an important role in future environmental problem-solving efforts. A key question for people considering convening multistakeholder partnerships is: What role should this be?

A perhaps obvious yet nonetheless important conclusion to draw from my analysis of partnership implications is that multistakeholder collaborative processes do not constitute the "silver bullet" that finally permits the harmonious and universally beneficial resolution of all environmental problems. As we have seen, they present distinct advantages to the problem-solving process, but they also limit what any solutions may accomplish. In addition, there are also certain types of problems for which collaborative processes are less well suited. They are not very appropriate, for instance, for addressing entrenched conflicts involving high political and economic stakes, as these situations are not very conducive to developing the trust, respect, cooperation, and willingness to explore other positions required in partnerships. Nor are they necessarily suitable for addressing those types of environmental problems for which an ecological modernization approach is a poor fit. This includes environmental problems characterized by substantial scientific uncertainty and long-term, high-consequence risks.[42]

It is also important to note that relatively little evidence currently exists that multistakeholder partnerships—or any other form of self-regulation, for that matter—present a viable substitute for state-sponsored regulatory approaches to environmental problem solving.[43] Nor is there much indication that collaboration-based strategies will be able to transcend many of the dilemmas facing traditional regulatory approaches. Multistakeholder partnerships are not exempt from the constraints of unequal representation or competing interests. They do not severely alter the underlying power dynamics and asymmetries that drive certain environmental problems. They do not ensure that consensus among society's diverse interests will be found, even if people learn new things about the environment, achieve intersubjective understandings, or explore new identities. Finally, they in no way guarantee that environmental conditions will be ameliorated, especially if fundamental changes to the way industrial society functions are required.

It therefore seems prudent to conclude that multistakeholder environmental partnerships may be most effective if treated as important supplements to, rather than replacements of, existing regulatory regimes. They are important tools in an increasingly diverse mix of environmental policy instruments, but they constitute only a partial solution. In terms of when to use them, the best strategy may be to pursue them in situations that play most to their strengths. This will involve cases where stakeholders are eager to act on behalf of the environment but have not had the institutional means of doing so in the past, where past environmental action has been stymied by the recurring exclusion of specific stakeholders, where environmental objectives are found to be relatively compatible with economic interests, and where stakeholders are willing to consider and respect other points of view in the search for consensus decisions.

By stating that multistakeholder partnerships constitute only a partial solution to today's environmental dilemmas, I am not claiming that they will never lead to breakthroughs in situations marked by heightened conflict, complexity, or uncertainty. I am simply acknowledging that their chances for success in these cases will be diminished. It is also possible that in the long run, the greatest contribution to be made by these partnerships will stem not from the actual decisions produced but from the personal transformations that they incite. In this manner, multistakeholder partnerships may be providing a valuable service to society every time they enable groups of stakeholders that have been characterized by histories of poor contact and communication to come together and engage in civil and constructive dialogue.

Improving Partnership Effectiveness—Recommended Actions

The impact that multistakeholder environmental partnerships will have on the future of environmental problem solving will depend not only on the situations in which they are used but also on how effectively they are carried out by the coordinators who design and manage them and by the participants who actually do the collaborating. This section draws on the preceding analysis of partnership implications to suggest six specific ways by which multistakeholder partnerships, as instruments of decision making, might be improved.[44] These recommendations include (1) attending to the sociohistoric dimension of collaboration, (2) promoting appropriate management of conflict and opposition, (3) providing the conditions that encourage personal transformation, (4) seeking appropriate third-party facilitation, (5) evaluating partnerships to encourage secondary benefits, and (6) maintaining realistic expectations. The overriding recommendation is to bolster partnership effectiveness in those areas where partnerships provide real advantages while minimizing the potential detriments that partnerships pose.

Attend to Sociohistoric Influences

One of the major goals of this book has been to highlight the role played by sociohistoric factors in multistakeholder collaboration processes. As illustrated in the preceding chapters, sociohistoric differences, when left unaddressed, can lead to misunderstandings, miscommunication, and indeed conflict among diverse participants. When partnership participants lose touch with what is being said or meant by their interlocutors, they often resort to default arguments and caricatures of other stakeholders. This, in turn, can shift the process away from efforts at dialogue, mutual discovery, and the search for commonalities and toward a return to the conventional defense of entrenched, self-interested positions.

Although it is not easy to predict which sociohistoric differences will be more likely to result in misinterpretation or discord in any particular setting,[45] efforts can and should be made by partnership participants and coordinators alike to pay more attention to the sociohistoric dimension of the collaborative process. Participants should strive to be mindful of sociohistoric differences where they exist and expose them when possible.[46] These efforts should also commence at the onset of partnership deliberations and continue throughout the collaborative process.

Participants can pursue this mindfulness in a variety of manners. Participants can attempt to be more aware of their own perceptions of the environmental problems at issue, their biases toward particular solutions, and how these preferences compare with those of other stakeholders. They can continually question their assumptions of other stakeholders and make greater efforts to be sensitive toward how other stakeholders might see them. They can also be conscious of how their understandings of and expectations for their partnerships might differ from those of other stakeholders. Finally, participants can be more attentive to the possibilities for personal transformation in these collaborative processes. This includes acknowledging where room for potential change exists as well as recognizing how people, including themselves, may have shifted in terms of views, preferences, or behaviors over the course of partnering. Such shifts are important because they can have a profound impact on partnership outcomes.

The potential result of paying more attention to the sociohistoric dimension of collaborative processes is improved partnership effectiveness. This effectiveness may take several forms. First, attending to sociohistoric differences can help pave the way for improved intersubjective understandings between stakeholders. This, then, permits the production of more confident and coherent decisions.[47]

Second, increased awareness of the sociohistoric forces at play can encourage the production of innovative solutions. The fact that different participants see the world in varying ways is itself a key resource for partnerships. The differences that exist among stakeholders' alternative sociohistoric-based perspectives and approaches constitute the "potential energy" (to borrow a concept from physics) out of which novel, creative ideas can emerge.

Finally, focusing on the sociohistoric dimension of collaboration encourages stakeholders to look beyond their interests or desired outcomes as they participate in these processes. It invites them to be more in-the-moment in their interactions and to acknowledge the human perceptions, beliefs, and relations at play. Indeed, it invites them to experience the process that is "partnering for the environment" in all of its complexity and grandeur. This approach provides an opportunity for partnership participants and coordinators alike to overcome the limits of the interest-based, means-end oriented perspective that predominates in this domain. According to some scholars, overcoming this instrumental rationality viewpoint will be critical to resolving many of the major conflicts impeding effective environmental governance today.[48]

Promote Appropriate Management of Conflict and Opposition

Multistakeholder environmental partnerships often bring together stakeholders who have had little or no contact in the past. They also encourage these stakeholders to cooperate—again, often for the first time—for the purpose of realizing common goals. Conflict management strategies promoting nonconfrontational behaviors should be encouraged in these instances to the extent that they permit participants to get to know one another, learn from each other's perspectives, and search for common ground and mutual gain. In situations where conflict and contestation has been the rule in the past, nonconfrontational behavior should also be fostered if it can help produce consensus-based decisions. While it is possible that the decisions produced in these instances will have only limited direct impact on the environmental issues of concern, there may still be value in producing consensus decisions because the very act of doing so demonstrates for the participants a manner of action that differs greatly from the mistrust, opposition, and gridlock that characterize so many other environmental policy venues.

Partnering just for the sake of having everyone get along, however, is not sufficient. Environmental partnerships must also be directed toward achieving significant environmental objectives. Moreover, partnerships must avoid suppressing the expression and exploration of conflicting positions merely to facilitate consensus. As noted before, differences of opinion and competing interests will always exist in these settings, and although these may limit what any partnership might accomplish, they also provide the fodder from which breakthroughs may occur.

Where oppositional behavior is inappropriate in multistakeholder partnerships is when particular participants, for reasons of individual or organizational self-interest, attempt to subvert partnerships from accomplishing their commonly agreed upon goals. Not only does this waste the time and money of everyone else involved, but it also undermines the possibility of future collaborative action. This is not to say, however, that participants who collaborate in partnerships may not pursue oppositional behaviors external to them. Indeed, the fact that partnerships are spaces for cooperation should not diminish or delegitimize activist or confrontational approaches within the broader environmental policy arena. Making this distinction between appropriate collaborative behavior within partnerships and appropriate conflictual behavior outside of them is a key means by which partnerships may guard against having their nonconfrontational nature exploited by special interests seeking only to manage opposition to their own private causes.

Provide the Conditions that Encourage Personal Transformation

The capacity for partnerships to induce change in and among the participating actors is another area around which partnership effectiveness and impact may be enhanced. In environmental partnerships, stakeholders enter into the collaborative process with necessarily less than complete information or knowledge regarding the issues of concern. By exposing these stakeholders to different people bearing different perspectives, partnerships create a dynamic context for environmental action. They provide occasions for critical self-reflection and, hence, opportunities for participants to perceive themselves, each other, and their respective interests in altered ways. They create possibilities for producing common ground from which solutions may be derived. They invite the generation of results that are different from what participants may have foreseen at the onset and that achieve more than what any one participant could accomplish alone. Finally, partnerships enable participants to develop a sense of collective identity with their fellow partners and a greater sense of ownership concerning the decisions made and the actions taken.

Simply acknowledging that these benefits exist, however, is not enough. Stakeholder processes need to be managed so as to promote them. Partnership organizers need to recognize that more participants will experience personal transformation and do so to a greater degree if the conditions for such change are favorable. In the case of multistakeholder environmental partnerships, the possibilities for personal transformation will increase in correlation to the number of different perspectives and interests represented and the amount of time that participants have to explore each other's positions. A smaller partnership that is on a short time frame and that comprises participants who are already of like minds and preoccupations will be less effective in stimulating such effects as double-loop learning, the production of innovative ideas, and the formation of altered identities.

In addition, as people need to *participate* in these partnerships to benefit from their transformative qualities, organizers need to be careful not to unnecessarily restrict the number of stakeholders who get to attend. This is particularly true with regard to first-time participants. A major constraint facing partnerships in this regard is the trend within modern bureaucratic organizations toward increasing levels of expertism. The result is that environmental groups, businesses, and governmental organizations will tend to send the same multistakeholder collaboration experts to all of their partnership activities. The problem is that this relegates the possibility for personal transformation to a limited group of participants who are themselves less likely than first-time partners to experience significant change.

These considerations translate into three main recommendations:

- First, partnership organizers interested in fostering personal transformations should strive to maximize rather than minimize representation of interests and perspectives in a multistakeholder partnership, balancing this, of course, against time, cost, and other procedural constraints. Decisions to limit the size of a partnership should be weighed against the long-term personal changes that may be induced by broader stakeholder participation.
- Second, organizers need to avoid assembling the same stakeholders for every new partnership initiative. This does not mean, however, that every partnership should seek to involve only first-time participants at the expense of those with significant expertise in collaborative processes. Rather, the best solution may be to strive for a mixture of actors that includes experienced partners who embody the model of good partnership behavior and who already enjoy strong relationships with other stakeholders as well as participants who are newer to the process and therefore more likely to experience change.
- Third, organizations must endeavor to provide sufficient time in the collaborative setting for participants to get to know, learn from, and create with each other. A truncated collaborative process will work against the development of personal transformations.

Seek Third-Party Facilitation

To pursue these suggestions requires a level of expertise that some partnership conveners, coordinators, and participants may not have. In these cases, it may be helpful to seek help in the form of third-party facilitation. Professional facilitators can provide assistance in a variety of manners.[49] First, they can play a crucial role in helping to make explicit the sociohistoric differences that exist among the participating stakeholders. Facilitators can encourage stakeholders to look beyond their own positions and interests to become more aware of some of the underlying beliefs and experiences that drive their actions and desires. Facilitators can also use their own awareness of the sociohistoric forces at play to help clear up misunderstandings or to work through conflicts stemming from these differences. Second, facilitators can assume the important task of encouraging good partnership behaviors, whether this includes respecting other people's perspectives, trusting one another, or operating in a nonconfrontational manner. They can do so by teaching participants how best to act in partnerships, by modeling this type of behavior, and by encouraging good partnership practices when they appear. Third, facilitators can help to manage conflict when it arises so as to avoid its destructive qualities and enhance its creative potential. Finally, facilitators can play the critical role of helping to foster personal transformations on the part of participating actors. They can assist participants in the recognition that change is not only acceptable but also beneficial. They can encourage mutual education, the need for innovation, and the exploration of new ways of seeing things, each other, and oneself. They can also make sure that partnerships remain safe spaces for such changes to occur, for example, by establishing ground rules requiring confidentiality.

Third-party facilitation alone will not produce successful partnership outcomes. It can be extremely helpful, however, in helping stakeholder participants to do so.

Evaluate Partnership Performance to Encourage Secondary Benefits

In the past, analyses evaluating the performance of multistakeholder environmental partnerships have been largely directed toward determining their effectiveness in achieving their original environmental objectives.[50] Partnerships have other secondary or indirect effects, however, that can also have a pronounced impact not only on short-term environmental decisions but also on the capacity for effective environmental action in the long run.[51] One such effect concerns the personal transformations that partnerships induce. These transformations can take the form of improved knowledge and understanding of the environmental issues at stake, better communication and more trust among stakeholders, the creation of innovative ideas, the production of interpersonal and interorganizational relationships, enhanced skills for operating in and advancing collaborative processes, increased levels of ownership of partnership outcomes, or a rise in the level of commitment by participants toward the betterment of society.

These types of personal transformations are not easy to evaluate in terms of their effects.[52] They are difficult to quantify in terms of costs and benefits, and their impact may be long term and extend beyond the partnership setting back to where the participants live and work. Nevertheless, they are important because they contribute to the capacity for future environmental problem solving.

To foster the potential benefits that derive from such incidental effects, partnership evaluations should be broadened to include them. Although not comprehensive, table 7.1 contains a list of potential topics, along with related questions, that provide a first step toward the development of a useful set of criteria for evaluating secondary, indirect partnership products.

Table 7.1. Potential Criteria for Evaluating Secondary Partnership Benefits

Criteria Topics	Associated Questions
Learning:	• Did the participants believe that they learned anything new in the partnership process? • What were the major things learned both regarding the environmental issues of concern and the other stakeholders involved? • Did this constitute single- or double-loop learning? • Did other participants share in this learning?
Conflict and conflict management:	• What conflicts arose or emerged during the collaborative process? • To what extent were participants able to work through these conflicts to reach agreement? • What made this possible (or not)?
Innovation:	• What innovative ideas or decisions were produced by the partnership that constitute a marked shift from how environmental concerns have been addressed in the past?
Social relations and collaborative capacities:	• What novel institutional capacities (new professional networks, new social relations, and new aptitudes for cooperative action) were generated that might improve the efficacy of future efforts (collaborative or otherwise) at environmental problem solving?
Identity formation:	• What level of collective identity was achieved that indicates the degree of ownership and responsibility for the decisions made and the actions taken? • What other individual-level forms of identity were induced, and how might these affect future environmental conflicts and problem solving?
Partnership process (to encourage secondary benefits):	• To what degree was the partnership organized and operated to facilitate the above types of transformations?

Maintain Realistic Expectations

A final message to be drawn from this prescriptively oriented section regards the necessity of maintaining realistic expectations for what multistakeholder environmental partnerships can and cannot accomplish. The biggest threat to these processes may come not from efforts to subvert or co-opt them but from failed outcomes resulting from their misapplication. Multistakeholder partnerships are better suited for certain problems than for others. Consequently, producing successful outcomes will depend not only on the efforts of the participants but also on the wisdom of the decisions to initiate the partnership in the first place. Partnership conveners and participants alike should expect from these processes only what they can reasonably achieve.

Possible Futures: Multistakeholder Partnerships in a Changing World

In this book, I have presented a portrait of multistakeholder environmental partnerships that stems from the analysis of a small set of case studies operating in Europe and the United States in the middle and late 1990s. As we move into the twenty-first century, the role, characteristics, and potential of these types of partnerships may well change. Imagining what forms these changes might take is the topic of this final section.

Changing Contexts

There are a variety of contextual factors likely to contribute to the evolution of multistakeholder environmental partnerships. One such factor involves the state of the natural environment. It is a given that local, regional, and global environmental conditions will change in the future. Some will improve, while others will get worse. The form of these environmental changes (i.e., whether they are beneficial or detrimental) and the extent to which they occur may cause people to reevaluate their interests in environmental issues, alter the degree to which they choose to engage, and revise their support for or opposition to collaborative approaches to environmental problem solving. This will affect the degree to which multistakeholder environmental partnerships are called upon to meet these challenges. Moreover, new or previously unrecognized problems might also arise. The environmental partnerships of the future will no doubt alter their foci to address these new issues.

A second potential factor concerns changes to the broader political-economic contexts defining Western societies. Capitalism, as it has done in the past, will continue to evolve over time. The degree to which neoliberal tendencies continue to prevail in the capitalist structures of the future will affect the support that voluntary, collaborative environmental policy instruments will receive.

Shifting power relations among society's diverse stakeholders constitutes a third possible factor leading to change. The inclusion of stakeholders in partnerships, their willingness to participate, and their ability to affect partnership outcomes will depend upon the credibility, legitimacy, and prestige that they will be able to harness relative to other stakeholders in the future. It remains to be seen if the corporate sector will be able to uphold its recent gains in the environmental policy domain or whether past deregulatory trends will continue to erode the authority of governmental agencies or the environmental community's capacity to wield influence.

A fourth potential source of change involves the ongoing evolution of environmentalism. Historically, the environmental movement in the industrialized West can be viewed as a series of broad, overlapping waves.[53] The first wave commenced around the turn of the twentieth century and ushered in an era of land and wildlife conservation. The essence of this wave was rational planning by governments to promote efficient development and use of natural resources.[54] The second wave arrived in the 1960s and, as discussed in chapter 2, was marked by the production of landmark legislation prohibiting or limiting the pollution of air, land, or water. The pivotal players in the second wave were large national- and international-level environmental groups that not only lobbied government and the business community on behalf of environmental causes but also pursued more contentious protest and legal actions against these actors. The Greenpeace Brent Spar campaign nicely exemplifies this type of environmentalist action. The third wave of environmentalism emerged in the 1980s and has been gathering momentum ever since. It arose out of the backlash that developed against some of the regulatory successes that had been achieved in the second wave. It was founded on the idea that the environment may best be protected by pursuing voluntary, market-based incentives rather than command-and-control-type regulations and by having the parties with a stake in these issues work things out collaboratively rather than in an adversarial fashion. The Quincy Library Group partnership and the four case studies examined in this book are distinctly third wave forms of environmental action.

What the environmental movement will look like in the future, however, remains uncertain. Some scholars argue that the beginnings of a fourth wave have already taken root.[55] This wave, due in large part to the enormous diversity of organizations, ideologies, and issues that compose it, has no single or unique defining quality. As Mark Dowie describes it, "It is part wilderness preservation, part toxic abatement, part ecological economics, part civil rights, part human rights, part secular, part religious, and parts of many ecologies."[56] It is, nonetheless, a reaction to the other waves in that it views the progress produced by these other strands of environmentalism to be too exclusive, too slow, and too accommodating. The fourth wave is more multiracial, multiethnic, multiclass, multicultural, and more committed to democratic process than its predecessors. It is also more militant and energized at the grass-roots level. Examples of fourth wave activists include environmental justice-oriented organizations addressing the needs of people of color, the burgeoning number of NIMBY-based organizations galvanized by local environmental concerns, and the many splinter groups that have been forming in reaction to perceived complacency within the mainstream environmental movement.

The arrival of such a wave has several possible implications for environmental partnerships. As noted above, it may broaden the definition of who is to be regarded as a legitimate stakeholder. It may also influence the types of issues deemed worthy of consideration. In addition, it may alter people's views of whether multistakeholder collaborative processes constitute an appropriate response for dealing with contemporary environmental problems. Successful partnership attention to fourth wave issues may lead to increased environmental community support for multistakeholder collaboration. Failure in this regard, however, might also lead the environmental community to abandon partnership efforts, thus serving to delegitimize collaborative processes more broadly.

A final factor that may contribute significantly to the evolution of multistakeholder environmental partnerships and their effects concerns changes to the individuals who initiate and populate such initiatives. This includes changes to the sociohistoric characteristics distinguishing these individuals. As people are faced with new sets of constraints in their daily lives, they will alter their actions accordingly. And as people start acting differently in the world and undergoing new experiences, the meaning systems, expectations, and other sociohistoric features that have guided their behaviors in the past will often change as well. Evolving environmental, political, economic, or social constraints, for instance, may lead people to change the way that they respond to environmental issues. This, then, may lead some individuals to modify their understandings of the natural environment and the key issues facing it. Such changes are important for partnerships because they lead to new *sociohistoric differences* among participating stakeholders. These new sociohistoric differences have the capacity to affect stakeholder communications, interactions, and relations and, consequently, the agreements and decisions that these partnerships might produce.

Let us ground this point by exploring possible changes to a particular sociohistoric feature. Consider the example of the discourse of ecological modernization.[57] As described earlier, this discourse presumes the existence of win-win solutions and promotes the goal of sustainable development. What is particular about the discourse of ecological modernization, however, is that these "wins" are largely being limited to the economic and ecological spheres. Consequently, in the discourse of ecological modernization, sustainable development is mainly interpreted along economic-environmental lines.

With the rise of the fourth wave of environmentalism, ecological modernization may increasingly be confronted by competing discourses demanding that issues of social equity and justice be better incorporated into efforts to achieve economic and ecological sustainability.[58] This is precisely what happened during the buildup to the 2002 World Summit on Sustainable Development. Here, great attention was placed on the disparity between rich and poor nations and on the right of the disadvantaged countries of the "south" to eradicate poverty and become more developed.[59]

Ecological modernization is notable as a discourse for its ability to appropriate key ideas from environmentalism.[60] The possibility thus exists that proponents of ecological modernization may end up broadening the discourse to incorporate this emphasis on social equity. This appropriation would have the effect of bolstering the stature of ecological modernization vis-à-vis fourth wave discourses while at the same time ensuring the retention of sustainable development as one of ecological modernization's key concepts. The result would be a new version of ecological modernization that might lead its users to expand their conception of environmental problems to include a greater social dimension. At the same time, it might also result in a partial deradicalization of the notion of social equity. Making the concept more palatable to people who had formerly resisted it might diminish its meaning for those fourth wave groups that were promoting the idea in the first place.

On the Nexus between Conflict and Cooperation

I mention these possible changes not as an attempt to predict the future but as a way of demonstrating the great diversity of changes that may lie ahead. Regardless of what these changes might be, it is a good bet that the prevailing paths for addressing tomorrow's environmental problems will remain unchanged. One will be the path of conflict; the other will be the path of cooperation. Both of these modes of action have their advantages and disadvantages, and many of these have been highlighted in these pages. It is unlikely, however, that either mode alone will be sufficient for resolving the environmental dilemmas facing contemporary industrial societies. It is rather the dynamic tension between the two that may spark the necessary responses. Multistakeholder environmental partnerships—as creative, informative, and personally transformative processes in which this relationship between conflict and cooperation gets played out—will likely play a key role in these efforts.

Notes

1. United Nations (2002a).
2. My view of environmental governance involves the collective actions of not only governmental bodies but of the business community, NGOs, and citizens groups as well.
3. Baba (1988).
4. Bingham (1986), Blackburn and Bruce (1995), Brown et al. (1995), Daniels and Walker (2001), Dukes (1996), Dukes et al. (2000), Glasbergen (1995b), Gray (1989),

Gulliver (1979), Ross (1993a, 1993b), Susskind and Cruikshank (1987), Winslade and Monk (2000).

5. Following cultural anthropological conventions, I use pseudonyms for the partnerships, organizations, and individuals discussed in this analysis. See discussion at the beginning of chapter 3.

6. Hajer (1995, 30). See also Blowers (1998) and Dryzek (1997).

7. Although this research on multistakeholder environmental partnerships was never meant to be rigorously comparative, I can say that all four of the case studies showed many more similarities than they did differences. This was apparent, for instance, in some of the discourses—such as those of ecological modernization, administrative rationality, and green radicalism—that tended to predominate in all of the cases studies.

8. Stake (1994).

9. This should be a very interesting and potentially fertile area for future research on this topic.

10. An additional potential weakness arises from the interpretive basis of my approach. This ties in to a more general debate over the legitimacy of interpretive science, however, and is thus beyond the scope of this particular exposition. See Poncelet (1998) for more discussion on this point.

11. See also Ross (1993a) on this point.

12. See also Ross (1993a) on this point.

13. De Bruijn and Tukker (2002), Hartman et al. (1999).

14. Many other scholars of dispute resolution have made this same argument. See, for instance, Daniels and Walker (2001), Dukes (1996), Kriesberg (1998), and Maser (1996).

15. Fisher (1983).

16. See also Bush and Folger (1994), Dukes (1996), Dukes et al. (2000), Gulliver (1979), Ross (1993a, 1993b), and Winslade and Monk (2000) on this point.

17. See also Amy (1987, 1990), Dukes (2001), McKinney (1988), Nader (1996), Smith (1993), and Varela (2000) on this point.

18. See also Blowers (1998) on this point.

19. J. O'Connor (1994).

20. See, for example, Collier (1998a), Eckersley (1995b), and Polanyi (1957).

21. See, for example, Buttel (1998), Cahn (1995), M. O'Connor (1994), Schnaiberg and Gould (1994), and Sweezy and Magdoff (1989).

22. The term "hegemonic" refers to the culturally based means by which an established order can maintain power in society (Gramsci 1971, 56ff). This is as opposed to the more visible apparatus of state coercion.

23. Levy (1997) makes a similar argument with regard to the process of environmental management.

24. Amy (1987, 1990), McCloskey (1996).

25. My argument here parallels Nader's (1995, 1996) observation that powerful political and economic actors in society are fostering a "harmony ideology" that has the effect of producing a "civilized" citizenry that is more willing to negotiate than to fight. Nader (1990, 2) defines "harmony ideology" as comprising "an emphasis on conciliation, recognition that resolution of conflict is inherently good and that its reverse—continued conflict or controversy—is bad or dysfunctional, a view of harmonious behavior as more civilized than disputing behavior, [and] the belief that consensus is of greater survival value than controversy."

26. See, for example, Harvey (1996) and Buttel (1992).

27. See also Hartman et al. (1999) on this point.

28. Christoff (1996), Dryzek (1995) and Hajer (1995) make similar arguments.

29. Holland and Lave (2001).

30. See Driessen (1998) on this point.

31. See Cardskadden and Lober (1998), Clutterbuck (1981), McIntosh et al. (1998), and Post et al. (1999) for more on the growing efforts by corporations to manage a broader range of stakeholders.

32. Stafford and Hartman (1996).

33. Cardskadden and Lober (1998), Hart (1997), Hartman and Stafford (1997), Hartman et al. (1999).

34. Guldbrandsen and Holland (2001) describe corporations as "super-citizens" in this respect.

35. For more on the burgeoning topic of corporate citizenship, see Kulik (1999), McIntosh et al. (1998), Rondinelli and Berry (2000), and Tichy et al. (1997).

36. Rowell (1996); see also Levy (1997).

37. Amy (1987), Ernste (1998), Nader (1995).

38. This increased sharing of power does not mean that governmental actors must compromise their constitutionally given authority and responsibility to govern.

39. Eurobarometer (1995) data, for instance, shows 62 percent of the EU public as finding environmental groups to be credible actors in the environmental arena as compared to 13 percent for public authorities and 2 percent for industry. In the United States, recent Gallop Poll data (Dunlap 2000) shows around 75 percent of Americans to have either a great deal or a moderate amount of trust that national and local environmental organizations will adequately protect the environment. This trust level decreased to 72 percent for federal and state agencies, 59 percent for local environmental agencies, 48 percent for small businesses, and 37 percent for large corporations.

40. Nader (1995).

41. See Harvey (1996) on this point.

42. See Blowers (1998) for a more detailed description of some of the environmental problems for which ecological modernization is less well suited.

43. Andrews (1998), Biekart (1998), Starkey (1998).

44. In this book, I limit my discussion of success factors to those that derive directly from the findings presented. A broader analysis would no doubt include other suggestions for improving partnership performance, such as making sure that all pertinent interests are adequately represented, that these stakeholders have been included from the beginning, and that leadership qualities are present. For other writings on the topic of multistakeholder collaboration success factors, see, for instance, De Bruijn and Tukker (2002), Gray (1989), Long and Arnold (1995), Sagawa and Segal (2000), Susskind and Cruikshank (1987) and Wondolleck and Yaffee (2000).

45. Ross (1993a).

46. See also Littlejohn and Domenici (2001) regarding the importance of self-awareness in collaborative dispute resolution processes.

47. See also Daniels and Walker (2001) on this point.

48. Dukes (1996), Winslade and Monk (2000).

49. For more on the potential benefits of professional facilitation, see Bush and Folger (1994), Kaner (1996), Maser (1996), and Maser et al. (1998).

50. Innes (1999). For an example of this type of evaluation, see Yosie and Herbst

(1998).

51. Long and Arnold (1995) refer to these as the "soft" components of evaluation. See also Innes (1999) and Stern and Hicks (2000) on this point.

52. Innes (1999).

53. Dowie (1995), Dalton (1994).

54. Costain and Lester (1995).

55. Dowie (1995), Gottlieb (1993); see also Guha and Martinez-Alier (1997), Martinez-Alier (2002).

56. Dowie (1995, 207).

57. See also Blowers (1998) and Harvey (1996) on the possibility of change to ecological modernization.

58. I am not arguing here that the concept of sustainable development lacks a notion of social equity. Indeed, social equity has been an integral component of sustainable development since the term's introduction in *Our Common Future* published by the World Commission on Environment and Development (1987). Rather, my point is that social equity has not been an important facet of the discourse of ecological modernization.

59. European Commission (2001b), Martinez-Alier (2002), United Nations (2002b).

60. Harvey (1996).

Appendix A

Supplementary Methodological Information

Environmental Partnership Selection Criteria

To be selected as a case study, potential partnerships had to satisfy the following criteria. They all had to meet the definition of multistakeholder environmental partnerships presented in chapter 1. They all had to operate actively with regularly scheduled meetings throughout the one- or two-year research periods. Finally, they all had to proceed in either English or French, languages in which I am fluent.

Forms of Data

The data collected took the following main forms: field notes from partnership meetings and other related events attended, audiotapes and notes from interviews performed, and written materials produced by the partnerships and by the partner organizations themselves. Four principal types of information inferred from the data collected serve as the basis for my analysis of environmental partnership processes. These include pertinent cultural models of both the partnership process and the environmental problems at issue; prominent discourses and the extent to which they are privileged; key meaning systems, practices, group processes, and notions of identity produced; and the relative position of power and influence of each participant individual and/or organization within the environmental domain. The cultural models and discourses were inferred via the discourse-analytic technique of focusing on key metaphors, terms, repetitions, generalizations, and evaluative statements.[1] My basic strategy for moving from the data to the above items was that typically used with ethnographic materials:

analytic induction—a strategy in which causal explanations for phenomena are continually reformulated as new data are obtained and analyzed.[2] In pursuing an inductive approach, my intent was to allow the data collected, rather than the theoretical concepts also informing the study, to drive the analysis.

Interview Selection Criteria and Design

The interviews were strategically selected so as to adequately represent the three major sectors involved, the variation in size of the participating organizations, and the range of level of participation in the partnerships. An average of twenty-five taped interviews lasting approximately ninety minutes apiece was conducted for each partnership. The interviews were open-ended and designed so as to elicit naturally occurring speech on a range of topics, including personal and organizational background, stakeholder processes in general, and the case-study partnership in specific. Refer to appendix B for the interview protocol that was used to guide these discussions.

Notes

1. Price (1987), Quinn and Holland (1987).
2. Denzin (1989), Glaser and Strauss (1967).

Appendix B

Interview Questions

Standard Interview Questions Modified
for Each of the Case-study Partnerships

A. Personal and Organizational Information
   1. Description of your organization
       a. What is the name of your organization? Where is it located? What is its history? What is your position in the organization? Where are you stationed?
       b. What is the function, and what are the overall goals of your organization?
       c. What are your and/or your organization's environmental interests/goals? How important are these relative to other priorities?
       d. Is your organization considered to be a major player in the environmental arena? Who are the other major players?
   2. Personal work history.
   3. What nationality are you? How has this influenced your environmental interests?

B. Partnership/Collaborative Action
   1. Have you been involved in any partnerships in the past? How successful have these been?
   2. How important is participating in partnerships for your organization?
   3. What does "partnership" mean to you and/or to your organization?
   4. What are the advantages and disadvantages of the partnership process?
   5. What does participating in partnerships bring you personally?

    6.   Should all of the participants in the partnership process be equal?

C.   The Particular Case-study Partnership
    1.   What are your activities and responsibilities in the partnership?
    2.   How did you become involved in the partnership, and why did you choose to participate?
    3.   What do you see as the goal or purpose of the partnership?
    4.   The issue:
        a.   What are the problems to which the partnership is responding?
        b.   What is at stake for your organization and your sector regarding the partnership and the environmental issues it encompasses?
        c.   What is at stake for the other sectors?
    5.   Discuss some of the key terms being used in the partnership (e.g., sustainable development, biodiversity, stewardship). Why have these become a focus for the partnership?
    6.   In your opinion, what should be the result of the partnership?
    7.   What are the benefits of the partnership? How does it benefit you personally? Your organization? Your sector? The other sectors? Society? The environment?
    8.   In your opinion, what must be done to ensure the success of the partnership?

D.   Feedback on Partnership Action to Date
    1.   What are your reactions to the partnership's activities/actions to date?
    2.   In theory, who should be the most important participants in the partnership, and, in actuality, which partners are playing the most important roles?
    3.   Do you believe that you and/or your organization's views and interests are understood by the other participants?

E.   Organizational Documents
    1.   Could I get copies of documents produced by your organization regarding the partnership and/or environmental affairs/issues in general?

Appendix C

Quotation System

My strategy for quoting is as follows. Each interview quotation is followed by a code consisting of a series of letters followed by two numbers separated by periods. The letters indicate the partnership from which the quote was taken. The first number refers to where the interview falls into the chronological sequence of interviews conducted. The final number indicates the page number from my interview notes upon which the quotation may be found. Therefore, the code GBP.11.7 indicates a quote coming from page 7 of the eleventh interview conducted for the GBP partnership. This coding was developed to help protect the identities of the participants.

All of the interview quotations from the GBP and TRC partnerships, as well as some of those from the EUPEC initiative, are my own translations from French. I have attempted to translate as literally as possible. To enhance the readability of quotations from all four of the case studies, I have taken the liberty to compensate for incorrect grammar, partial sentences, and idiomatic language when necessary. Interpolations are enclosed in brackets and have been added both for clarification and again to conceal the identity of particular organizations or individuals.

Bibliography

Abbott, Alison. 1996. "Brent Spar: When Science Is Not to Blame." *Nature* 380, no. 6569: 13-14.

Abelson, Robert P. 1996. "The Secret Existence of Expressive Behavior." Pp. 25-36 in *The Rational Choice Controversy: Economic Models of Politics Revisited*, edited by J. Friedman. New Haven, CT: Yale University Press.

Achterberg, Wouter. 1996. "Sustainability and Associative Democracy." Pp. 157-174 in *Democracy and the Environment: Problems and Prospects*, edited by W. Lafferty and J. Meadowcroft. Brookfield, VT: Edward Elgar Publishing Company.

Almond, Gabriel A., and Sidney Verba. 1963. *Civic Culture: Political Attitudes and Democracy in Five Nations*. Princeton, NJ: Princeton University Press.

American Heritage Dictionary. 1997. *The American Heritage Dictionary of the English Language*. Boston, MA: Houghton Mifflin Company.

Amin, Ash, ed. 1994. *Post-Fordism: A Reader*. Oxford: Blackwell Publishers.

Amy, Douglas J. 1987. *The Politics of Environmental Mediation*. New York: Columbia University Press.

———. 1990. "Environmental Dispute Resolution: The Promise and the Pitfalls." Pp. 211-234 in *Environmental Policy in the 1990s: Toward a New Agenda*, edited by N. Vig and M. Kraft. Washington, DC: Congressional Quarterly, Inc.

Anderson, Terry L., ed. 1997. *Breaking the Environmental Policy Gridlock*. Stanford, CA: Hoover Institution Press.

Anderson, Terry L., and Donald R. Leal. 1991. *Market Environmentalism*. San Francisco, CA: Pacific Institute for Public Policy.

Andrews, Richard N. L. 1998. "Environmental Regulation and Business 'Self-Regulation.'" *Policy Sciences* 31: 177-197.

———. 1999. *Managing the Environment, Managing Ourselves: A History of American Environmental Policy*. New Haven, CT: Yale University Press.

Argyris, Chris, and Donald A. Schön. 1996. *Organizational Learning II: Theory, Method, and Practice*. Reading, MA: Addison-Wesley Publishing Company.

Arrow, Holly, Joseph E. McGrath, and Jennifer L. Berdahl. 2000. *Small Groups as Complex Systems: Formation, Coordination, Development, and Adaptation.* Thousand Oaks, CA: Sage Publications.

Atkinson, Paul, and Martyn Hammersley. 1994. "Ethnography and Participant Observation." Pp. 248-261 in *Handbook of Qualitative Research*, edited by N. Denzin and Y. Lincoln. Thousand Oaks, CA: Sage Publications.

Axelrod, Robert. 1984. *The Evolution of Cooperation.* New York: Basic Books, Inc.

Baba, Marietta L. 1988. "Two Sides to Every Story: An Ethnohistorical Approach to Organizational Partnerships." *City and Society* 2, no. 2: 71-104.

Bacow, Lawrence S., and Michael Wheeler. 1984. *Dispute Resolution.* New York: Plenum Press.

Baker, Susan. 1996. "Environmental Policy in the European Union: Institutional Dilemmas and Democratic Practice." Pp. 213-233 in *Democracy and the Environment: Problems and Prospects*, edited by W. Lafferty and J. Meadowcroft. Brookfield, VT: Edward Elgar Publishing Company.

Baker, Susan, Maria Kousis, Kick Richardson, and Stephan Young. 1997. "The Theory and Practice of Sustainable Development in EU Perspective." Pp. 1-40 in *The Politics of Sustainable Development: Theory, Policy and Practice within the European Union*, edited by S. Baker, M. Kousis, D. Richardson, and S. Young. London: Routledge.

Bakhtin, Mikhail M. 1981. *The Dialogic Imagination: Four Essays by M. M. Bakhtin*, edited by Michael Holquist, translated by Caryl Emerson and Michael Holquist. Austin: University of Texas Press.

Baron, David P. 2000. *Business and Its Environment.* 3rd ed. Upper Saddle River, NJ: Prentice Hall.

Bennie, Lynn G. 1998. "Brent Spar, Atlantic Oil, and Greenpeace." *Parliamentary Affairs* 51, no. 3 (July): 397(14).

Bennett, John W. 1990. "Ecosystems, Environmentalism, Resource Conservation, and Anthropological Research." Pp. 435-457 in *The Ecosystem Approach in Anthropology: From Concept to Practice*, edited by E. Moran. Ann Arbor: The University of Michigan Press.

Benson, Christina C. 1996. "The ISO 14000 International Standards: Moving beyond Environmental Compliance." *North Carolina Journal of International Law & Commercial Regulation* 22, no. 1: 306-364.

Berger, Peter, and Thomas Luckmann. 1967. *The Social Construction of Reality.* Harmondsworth: Penguin.

Berry, Michael A., and Dennis A. Rondinelli. 1998. "Proactive Corporate Environmental Management: A New Industrial Revolution." *Academy of Management Executive* 12, no. 2: 38-50.

Biekart, Jan Willem. 1998. "Negotiated Agreements in EU Environmental Policy." Pp. 165-189 in *New Instruments for Environmental Policy in the EU*, edited by J. Golub. London: Routledge.

Bingham, Gail. 1986. *Resolving Environmental Disputes: A Decade of Experience.* Washington, DC: The Conservation Foundation.

Blackburn, J. Walton, and Willa M. Bruce, eds. 1995. *Mediating Environmental Conflicts: Theory and Practice.* Westport, CT: Quorum Books.

Blackstock, Michael D. 2001. "Where Is the Trust: Using Trust-Based Mediation for First Nations Dispute Resolution." *Conflict Resolution Quarterly* 19, no. 1: 9-30.

Blowers, Andrew. 1998. "Power, Participation and Partnership: The Limits of Co-operative Environmental Management." Pp. 229-250 in *Co-operative Environmental*

Governance: Public-Private Agreements as a Policy Strategy, edited by P. Glasbergen. Dordrecht, The Netherlands: Kluwer Academic Publishers.

Bolton, Gary E., and Kalyan Chatterjee. 1996. "Coalition Formation, Communication, and Coordination: An Exploratory Experiment." Pp. 253-271 in *Wise Choices: Decisions, Games, and Negotiations*, edited by R. Zeckhauser, R. Keeney, and J. Sebenius. Boston, MA: Harvard Business School Press.

Borrini-Feyerabend, Grazia. 1999. "Collaborative Management of Protected Areas." Pp. 224-234 in *Partnerships for Protection: New Strategies for Planning and Management for Protected Areas*, edited by S. Stolton and N. Dudley. London: Earthscan Publications Ltd.

Bourdieu, Pierre. 1977. *Outline of a Theory of Practice*. Cambridge: Cambridge University Press.

———. 1982. "The Economics of Linguistic Exchanges." *Social Science Information*, no. 16: 645-668.

———. 1983. "The Field of Cultural Production, or: The Economic World Reversed." *Poetics* 12: 311-356.

———. 1985. "The Genesis of the Concepts of 'Habitus' and 'Field.'" *Sociocriticism* 2, no. 2: 11-24.

———. 1986. "The Forms of Capital." Pp. 241-258 in *Handbook of Theory and Research for the Sociology of Education*, edited by J. G. Richardson. New York: Greenwood Press.

———. 1990. *The Logic of Practice*. Stanford, CA: Stanford University Press.

Bourdieu, Pierre, and Loic J. D. Wacquant. 1992. *An Invitation to Reflexive Sociology*. Oxford: Polity Press.

Brewer, Marilynn B., and Wendi Gardner. 1996. "'Who Is This 'We'? Levels of Collective Identity and Self Representations.'" *Journal of Personality and Social Psychology* 71, no. 1: 83-93.

Brick, Philip, Donald Snow, and Sarah van de Wetering, eds. 2001. *Across the Great Divide: Explorations in Collaborative Conservation and the American West*. Washington, DC: Island Press.

Britan, Gerald M., and Ronald Cohen. 1980. "Toward an Anthropology of Formal Organization." Pp. 9-30 in *Hierarchy and Society: Anthropological Perspectives on Bureaucracy*, edited by G. Britan and R. Cohen. Philadelphia: Institute for the Study of Human Issues.

Brosius, J. Peter. 1999a. "Green Dots, Pink Hearts: Displacing Politics from the Malaysian Rain Forest." *American Anthropologist* 101, no. 1: 36-57.

———. 1999b. "Analyses and Interventions: Anthropological Engagements with Environmentalism." *Current Anthropology* 40: 277-309.

Brown, Valerie A. 1995. "Managing Environmental Conflicts." Pp. 13-72 in *Risks and Opportunities: Managing Environmental Conflict and Change*, edited by V. Brown, D. Smith, R. Wiseman, and J. Handmer. London: Earthscan Publications Ltd.

Brown, Valerie A., David I. Smith, Rob Wiseman, and John Handmer, eds. 1995. *Risks and Opportunities: Managing Environmental Conflict and Change*. London: Earthscan Publications Ltd.

Bruner, Jerome. 1990. *Acts of Meaning*. Cambridge, MA: Harvard University Press.

Buchholz, Rogene A. 1998. *Principles of Environmental Management: The Greening of Business*. 2nd ed. Upper Saddle River, NJ: Prentice Hall.

Bush, Robert A. B., and Joseph P. Folger. 1994. *The Promise of Mediation: Responding to Conflict through Empowerment and Recognition*. San Francisco, CA: Jossey-Bass.

Butt Philip, Alan. 1995. "David versus Goliath? The Challenge for Environmentalists in the Making and the Implementation of EU Environmental Policy." Paper presented at the European Community Studies Association Biennial International Conference, Charleston, South Carolina, May 1995.

Butt Philip, Alan, and Martin Porter. 1997. "Business Alliance, Network Construction and Agenda Definition: Recent Development in Lobbying Activities in Brussels and Strasbourg." Paper presented at the Fifth Biennial International Conference of the European Community Studies Association, Seattle, WA, May-June 1997.

Buttel, Frederick H. 1992. "Environmentalization: Origins, Processes, and Implications for Rural Social Change." *Rural Sociology* 57, no. 1: 1-27.

———. 1998. "Some Observations on States, World Orders, and the Politics of Sustainability." *Organization & Environment* 11, no. 3: 261-286.

Cahn, Matthew Alan. 1995. *Environmental Deceptions: The Tension between Liberalism and Environmental Policymaking in the United States.* Albany, NY: State University of New York Press.

Calhoun, Craig. 1992. "Habermas and the Public Sphere." Pp. 1-48 in *Habermas and the Public Sphere,* edited by C. Calhoun. Cambridge, MA: The MIT Press.

Callicott, J. Baird. 1994. *Earth's Insights: A Multicultural Survey of Ecological Ethics from the Mediterranean Basin to the Australian Outback.* Berkeley: University of California Press.

Cardskadden, H., and Douglas J. Lober. 1998. "Environmental Stakeholder Management as Business Strategy: The Case of the Corporate Wildlife Habitat Enhancement Programme." *Journal of Environmental Management* 52: 183-202.

Carr, Deborah S., Steven W. Selin, and Michael A. Schuett. 1998. "Managing Public Forests: Understanding the Role of Collaborative Planning." *Environmental Management* 22, no. 5: 767-776.

Chia, Ho-Beng, Chee-Leaon Chong, Joo-Eng Lee-Partridge, Chantel Chu Shi Hwee, and Sharon Franciesca Kow Wei-Fei. 2001. "Enacting and Reproducing Social and Individual Identity through Mediation." *Conflict Resolution Quarterly* 19, no. 1: 49-74.

Christoff, Peter. 1996. "Ecological Modernisation, Ecological Modernities." *Environmental Politics* 5, no. 3: 476-500.

Clery, Daniel. 1996. "Science Intrudes on Brent Spar Saga." *Science* 272, no. 5266: 1,258-1,259.

Clutterbuck, David. 1981. *How to Be a Good Corporate Citizen: A Manager's Guide to Making Social Responsibility Work—and Pay.* London: McGraw-Hill Book Company Limited.

Cobb, Sara. 1993. "Empowerment and Mediation: A Narrative Perspective." *Negotiation Journal* 9, no. 3: 245-255.

Coen, David. 1997. "The Evolution of the Large Firm as a Political Actor in the European Union." *Journal of European Public Policy* 4, no. 1: 91-108.

Coenen, Frans H. J. M., Dave Huitema, and Laurence J. O'Toole Jr., eds. 1998. *Participation and the Quality of Environmental Decision Making.* Dordrecht, The Netherlands: Kluwer Academic Publishers.

Collier, Ute. 1998a. "The Environmental Dimensions of Deregulation: An Introduction." Pp. 3-22 in *Deregulation in the European Union: Environmental Perspectives,* edited by U. Collier. New York and London: Routledge.

———, ed. 1998b. *Deregulation in the European Union: Environmental Perspectives.* New York and London: Routledge.

Conley, Alex. 2001. "Selected Resources in Collaborative Conservation." Pp. 251-264 in *Across the Great Divide: Explorations in Collaborative Conservation and the American West*, edited by P. Brick et al. Washington, DC: Island Press.

Costain, W. Douglas, and James P. Lester. 1995. "The Evolution of Environmentalism." Pp. 15-38 in *Environmental Politics and Policy: Theories and Evidence*, edited by J. Lester. Durham, NC: Duke University Press.

Costanza, Robert. 1989. "What Is Ecological Economics?" *Ecological Economics* 1: 1-7.

Cowles, Maria Green. 1995. "The 'Business' of Agenda-Setting in the European Union." Paper presented at the European Community Studies Association Biennial International Conference, Charleston, SC, May 1995.

Crowfoot, James E., and Julia M. Wondolleck. 1990a. "Environmental Dispute Settlement." Pp. 17-31 in *Environmental Disputes: Community Involvement in Conflict Resolution*, edited by J. Crowfoot and J. Wondolleck. Washington, DC: Island Press.

———, eds. 1990b. *Environmental Disputes: Community Involvement in Conflict Resolution*. Washington, DC: Island Press.

———. 1990c. "Citizen Organizations and Environmental Conflict." Pp. 1-16 in *Environmental Disputes: Community Involvement in Conflict Resolution*, edited by J. Crowfoot and J. Wondolleck. Washington, DC: Island Press.

Crumley, Carole L., ed. 2001. *New Directions in Anthropology and Environment: Intersections*. Walnut Creek, CA: AltaMira Press.

Culbertson, Katherine. 1995. "Greenpeace Admits Goof on Brent Spar, Still Opposes Original Plan for Disposal." *The Oil Daily* 45, no. 170 (September 6): 3-4.

Curtis, Allan. 1998. "Agency-Community Partnership in Landcare: Lessons for State-Sponsored Citizen Resource Management." *Environmental Management* 22, no. 4: 563-574.

Dalton, Russell J. 1993. "The Environmental Movement in Western Europe." Pp. 41-68 in *Environmental Politics in the International Arena: Movements, Parties, Organizations, and Policy*, edited by S. Kamieniecki. Albany: State University of New York Press.

———. 1994. *The Green Rainbow: Environmental Groups in Western Europe*. New Haven, CT: Yale University Press.

Daniels, Steven E., and Gregg B. Walker. 2001. *Working through Environmental Conflict: The Collaborative Learning Approach*. Westport, CT: Praeger Publishers.

De Bruijn, Theo J. N. M., and Arnold Tukker, eds. 2002. *Partnership and Leadership: Building Alliances for a Sustainable Future*. Dordrecht, The Netherlands: Kluwer Academic Publishers.

De Jongh, Paul E., and Sean Captain. 1999. *Our Common Journey: A Pioneering Approach to Cooperative Environmental Management*. London: Zed Books.

Dente, Bruno. 1995. "The Globalization of Environmental Policy and the Search for New Instruments." Pp. 1-20 in *Environmental Policy in Search of New Instruments*, edited by B. Dente. Dordrecht, The Netherlands: Kluwer Academic Publishers.

Denzin, Norman K. 1989. *The Research Act: A Theoretical Introduction to Sociological Methods*. 3rd ed. Englewood Cliffs, NJ: Prentice Hall.

Dowie, Mark. 1995. *Losing Ground: American Environmentalism at the Close of the Twentieth Century*. Cambridge, MA: The MIT Press.

Driessen, Peter. 1998. "The Scope of Co-operative Management." Pp. 251-267 in *Co-operative Environmental Governance: Public-Private Agreements as a Policy Strategy*, edited by P. Glasbergen. Dordrecht, The Netherlands: Kluwer Academic Publishers.

Dryzek, John S. 1992. "Ecology and Discursive Democracy: Beyond Liberal Capitalism and the Administrative State." *Capitalism, Nature, Socialism* 3, no. 2: 18-42.
———. 1995. "Democracy and Environmental Policy Instruments." Pp. 294-303 in *Markets, the State, and the Environment: Towards Integration*, edited by R. Eckersley. Melbourne: MacMillan Education Australia Pty Ltd.
———. 1996. "Strategies of Ecological Democratization." Pp. 108-123 in *Democracy and the Environment: Problems and Prospects*, edited by W. Lafferty and J. Meadowcroft. Brookfield, VT: Edward Elgar Publishing Company.
———. 1997. *The Politics of the Earth: Environmental Discourses.* Oxford: Oxford University Press.
Dukes, E. Franklin. 1996. *Resolving Public Conflict: Transforming Community and Governance.* Manchester: Manchester University Press.
———. 2001. "Integration in Environmental Conflict." *Conflict Resolution Quarterly* 19, no. 1: 103-115.
Dukes, E. Franklin, Marina A. Piscolish, and John B. Stephens. 2000. *Reaching for Higher Ground in Conflict Resolution: Tools for Powerful Groups and Communities.* San Francisco, CA: Jossey-Bass, Inc.
Dunlap, Riley E. 2000. "Americans Have Positive Image of the Environmental Movement: Majorities Agree with Movement's Goals, and Trust It to Protect the Nation's Environment." *Gallop Poll Monthly* 415 (April): 19-25.
Eckersley, Robyn. 1995a. "Markets, the State and the Environment: An Overview." Pp. 7-45 in *Markets, the State, and the Environment: Towards Integration*, edited by R. Eckersley. Melbourne: MacMillan Education Australia Pty Ltd.
———, ed. 1995b. *Markets, the State, and the Environment: Towards Integration.* Melbourne: MacMillan Education Australia Pty Ltd.
The Economist. 1996. "Still Sparring." *The Economist* 340, no. 7975 (July 20): 52.
Ehrenfeld, David. 1997. "The Management Explosion and the Next Environmental Crisis." Pp. 53-68 in *People, Land, and Community: Collected E. F. Schumacher Society Lectures*, edited by H. Hannum. New Haven, CT: Yale University Press.
Eiderström, Eva. 1998. "Ecolabels in EU Environmental Policy." Pp. 190-214 in *New Instruments for Environmental Policy in the EU*, edited by J. Golub. New York: Routledge.
Ellickson, Robert C. 1991. *Order without Law: How Neighbors Settle Disputes.* Cambridge, MA: Harvard University Press.
Endicott, Eve, ed. 1993. *Land Conservation through Public/Private Partnerships.* Washington, D.C.: Island Press.
Ernste, Huib. 1998. "Environmental Governance and Modern Management Paradigms in Government and Private Industry." Pp. 43-64 in *Co-operative Environmental Governance: Public-Private Agreements as a Policy Strategy*, edited by P. Glasbergen. Dordrecht, The Netherlands: Kluwer Academic Publishers.
Escobar, Arturo. 1995. *Encountering Development: The Making and Unmaking of the Third World.* Princeton, NJ: Princeton University Press.
Eurobarometer. 1995. "Report on Standard Eurobarometer." *Eurobarometer: Public Opinion in the European Union*, no. 43.
European Commission. 1993. *Towards Sustainability: A European Community Programme of Policy and Action in Relation to the Environment and Sustainable Development.* Luxembourg: Office for Official Publications of the European Communities.

——. 1997. *Statements on Sustainable Development. The General Consultative Forum on the Environment, 1993-96.* Luxembourg: Office for Official Publications of the European Communities.

——. 2001a. *European Consultative Forum on the Environment and Sustainable Development: Activity and Self-Assessment Report 1997-2001.* Luxembourg: Office for Official Publications of the European Communities.

——. 2001b. *Ten Years after Rio: Preparing for the World Summit on Sustainable Development in 2002.* Communication from the Commission to the Council and European Parliament, COM(2001) 53 final.

European Parliament/Council of the European Union. 2002. "Decision No. 1600/2002/EC of the European Parliament and of the Council of the European Union of 22 July 2002 laying down the Sixth Community Environmental Action Programme." *Official Journal of the European Communities* L 242 (10.9.2002): 1-15.

Feigenbaum, Armand V. 1988. "Total Quality Developments into the 1990s—An International Perspective." Pp. 3-10 in *Total Quality Management: An IFS Executive Briefing,* edited by R. Chase. New York: Springer-Verlag.

Fiorino, Daniel J. 1996. "Environmental Policy and the Participation Gap." Pp. 194-212 in *Democracy and the Environment: Problems and Prospects,* edited by W. Lafferty and J. Meadowcroft. Brookfield, VT: Edward Elgar Publishing Company.

Fisher, Roger. 1983. "Negotiating Power." *American Behavioral Scientist* 27, no. 2: 149-166.

Fisher, Roger, William Ury, and Bruce Patton. 1991. *Getting to Yes: Negotiating Agreement without Giving In.* 2nd ed. New York: Penguin Books.

Folger, Joseph P., Marshall S. Poole, and R. K. Stutman. 1997. *Working through Conflict.* 3rd ed. New York: Longman.

Foucault, Michel. 1970. *The Discourse on Language. Appendix to The Archaeology of Knowledge.* New York: Pantheon.

Forester, John. 1993. *Critical Theory, Public Policy, and Planning Practice: Toward a Critical Pragmatism.* Albany, NY: SUNY Press.

——. 1996. "Beyond Dialogue to Transformative Learning: How Deliberative Rituals Encourage Political Judgement in Community Planning Processes." *Poznan Studies in the Philosophy of the Sciences and the Humanities* 46: 295-333.

——. 1999. *The Deliberative Practitioner: Encouraging Participatory Planning Processes.* Cambridge, MA: The MIT Press.

Freeman, Jo, and Victoria Johnson, eds. 1999. *Waves of Protest: Social Movements since the Sixties.* Lanham, MD: Rowman & Littlefield Publishers.

Frey, Lawrence R., ed. 1994. *Group Communication in Context: Studies of Natural Groups.* Hillsdale, NJ: Lawrence Erlbaum Associates.

Friedmann, John. 1987. *Planning in the Public Domain: From Knowledge to Action.* Princeton, NJ: Princeton University Press.

Gamman, John K. 1994. *Overcoming Obstacles in Environmental Policymaking: Creating Partnerships through Mediation.* Albany: State University of New York Press.

Geertz, Clifford. 1973. *The Interpretation of Culture.* New York: Basic Books, Inc.

George, Alexander L. 1979. "Case Studies and Theory Development: The Method of Structured, Focused Comparison." Pp. 43-68 in *Diplomacy: New Approaches to History, Theory, and Policy,* edited by P. Lauren. New York: The Free Press.

Giddens, Anthony. 1984. *The Constitution of Society: Outline of the Theory of Structuration.* Cambridge: Polity Press.

Gidron, Benjamin, Ralph M. Kramer, and Lester M. Salamon. 1992. *Government and the Third Sector: Emerging Relationships in Welfare States.* San Francisco: Jossey-Bass Publishers.

Gill, Stephen. 1995. "Globalisation, Market Civilisation, and Disciplinary Neoliberalism." *Millennium: Journal of International Studies* 24, no. 3: 399-423.

Glasbergen, Pieter. 1995a. "Environmental Dispute Resolution as a Management Issue: Towards New Forms of Decision Making." Pp. 1-18 in *Managing Environmental Disputes: Network Management as an Alternative,* edited by P. Glasbergen. Dordrecht, The Netherlands: Kluwer Academic Publishers.

———, ed. 1995b. *Managing Environmental Disputes: Network management as an Alternative.* Dordrecht, The Netherlands: Kluwer Academic Publishers.

———. 1996a. "Learning to Manage the Environment." Pp. 175-193 in *Democracy and the Environment: Problems and Prospects,* edited by W. Lafferty and J. Meadowcroft. Brookfield, VT: Edward Elgar Publishing Company.

———. 1996b. "Introduction." Pp. 1-10 in *Environmental Problems as Conflicts of Interest,* edited by P. Sloep and A. Blowers. London: Arnold.

———. 1998a. "The Question of Environmental Governance." Pp. 1-18 in *Co-operative Environmental Governance: Public-Private Agreements as a Policy Strategy,* edited by P. Glasbergen. Dordrecht, The Netherlands: Kluwer Academic Publishers.

———. 1998b. "Partnership as a Learning Process: Environmental Covenants in the Netherlands." Pp. 133-156 in *Co-operative Environmental Governance: Public-Private Agreements as a Policy Strategy,* edited by P. Glasbergen. Dordrecht, The Netherlands: Kluwer Academic Publishers.

———, ed. 1998c. *Co-operative Environmental Governance: Public-Private Agreements as a Policy Strategy.* Dordrecht, The Netherlands: Kluwer Academic Publishers.

Glaser, Barney G., and Anselm L. Strauss. 1967. *The Discovery of Grounded Theory.* Chicago: Aldine Publishing Co.

Gobin, Corinne. 1986. *L'Etat Belge et le Problèmatique de l'Environnement.* Brussels: Centre de Recherche et d'Information Socio-Politique.

Goldsmith, Alex. 1995. "Best of Enemies." *Tomorrow* 5, no. 2: 24-26.

Golub, Jonathan. 1998. "New Instruments for Environmental Policy in the EU: Introduction and Overview." Pp. 1-29 in *New Instruments for Environmental Policy in the EU,* edited by J. Golub. New York: Routledge.

Gordon, John, and Jane Coppock. 1997. "Ecosystem Management and Economic Development." Pp. 37-48 in *Thinking Ecologically: The Next Generation of Environmental Policy,* edited by M. Chertow and D. Esty. New Haven, CT: Yale University Press.

Gottlieb, Robert. 1993. *Forcing the Spring: The Transformation of the American Environmental Movement.* Washington, DC: Island Press.

Gould, Kenneth A., Allan Schnaiberg, and Adam S. Weinberg. 1996. *Local Environmental Struggles: Citizen Activism in the Treadmill of Production.* Cambridge: Cambridge University Press.

Grabosky, Peter N. 1995. "Governing at a Distance: Self-Regulating Green Markets." Pp. 197-228 in *Markets, the State, and the Environment: Towards Integration,* edited by R. Eckersley. Melbourne: MacMillan Education Australia Pty Ltd.

Gramsci, Antonio. 1971. *Selections from the Prison Notebooks,* edited by Q. Hoare and G. N. Smith, translated by Q. Hoare and G. N. Smith. New York: International Publishers.

Gray, Barbara. 1989. *Collaborating: Finding Common Ground for Multiparty Problems.* San Francisco: Jossey-Bass.

Green, Donald P., and Ian Shapiro. 1994. *Pathologies of Rational Choice Theory: A Critique of Applications in Political Science*. New Haven, CT: Yale University Press.

Group of Lisbon. 1993. *Limits to Competition*. Lisbon: Gulbenkian Foundation.

Grove-White, Robin. 1993. "Environmentalism: A New Moral Discourse for Technological Society?" Pp. 18-30 in *Environmentalism: The View from Anthropology*, edited by K. Milton. ASA Monographs 32. New York: Routledge.

———. 1996. "Brent Spar Rewrote the Rules." *New Statesman* 126, no. 4339 (June 20): 17-19.

Guha, Ramachandra, and Juan Martinez-Alier, eds. 1997. *Varieties of Environmentalism: Essays North and South*. London: Earthscan Publications Ltd.

Guldbrandsen, Thaddeus C., and Dorothy C. Holland. 2001. "Encounters with the Supercitizen: Neoliberalism, Environmental Activism, and the American Heritage Rivers Initiative." *The Anthropological Quarterly* (Special issue, edited by Krista Harper) 74, no. 3: 124-134.

Gulliver, Phillip H. 1979. *Disputes and Negotiations: A Cross-Cultural Perspective*. New York: Academic Press, Inc.

Habermas, Jürgen. 1984. *The Theory of Communicative Action: Reason and the Rationalization of Society*. Vol. 1. Translated by Thomas McCarthy. Boston, MA: Beacon Press.

———. 1992. "Further Reflections on the Public Sphere." Pp. 421-461 in *Habermas and the Public Sphere*, edited by C. Calhoun. Cambridge, MA: The MIT Press.

Hagland, Paul. 1991. "Environmental Policy." Pp. 259-272 in *The State of the European Community: Policies, Institutions and Debates in the Transition Years*, edited by L. Hurwitz and C. Lequesne. Boulder, CO: Lynne Rienner Publishers.

Hajer, Maarten. 1995. *The Politics of Environmental Discourse: Ecological Modernization and the Policy Process*. Oxford: Clarendon Press.

Hannigan, John A. 1995. *Environmental Sociology: A Social Constructionist Perspective*. London and New York: Routledge.

Hardin, Garrett. 1968. "The Tragedy of the Commons." *Science* 162: 1243-1248.

Hart, Stuart L. 1997. "Beyond Greening: Strategies for a Sustainable World." *Harvard Business Review* 75, no. 1: 66-76.

Hartman, Cathy L., and Edwin R. Stafford. 1997. "Green Alliances: Building New Business with Environmental Groups." *Long Range Planning* 30, no. 2: 184-196.

Hartman, Cathy L., Peter S. Hoffman, and Edwin R. Stafford. 1999. "Partnerships: A Path to Sustainability." *Business Strategy and the Environment* 8: 255-266.

Harvey, David. 1989. *The Condition of Postmodernity: An Enquiry into the Origins of Cultural Change*. Oxford: Basil Blackwell.

———. 1996. *Justice, Nature and the Geography of Difference*. Cambridge, MA: Blackwell Publishers, Inc.

Hawkins, Russel, and Leah Benedict. 1990. "Making Environmental Partnerships Work." *MIS Report* (Special report, edited by R. Hawkins and L. Bendict) 22, no. 9: 1-24.

Healey, Patsy. 1997. *Collaborative Planning: Shaping Places in Fragmented Societies*. Vancouver: University of British Columbia Press.

Herzfeld, Michael. 1992. *The Social Production of Indifference: Exploring the Symbolic Roots of Western Bureaucracy*. Chicago: The University of Chicago Press.

Hogg, Michael A. 1996. "Social Identity, Self-Categorization, and the Small Group." Pp. 227-253 in *Understanding Group Behavior: Small Group Processes and Interpersonal Relations*. Vol. 2. Edited by Erich H. Witte and James H. Davis. Mahwah, NJ: Lawrence Erlbaum Associates, Publishers.

Holland, Dorothy C., William S. Lachicotte, Debra Skinner, and Carole Cain. 1998. *Identity and Agency in Cultural Worlds*. Cambridge, MA: Harvard University Press.

Holland, Dorothy C., and Jean Lave. 2001. "History in Person: An Introduction." Pp. 3-33 in *History in Person: Enduring Struggles, Contentious Practice, Intimate Identities*, edited by D. Holland and J. Lave. Santa Fe, NM: School of American Research Press.

Horkheimer, Max, and Theodor W. Adorno. 1972. *The Dialectic of Enlightenment*, translated by John Cumming. New York: Herder and Herder.

Innes, Judith E. 1995. "Planning Theory's Emerging Paradigm: Communicative Action and Interactive Practice." *Journal of Planning Education and Research* 14, no. 3: 183-190.

————. 1999. "Evaluating Consensus Building." Pp. 631-675 in *The Consensus Building Handbook: A Comprehensive Guide to Reaching Agreement*, edited by Lawrence Susskind, Sarah McKearnan, and Jennifer Thomas-Larmer. Thousand Oaks, CA: Sage Publications.

Jänicke, Martin. 1996. "Democracy as a Condition for Environmental Policy Success: The Importance of Non-Institutional Factors." Pp. 71-85 in *Democracy and the Environment: Problems and Prospects*, edited by W. Lafferty and J. Meadowcroft. Brookfield, VT: Edward Elgar Publishing Company.

Jessop, Bob. 1994. "Post-Fordism and the State." Pp. 251-279 in *Post-Fordism: A Reader*, edited by A. Amin. Oxford: Blackwell Publishers.

Johnson, Richard. 1987. "What Is Cultural Studies Anyway?" *Social Text: Theory/Culture/Ideology* 16: 38-80.

Johnson, Stanley P. 1993. *The Earth Summit: The United Nations Conference on Environment and Development*. International Law and Policy Series. London: Graham & Trotman Ltd.

Kaliner, Joshua. 1997. *The Corporate Planet: Ecology and Politics in an Age of Globalization*. San Francisco, CA: Sierra Club Books.

Kaner, Sam. 1996. *Facilitator's Guide to Participatory Decision Making*. Gabriola Island, BC: New Society Publishers.

Kearns, Kenneth D., and Anna L. West. 1996. "Innovations in Public Affairs Programming: Collaborative Planning and Beyond." Pp. 355-370 in *Practical Public Affairs in an Era of Change: A Communications Guide for Business, Government, and College*, edited by L. B. Dennis. Lanham, MD: University Press of America, Inc.

Kemmis, Daniel. 1990. *Community and the Politics of Place*. Norman: University of Oklahoma Press.

Kempton, Willett. 1991. "Lay Perspectives on Global Climate Change." *Global Environmental Change: Human and Policy Dimensions* 1, no. 3: 183-208.

Kempton, Willett, James S. Boster, and Jennifer A. Hartley. 1995. *Environmental Values in American Culture*. Cambridge, MA: The MIT Press.

Kempton, Willett, and Paul P. Craig. 1993. "European Perspectives on Global Climate Change." *Environment* 35, no. 3: 16-20, 41-45.

Kiester, Edwin, Jr. 1999. "A Town Buries the Axe." *Smithsonian* 30, no. 4: 70-79.

Krämer, Ludwig. 1989. "Enforcement of Community Legislation on the Environment." *RSA Journal*, 137: 243-248.

Kressel, Kenneth, and Dean Pruitt. 1989. *Mediation Research: The Process and Effectiveness of Third Party Intervention*. San Francisco, CA: Jossey-Bass Publishers.

Kriesberg, Louis. 1998. *Constructive Conflicts: From Escalation to Resolution*. Lanham, MD: Rowman & Littlefield Publishers, Inc.

Kriesi, Hanspeter, Ruud Koopmans, Jan Willem Duyvendak, and Marco G. Giugni. 1995. *New Social Movements in Western Europe: A Comparative Analysis*. Minneapolis: University of Minnesota Press.

Kulik, Todd. 1999. *The Expanding Parameters of Global Corporate Citizenship*. New York: The Conference Board, Inc.

Lafferty, William M., and James Meadowcroft. 1996. "Democracy and the Environment: Prospects for Greater Congruence." Pp. 256-272 in *Democracy and the Environment: Problems and Prospects*, edited by W. Lafferty and J. Meadowcroft. Brookfield, VT: Edward Elgar Publishing Company.

Lakoff, George. 1984. *Classifiers as a Reflection of Mind: A Cognitive Model Approach to Prototype Theory*. Berkeley Cognitive Science Report No. 19. Berkeley: University of California Institute of Human Learning.

Laraña, Enrique, Hank Johnston, and Joseph R. Gusfield, eds. 1994. *New Social Movements: From Ideology to Identity*. Philadelphia: Temple University Press.

Levy, David L. 1997. "Environmental Management as Political Sustainability." *Organization & Environment* 10, no. 2: 126-147.

Liberatore, Angela. 1995. "The Social Construction of Environmental Problems." Pp. 59-83 in *Perspectives on Environmental Problems*, edited by P. Glasbergen and A. Blowers. London: Arnold.

Liefferink, Duncan, and Arthur P. J. Mol. 1998. "Voluntary Agreements as a Form of Deregulation? The Dutch Experience." Pp. 181-197 in *Deregulation in the European Union: Environmental Perspectives*, edited by U. Collier. New York: Routledge.

Littlejohn, Stephen W., and Kathy Domenici. 2001. *Engaging Communication in Conflict: Systemic Practice*. Thousand Oaks, CA: Sage Publications, Inc.

Litfin, Karen T. 1994. *Ozone Discourses: Science and Politics in Global Environmental Cooperation*. New York: Columbia University Press.

Livesey, Sharon M. 1999. "McDonald's and the Environmental Defence Fund: A Case Study of a Green Alliance." *Journal of Business Communication* 36, no. 1: 5-39.

Lober, Douglas J. 1997. "Explaining the Formation of Business-Environmentalist Collaborations: Collaborative Windows and the Paper Task Force." *Policy Sciences* 30: 1-24.

Lodge, Juliet. 1989. "Environment: Towards a Clean Blue-Green EC?" Pp. 319-326 in *The European Community and the Challenge of the Future*, edited by J. Lodge. New York: St. Martin's Press.

Long, Frederick J., and Matthew B. Arnold. 1995. *The Power of Environmental Partnerships*. Fort Worth, TX: Harcourt Brace & Company.

Luyken, Reiner. 1995. "Greenpeace: A House Divided." *World Press Review* 42, no. 9: 18-19.

Lynn, Frances M., and George J. Busenberg. 1995. "Citizen Advisory Committees and Environmental Policy: What We Know, What's Left to Discover." *Risk Analysis* 15, no. 2: 147-162.

Lynn, Frances M., Nevin Cohen, and Caron Chess. 2000. "The Chemical Industry's Community Advisory Panels: What's Been Their Impact?" *Environmental Science & Technology* 34, no. 10: 1881-1886.

Maarleveld, Marleen, and Constant Dangbégnon. 1999. "Managing Natural Resources: A Social Learning Perspective." *Agriculture and Human Values* 16: 267-280.

Maida, Peter R. 1995. "Mediation and the New Environmental Agenda." Pp. 17-35 in *Mediating Environmental Conflicts: Theory and Practice,* edited by J. W. Blackburn and W. M. Bruce. Westport, CT: Quorum Books.

Marks, Gary, and Doug McAdam. 1996. "Social Movements and the Changing Structure of Political Opportunity in the European Union." Pp. 95-120 in *Governance in the European Union,* edited by G. Marks, F. Scharpf, P. Schmitter, and W. Streeck. Thousand Oaks, CA: Sage Publications.

Marston, Ed. 2001. "The Quincy Library Group: A Divisive Attempt at Peace." Pp. 79-90 in *Across the Great Divide: Explorations in Collaborative Conservation and the American West,* edited by P. Brick et al. Washington, DC: Island Press.

Martinez-Alier, Joan. 2002. *The Environmentalism of the Poor.* A Report for the United Nations Research Institute for Social Development (UNRISD) for the World Summit on Sustainable Development (WSSD).

Maser, Chris. 1996. *Resolving Environmental Conflict: Towards Sustainable Community Development.* Delray Beach, FL: St. Lucie Press.

Maser, Chris, Russ Beaton, and Kevin Smith. 1998. *Setting the Stage for Sustainability: A Citizen's Handbook.* Boca Raton, FL: Lewis Publishers.

Mazza, Patrick. 1997. "Cooptation or Constructive Engagement?: Quincy Library Group's Effort to Bring Together Loggers and Environmentalists under Fire." *Cascadia Planet.* www.tnews.com/text/quincy_library.html

McCloskey, Michael. 1996. "The Skeptic: Collaboration Has Its Limits." *High Country News* (May 13): 7.

McCormick, John. 2001. *Environmental Policy in the European Union.* New York: Palgrave.

McIntosh, Malcolm, Deborah Leipziger, Keith Jones, and Gill Coleman. 1998. *Corporate Citizenship: Successful Strategies for Responsible Companies.* London: Financial Times Professional Limited.

McKinney, Matthew J. 1988. "Water Resources Planning: A Collaborative, Consensus-Building Approach." *Society and Natural Resources* 1: 335-350.

McNeely, Jeffrey A., ed. 1995. *Expanding Partnerships in Conservation.* Washington, DC: Island Press.

Meadowcroft, James. 1998. "Co-operative Management Regimes: A Way Forward?" Pp. 21-42 in *Co-operative Environmental Governance: Public-Private Agreements as a Policy Strategy,* edited by P. Glasbergen. Dordrecht, The Netherlands: Kluwer Academic Publishers.

Milliman, John, and Ann Feyerherm. 1999. "Responding to Community Expectations on Corporate Environmental Performance: How to Develop Effective Citizen Advisory Panels." *Corporate Environmental Strategy* 6, no. 2: 164-174.

Milton, Kay, ed. 1993. *Environmentalism: The View from Anthropology.* London: Routledge.

Ministère de la Region Wallonne. 1995. *Votre Jardin au Naturel.* Jambes: Direction Générale des Ressources Naturelles et de l'Environnement.

Ministre de l'Environnement, des Ressources Naturelles, et de l'Agriculture. 1995. *Plan d'Environnement pour le Développement durable en Région wallonne.* Bruxelles: Le Gouvernement Wallon.

Mol, Arthur P. J. 1996. "Ecological Modernisation and Institutional Reflexivity: Environmental Reform in the Late Modern Age." *Environmental Politics* 5, no. 2: 302-323.

Moote, Ann, Alex Conley, Karen Firehock, and E. Franklin Dukes. 2000. *Assessing Research Needs: Summary of a Workshop on Community-Based Collaboratives.* Tuscon, AZ: Udall Center Publications 00-5.

Moote, Margaret A., Mitchel P. McClaran, and Donna K. Chickering. 1997. "Theory in Practice: Applying Participatory Democracy Theory to Public Land Planning." *Environmental Management* 21, no. 6: 877-889.

Moran, Alan. 1995. "Tools of Environmental Policy: Market Instruments versus Command-and-Control." Pp. 73-85 in *Markets, the State, and the Environment: Towards Integration,* edited by R. Eckersley. Melbourne: MacMillan Education Australia Pty Ltd.

Nader, Laura. 1990. *Harmony Ideology: Justice and Control in a Zapotec Mountain Village.* Stanford, CA: Stanford University Press.

———. 1995. "Civilization and Its Negotiations." Pp. 39-64 in *Understanding Disputes: The Politics of Argument,* edited by P. Caplan. Oxford: Berg Publishers.

———. 1996. "Coercive Harmony: The Political Economy of Legal Models." Pp. 1-13 in *Essays on Controlling Processes, 1996,* edited by L. Nader. Kroeber Anthropological Society Papers, Number 80.

Newton, David E. 1996. *Environmental Justice: A Reference Handbook.* Santa Barbara, CA: ACB-CLIO, Inc.

Nonini, Donald M. 1985. "Varieties of Materialism." *Dialectical Anthropology* 9, no. 1-4: 7-64.

Norton, Bryan G. 1992. "New Directions in Environmental Ethics." *World and I* 7: 72-87.

O'Connor, James. 1988. "Capitalism, Nature, Socialism: A Theoretical Introduction." *Capitalism, Nature, Socialism* 1: 11-38.

———. 1994. "Is Sustainable Capitalism Possible?" Pp. 176-197 in *Is Capitalism Sustainable? Political Economy and the Politics of Ecology,* edited by M. O'Connor. New York: The Guilford Press.

O'Connor, Martin, ed. 1994. *Is Capitalism Sustainable? Political Economy and the Politics of Ecology.* New York: The Guilford Press.

O'Connor, Martin, and Sybille van den Hove. 2001. "Prospects for Public Participation on Nuclear Risks and Policy Options: Innovations in Governance Practices for Sustainable Development in the European Union." *Journal of Hazardous Materials* 86: 77-99.

The Oil and Gas Journal. 1997. "The Greenpeace Method." *The Oil and Gas Journal* 95, no. 14 (April 7): 23.

O'Leary, Rosemary. 1995. "Environmental Mediation: What Do We Know and How Do We Know It?" Pp. 17-35 in *Mediating Environmental Conflicts: Theory and Practice,* edited by J. W. Blackburn and W. M. Bruce. Westport, CT: Quorum Books.

Osborne, David, and Ted Gaebler. 1992. *Reinventing Government: How the Entrepreneurial Spirit Is Transforming the Public Sector.* Reading, MA: Addison Wesley Publishing Company.

Ostrom, Elinor. 1990. *Governing the Commons: The Evolution of Institutions for Collective Action.* Cambridge: Cambridge University Press.

Ozawa, Connie P. 1993. "Improving Citizen Participation in Environmental Decision Making: The Use of Transformative Mediator Techniques." *Environment and Planning C: Government and Policy* 11: 103-117.

Paehlke, Robert. 1996. "Environmental Challenges to Democratic Practice." Pp. 18-38 in *Democracy and the Environment: Problems and Prospects,* edited by W. Lafferty and J. Meadowcroft. Brookfield, VT: Edward Elgar Publishing Company.

Paterson, Tony. 1995. "North Sea Shell Game." *World Press Review* 42, no. 9 (September): 18-19.

Paton, Bruce. 2000. "Voluntary Environmental Initiatives and Sustainable Industry. *Business Strategy and the Environment* 9, no. 5: 328-338.

Patterson, Thomas C. 1994. "Toward a Properly Historical Ecology." Pp. 223-247 in *Historical Ecology: Cultural Knowledge and Changing Landscapes*, edited by C. Crumley. Santa Fe, NM: School of American Research Press.

Peace, Adrian. 1993. "Environmental Protest, Bureaucratic Closure: The Politics of Discourse in Rural Ireland." Pp. 189-204 in *Environmentalism: The View from Anthropology*, edited by K. Milton. ASA Monographs 32. London: Routledge.

Peacock, James L. 1986. *The Anthropological Lens: Harsh Light, Soft Focus*. Cambridge: Cambridge University Press.

Pearce, W. Barnett. 1989. *Communication and the Human Condition*. Carbondale: Southern Illinois University Press.

Pearce, W. Barnett, and Vernon E. Cronen. 1980. *Communication, Action, and Meaning: The Creation of Social Realities*. New York: Praeger Publishers.

Pearce, W. Barnett, and Stephen W. Littlejohn. 1997. *Moral Conflict: When Social Worlds Collide*. Thousand Oaks, CA: Sage Publications.

Pellow, David. 1996. "New Models for Struggle: Environmental Decision-Making through Consensus." Northwestern University Institute for Policy Research Working Papers, WP-96-34.

Pinkerton, Evelyn, ed. 1989. *Co-Operative Management of Local Fisheries: New Directions for Improved Management and Community Development*. Vancouver, Canada: The University of British Columbia Press.

Piven, Frances Fox, and Richard A. Cloward. 1979. *Poor People's Movements: Why They Succeed, How They Fail*. New York: Vintage Books.

Polanyi, Karl. 1957. *The Great Transformation*. Boston: Beacon.

Pollack, Mark A. 1997. "Representing Diffuse Interests in EC Policymaking." *Journal of European Public Policy* 4, no. 4: 572-590.

Poncelet, Eric C. 1998. *Enduring Environmental Conflicts and Emerging Cultures of Cooperation: Partnerships in the European Union and Belgium*. Ann Arbor, MI: UMI Dissertation Services.

————. 2003. "Resisting Corporate Citizenship: Business-NGO Relations in Multistakeholder Environmental Partnerships." *Journal of Corporate Citizenship* 9: 97-115.

Poole, Marshall S., and Randy Y. Hirokawa. 1996. "Communication and Group Decision Making." Pp. 3-18 in *Communication and Group Decision Making*. 2nd ed. Edited by Randy Y. Hirokawa and Marshall S. Poole. Thousand Oaks, CA: Sage Publications.

Post, James E., Anne T. Lawrence, and James Weber. 1999. *Business and Society: Corporate Strategy, Public Policy, Ethics*. 9th ed. Boston: McGraw-Hill.

Prato, Giuliana B. 1993. "Political Decision-Making: Environmentalism, Ethics and Popular Participation in Italy." Pp. 174-188 in *Environmentalism: The View from Anthropology*, edited by K. Milton. ASA Monographs 32. London: Routledge.

President's Council on Sustainable Development (PCSD). 1996. *Sustainable America: A New Consensus of Prosperity, Opportunity, and a Healthy Environment*. Washington, DC: U.S. Government Printing Office.

————. 1999. *Towards a Sustainable America: Advancing Prosperity, Opportunity, and a Healthy Environment for the 21st Century*. Washington, DC: U.S. Government Printing Office.

Press, Allison, and Catherine Taylor. 1990. *Europe and the Environment: The European Community and Environmental Policy*. London: The Industrial Society.

Price, Laurie. 1987. "Ecuadorian Illness Stories: Cultural Knowledge in Natural Discourse." Pp. 313-342 in *Cultural Models in Language and Thought*, edited by D. Holland and N. Quinn. Cambridge: Cambridge University Press.

Punch, Maurice. 1994. "Politics and Ethics in Qualitative Research." Pp. 83-104 in *Handbook of Qualitative Research*, edited by N. Denzin and Y. Lincoln. Thousand Oaks, CA: Sage Publications.

Quinn, Naomi, and Dorothy Holland. 1987. "Culture and Cognition." Pp. 3-40 in *Cultural Models in Language and Thought*, edited by D. Holland and N. Quinn. Cambridge: Cambridge University Press.

Reinhart, Forest L. 2000. *Down to Earth: Applying Business Principles to Environmental Management*. Boston: Harvard Business School Press.

Rikhardsson, Pall, and Richard Welford. 1997. "Clouding the Crisis: The Construction of Corporate Environmental Management." Pp. 40-62 in *Hijacking Environmentalism: Corporate Responses to Sustainable Development*, edited by R. Welford. London: Earthscan Publications Ltd.

Röling, Niels G. 1994. "Communication Support for Sustainable Natural Resource Management." *IDS Bulletin* 25, no. 2: 125-133.

Röling, Niels G., and Annemarie E. Wagemakers. 1998. "A New Practice: Facilitating Sustainable Agriculture." Pp. 1-22 in *Facilitating Sustainable Agriculture: Participatory Learning and Adaptive Management in Times of Environmental Uncertainty*, edited by N. Röling and M. Wagemakers. Cambridge: Cambridge University Press.

Rolston, Holmes. 1986. *Philosophy Gone Wild: Essays in Environmental Ethics*. Buffalo, NY: Prometheus Books.

Rondinelli, Dennis A., and Michael A. Berry. 2000. "Environmental Citizenship in Multinational Corporations: Social Responsibility and Sustainable Development." *European Management Journal* 18, no. 1: 70-84.

Ross, Marc H. 1993a. *The Culture of Conflict: Interpretations and Interests in Comparative Perspective*. New Haven, CT: Yale University Press.

———. 1993b. *The Management of Conflict: Interpretations and Interests in Comparative Perspective*. New Haven, CT: Yale University Press.

Rowell, Andrew. 1996. *Green Backlash: Global Subversion of the Environmental Movement*. London: Routledge.

Roy, Beth. 1994. *Some Trouble with Cows: Making Sense of Social Conflict*. Berkeley, CA: University of California Press.

Ryan, Clare M. 1995. "Regulatory Negotiation: Learning from Experiences in the U.S. Environmental Protection Agency." Pp. 203-216 in *Mediating Environmental Conflicts: Theory and Practice*, edited by J. W. Blackburn and W. M. Bruce. Westport, CT: Quorum Books.

Sagawa, Shirley, and Eli Segal. 2000. *Common Interest, Common Good: Creating Value through Business and Social Sector Partnerships*. Boston: Harvard Business School Press.

Sagoff, Mark. 1988. *The Economy of the Earth*. Cambridge: Cambridge University Press.

Salamon, Lester M. 1995. *Partners in Public Service: Government-Nonprofit Relations in the Modern Welfare State*. Baltimore: The Johns Hopkins University Press.

Scheuing, Eberhard E. 1994. *The Power of Strategic Partnering*. Portland, OR: Productivity Press.

Schnaiberg, Allan, and Kenneth A. Gould. 1994. *Environment and Society: The Enduring Conflict*. New York: St. Martin's Press.

Schwarz, Michiel, and Michael Thompson. 1990. *Divided We Stand: Redefining Politics, Technology and Social Choice*. Philadelphia: University of Pennsylvania Press.

Seibold, David R., Renée A. Meyers, and Sunwolf. 1996. "Communication and Influence in Group Decision Making." Pp. 242-268 in *Communication and Group Decision Making*. 2nd ed. Edited by Randy Y. Hirokawa and Marshall S. Poole. Thousand Oaks, CA: Sage Publications.

Selin, Steve, and Deborah Chavez. 1995. "Developing a Collaborative Model for Environmental Planning and Management." *Environmental Management* 19, no. 2: 189-195.

Shailor, Jonathan G. 1994. *Empowerment in Dispute Mediation: A Critical Analysis of Communication*. Westport, CT: Praeger Publishers.

Silverstein, Michael. 1993. "What Does It Mean to Be Green?" *Business and Society Review*, no. 86: 16-23.

Simmons, Ian. 1993. *Interpreting Nature: Cultural Constructions of the Environment*. London and New York: Routledge.

Singh, Kanika. 1995. "Sparring with Shell." *Multinational Monitor* 16, no. 7-8 (July-August): 6.

Sloep, Peter B., and Andrew Blowers, eds. 1996. *Environmental Problems as Conflicts of Interests*. London: Arnold.

Smet, Miet. 1990. "Management and Control of Transfrontier Waste Movements in Belgium." *Marine Policy* (May): 228-235.

Smith, L. Graham. 1993. *Impact Assessment and Sustainable Resource Management*. London: Longman.

Smith, L. Graham, Carla Y. Nell, and Mark V. Prystupa. 1997. "The Converging Dynamics of Interest Representation in Resource Management." *Environmental Management* 21, no. 2: 139-146.

Smith, Turner T., and Roszell D. Hunter. 1992. "The European Community Environmental Legal System." *Environmental Law Reporter* 22: 10,106-10,135.

Snow, Donald. 2001. "Coming Home: An Introduction of Collaborative Conservation." Pp. 1-11 in *Across the Great Divide: Explorations in Collaborative Conservation and the American West*, edited by P. Brick, D. Snow, and S. van de Wetering. Washington, DC: Island Press.

Squires, Gregory D. 1996. "Partnership and the Pursuit of the Private City." Pp. 266-290 in *Readings in Urban Theory*, edited by S. Fainstein and S. Campbell. Cambridge: Blackwell.

Stafford, Edwin R., and Cathy L. Hartman. 1996. "Green Alliances: Strategic Relations between Businesses and Environmental Groups." *Business Horizons* 39 (March/April): 50-59.

Stafford, Edwin R., Michael J. Polonsky, and Cathy L. Hartman. 2000. "Environmental NGO-Business Collaboration and Strategic Building: A Case Analysis of the Greenpeace-Foron Alliance." *Business Strategy and the Environment* 9: 122-135.

Stake, Robert E. 1994. "Case Studies." Pp. 236-247 in *Handbook of Qualitative Research*, edited by N. Denzin and Y. Lincoln. Thousand Oaks, CA: Sage Publications.

Starkey, Richard. 1998. "Competitiveness, Deregulation and Environmental Protection." Pp. 23-41 in *Deregulation in the European Union: Environmental Perspectives*, edited by U. Collier. London: Routledge.

Stern, Alissa J., and Tim Hicks. 2000. *The Process of Business/Environmental Collaborations: Partnering for Sustainability*. Westport, CT: Quorum Books.

Stolton, Sue, and Nigel Dudley. 1999. *Partnerships for Protection: New Strategies for Planning and Management for Protected Areas*. London: Earthscan Publications Ltd.

Susskind, Lawrence, and Jeffrey Cruikshank. 1987. *Breaking the Impasse: Consensual Approaches to Resolving Public Disputes*. New York: Basic Books, Inc.

Susskind, Lawrence, Paul F. Levy, and Jennifer Thomas-Larmer. 2000. *Negotiating Environmental Agreements: How to Avoid Escalating Confrontation, Needless Costs, and Unnecessary Litigation*. Washington, DC: Island Press.

Susskind, Lawrence, Sarah McKearnan, and Jennifer Thomas-Larmer, eds. 1999. *The Consensus Building Handbook: A Comprehensive Guide to Reaching Agreement*. Thousand Oaks, CA: Sage Publications.

SustainAbility, Ltd., and *TOMORROW*—Global Environment Business. 1994. *The Green Keiretsu: An International Survey of Business Alliances and Networks for Sustainable Development*. London: SustainAbility, Ltd., and *TOMORROW*—Global Environment Business.

Swaffield, Simon. 1998. "Contextual Meanings in Policy Discourse: A Case Study of Language Use Concerning Resource Policy in the New Zealand High Country." *Policy Sciences* 31: 199-224.

Sweezy, Paul M., and Harry Magdoff. 1989. "Capitalism and the Environment." *Monthly Review* 41, no. 2: 1-10.

Switzer, Jacqueline V. 1994. *Environmental Politics: Domestic and Global Dimensions*. New York: St. Martin's Press.

Taschner, Karola. 1998. "Environmental Management Systems: The European Regulation." Pp. 215-241 in *New Instruments for Environmental Policy in the EU*, edited by J. Golub. London: Routledge.

Taylor, Michael. 1996. "When Rationality Fails." Pp. 223-234 in *The Rational Choice Controversy: Economic Models of Politics Revisited*, edited by J. Friedman. New Haven: Yale University Press.

Tichy, Noel M., Andrew R. McGill, and Lynda St. Clair. 1997. "Corporate Global Citizenship—Why Now?" Pp. 1-22 in *Corporate Global Citizenship: Doing Business in the Public Eye*, edited by N. Tichy, A. McGill, and L. St. Clair. San Francisco: The New Lexington Press.

Turner, John, and Jason Rylander. 1997. "Land Use: The Forgotten Agenda." Pp. 60-75 in *Thinking Ecologically: The Next Generation of Environmental Policy*, edited by M. Chertow and D. Esty. New Haven: Yale University Press.

Tversky, Amos. 1996. "Contrasting Rational and Psychological Principles of Choice." Pp. 5-21 in *Wise Choices: Decisions, Games, and Negotiations*, edited by R. Zeckhauser, R. Keeney, and J. Sebenius. Boston, MA: Harvard Business School Press.

United Nations. 2002a. *Report of the World Summit on Sustainable Development. Johannesburg, South Africa, 26 August – 4 September 2002*. New York: United Nations.

———. 2002b. *Global Challenge, Global Opportunity: Trends in Sustainable Development*. Published by the United Nations Department of Economic and Social Affairs for the World Summit on Sustainable Development, Johannesburg, South Africa, 26 August – 4 September 2002.

United States Department of Labor. 1998. *Partnership Handbook*. Washington, DC: United States Department of Labor.

Urban, Sabine, and Serge Vendemini. 1992. *European Strategic Alliances: Co-operative Corporate Strategies in the New Europe*. Translated by R. Ingleton. Oxford: Blackwell Publishers.

Ury, William L., Jeanne M. Brett, and Stephen B. Goldberg. 1988. *Getting Disputes Resolved: Designing Systems to Cut the Cost of Conflict*. San Francisco, CA: Jossey-Bass Publishers.

Van den Hove, Sybille. 2000. "Participatory Approaches to Environmental Policy-

Making: The European Commission Climate Policy Process as a Case Study." *Ecological Economics* 33: 457-472.

Varela, Maria. 2000. "Collaborative Conservation: Peace or Pacification? The View from Los Ojos." Pp. 228-235 in *Across the Great Divide: Explorations in Collaborative Conservation and the American West*, edited by P. Brick, D. Snow, and S. van de Wetering. Washington, DC: Island Press.

Venter, Andrew K., and Charles M. Breen. 1998. "Partnership Forum Framework: Participative Framework for Protected Area Outreach." *Environmental Management* 22, no. 6: 803-815.

Vogel, David. 1993. "Environmental Policy in the European Community." Pp. 181-198 in *Environmental Politics in the International Arena: Movements, Parties, Organizations, and Policy*, edited by S. Kamieniecki. Albany: State University of New York Press.

Warren, Lynda M. 1993. "The Precautionary Principle: Use with Caution!" Pp. 97-111 in *Environmentalism: The View from Anthropology*, edited by K. Milton. ASA Monographs 32. London: Routledge.

Weale, Albert. 1992. *The New Politics of Pollution*. Manchester and New York: Manchester University Press.

Weber, Edward P. 1998. "Successful Collaboration: Negotiating Effective Regulations." *Environment* 40, no. 9: 10-15, 32-37.

Weber, Max. 1946. *From Max Weber: Essays in Sociology*, edited by H. H. Gerth and C. Wright Mills. New York: Oxford University Press, Inc.

Weedon, Chris. 1997. *Feminist Practice and Poststructuralist Theory*. Oxford: Blackwell Publishers.

Weidner, Helmut. 1995. "Mediation as Policy Instrument for Resolving Environmental Disputes." Pp. 159-195 in *Environmental Policy in Search of New Instruments*, edited by B. Dente. Dordrecht, The Netherlands: Kluwer Academic Publishers.

Weizsäcker, Ernst U. von. 1994. *Earth Politics*. London: Zed Books Ltd.

Welford, Richard. 1996. "Environmental Issues and Corporate Environmental Management." Pp. 1-12 in *Corporate Environmental Management: Systems and Strategies*, edited by R. Welford. London: Earthscan Publications Ltd.

Welford, Richard, and Andrew Gouldson. 1993. *Environmental Management and Business Strategy*. London: Pitman Publishing.

Wertsch, James V. 1991. *Voices of the Mind: A Sociocultural Approach to Mediated Action*. Cambridge, MA: Harvard University Press.

White, James Boyd. 1990. *Justice as Translation: An Essay in Cultural and Legal Criticism*. Chicago: University of Chicago Press.

White, Lynn Jr. 1967. "The Historical Roots of Our Ecological Crisis." *Science* 155, no. 3767: 1,203-1,207.

Wildavsky, Aaron. 1987. "Choosing Preferences by Constructing Institutions: A Cultural Theory of Preference Formation." *American Political Science Review* 81:3-21.

Williams, Bruce A., and Albert R. Matheny. 1995. *Democracy, Dialogue, and Environmental Disputes: The Contested Languages of Social Regulation*. New Haven: Yale University Press.

Willis, Paul. 1977. *Learning to Labor: How Working Class Kids Get Working Class Jobs*. New York: Columbia University Press.

———. 1981. "Cultural Production Is Different from Cultural Reproduction Is Different from Social Reproduction Is Different from Reproduction." *Interchange* 12, no. 2-3: 48-67.

Winer, Michael B., and Karen L. Ray. 1994. *Collaboration Handbook: Creating,*

Sustaining, and Enjoying the Journey. St. Paul, MN: Amherst H. Wilder Foundation.

Winslade, John, and Gerald Monk. 2000. *Narrative Mediation: A New Approach to Conflict Resolution.* San Francisco, CA: Jossey-Bass, Inc.

Wondolleck, Julia M., and Clare M. Ryan. 1999. "What Hat Do I Wear Now?: An Examination of Agency Roles in Collaborative Processes." *Negotiation Journal* 15, no. 2: 117-133.

Wondolleck, Julia M., and Steven L. Yaffee. 2000. *Making Collaboration Work: Lessons from Innovation in Natural Resource Management.* Washington, DC: Island Press.

Woodhill, James, and Niels G. Röling. 1998. "The Second Wing of the Eagle: The Human Dimension in Learning Our Way to More Sustainable Futures." Pp. 46-72 in *Facilitating Sustainable Agriculture: Participatory Learning and Adaptive Management in Times of Environmental Uncertainty,* edited by N. Röling and M. Wagemakers. Cambridge: Cambridge University Press.

World Commission on Environment and Development (WCED). 1987. *Our Common Future.* Oxford: Oxford University Press.

Yaffee, Steven L., et al. 1996. *Ecosystem Management in the United States: An Assessment of Current Experience.* Washington, DC: Island Press.

Yosie, Terry F., and Timothy D. Herbst. 1998 "Using Stakeholder Processes in Environmental Decision Making: An Evaluation of Lessons Learned, Key Issues, and Future Challenges." Tec-Com, Inc. Publishers. *Riskworld.* www.riskworld.com/ Nreports/1998/STAKEHOLD/HTML/nr98aa07.htm

Young, Stephen. 1997. "Community-Based Partnerships and Sustainable Development: A Third Force in the Social Economy." Pp. 217-236 in *The Politics of Sustainable Development: Theory, Policy and Practice within the European Union,* edited by S. Baker, M. Kousis, D. Richardson, and S. Young. London: Routledge.

Index

Note: Page numbers for figures and tables appear in italics.

About the Author

Eric C. Poncelet earned his Ph.D. in cultural anthropology from the University of North Carolina, Chapel Hill, in 1998. His research has focused on multistakeholder environmental collaboration in the European Union and the United States. Currently, he is an associate mediator at CONCUR, Inc.—a California-based firm providing services in agreement-focused facilitation, joint fact-finding, and strategic planning. At CONCUR, Dr. Poncelet designs, manages, and facilitates collaborative processes directed toward resolving natural resource management-based disputes in the areas of water resources protection, fisheries management, and species preservation. He also provides training on the topics of effective environmental negotiation, facilitation, and process design. His articles on multistakeholder environmental collaboration appear in such journals as *Environmental Management, Policy Sciences,* and the *Journal of Corporate Citizenship.* He is also a registered professional mechanical engineer and has worked as a power systems engineer in the energy sector.